Machiavelli
for
Women

Machiavelli

for

Women

*Defend Your Worth, Grow Your Ambition,
and Win the Workplace*

STACEY VANEK SMITH

GALLERY BOOKS

NEW YORK   LONDON   TORONTO   SYDNEY   NEW DELHI

G

Gallery Books
An Imprint of Simon & Schuster, Inc.
1230 Avenue of the Americas
New York, NY 10020

First Gallery Books hardcover edition September 2021

GALLERY BOOKS and colophon are registered trademarks
of Simon & Schuster, Inc.

For information about special discounts for bulk purchases,
please contact Simon & Schuster Special Sales at 1-866-506-1949
or business@simonandschuster.com.

The Simon & Schuster Speakers Bureau can bring authors to your live event.
For more information or to book an event, contact the Simon & Schuster Speakers
Bureau at 1-866-248-3049 or visit our website at www.simonspeakers.com.

Manufactured in the United States of America

1 3 5 7 9 10 8 6 4 2

Library of Congress Cataloging-in-Publication Data

Names: Vanek Smith, Stacey, author.
Title: Machiavelli for women : defend your worth, grow your ambition,
and win the workplace / Stacey Vanek Smith.
Description: New York : Gallery Books, 2021.
Identifiers: LCCN 2020049503 (print) | LCCN 2020049504 (ebook) | ISBN
9781982121754 (hardcover) | ISBN 9781982121778 (ebook)
Subjects: LCSH: Women—Life skills guides. | Women's rights. |
Women—Employment. | Machiavelli, Niccolò, 1469–1527.
Classification: LCC HQ1155 .V364 2021 (print) | LCC HQ1155 (ebook) |
DDC331.4—dc23
LC record available at https://lccn.loc.gov/2020049503
LC ebook record available at https://lccn.loc.gov/2020049504

ISBN 978-1-9821-2175-4
ISBN 978-1-9821-2177-8 (ebook)

For my beautiful mother,
my grandmothers,
and all the women who came before

Contents

Note on Translations

In studying *The Prince*, I mainly used two translations. The first was the *Dover Thrift Editions* version, translated by N. H. Thomson. I loved this translation for the beauty of its language. I also relied heavily on the *Millennium Publications* edition, translated by W. K. Marriott. I valued the clarity of this translation. I have used quotes from these two editions interchangeably throughout the book. When a quote is from the *Dover Thrift Editions* translation, I include "DTE" after the quote. When it is from the *Millennium Publications* edition, I indicate that with "MPE." In a couple of cases, I've used alternate translations and I have cited these in the endnotes.

Introduction

I first read *The Prince* in college. I was taking a political philosophy class and we were reading all the greatest hits: Plato, Hobbes, Marx, Machiavelli.

I hated *The Prince*.

How to seize power. How to hold on to power. Should you build a fortress? Should you slaughter the locals when you conquer a new territory? (Apparently, it largely depends on whether you enjoy the same foods.) It was all so brutish and bloody and cynical and depressing. I preferred Cicero and Rousseau. They wrote such beautiful, soaring treatises on society and man's place in it. Man—it *was* always man—was noble, godlike, and so full of beauty, grace, and goodness that if you just set him free to explore his own nature—let him do him—the world would blossom into a glittering, shining place of learning, leisure, art, and brotherhood.

Machiavelli, on the other hand, describes humans as "thankless, fickle, false . . . [and] greedy . . . a sorry breed . . ." (Chapter XVII, DTE). He condones, at different moments in *The Prince*, lying, bragging, the killing of children, and pretending to be friends with someone and then stabbing them in the back. At one point in the book he does a truly chilling cost-benefit analysis of whether to exterminate the local population once you've taken control of a new land. To his credit, he comes out against it . . . but just barely. *The Prince* was the opposite of inspiring or uplifting. It was cynical, depressing, and did absolutely nothing for my eighteen-year-old soul.

Fast-forward twenty-five years: I've worked in journalism organizations all over the country—starting at the *Idaho Statesman* as a copy editor, moving on to *Idaho Weddings* and *Boise* magazine, then to journalism school in New York. From there I went to the public radio show *Marketplace*, then (a decade later) to NPR's *Planet Money* podcast. A few years ago, I helped NPR launch *Planet Money*'s daily *The Indicator* podcast, and serve as the host of the show. I've worked through the housing crisis, the Great Recession and recovery, the podcast bubble, and the coronavirus pandemic and recession. I've seen countless reshufflings, promotions, layoffs, demotions, firings, furloughs, Me Too scandals, backstabbings, and politicking. Watching it all play out, I have never once found myself thinking about Cicero or Rousseau, but I have found myself thinking about Machiavelli. A lot. I think that cynical, brutish Italian was onto something.

Granted, women taking advice from Machiavelli might seem strange. Like, do we really need another old white guy mansplaining power to us? "Hey, ladies, *here* is how you can finally be the coldhearted, murderous tyrant you always dreamed you could be!" I mean . . . no. But I would argue murderous tyranny is not what Machiavelli is about at all. Machiavelli was an incredibly clear-eyed, original thinker who might just be history's first true champion of real talk. For that reason, there could be no better guide for women in the workplace. If there's something that is in short supply amid all the outrage and girl power rhetoric, it is data, research, and real solutions. Machiavelli was a big believer in those things, and he might have been the greatest of all time at figuring out what obstacles stood in the way of people getting into leadership positions and how they could overcome those obstacles.

In the five hundred years since Machiavelli wrote *The Prince*, a lot of things have changed: We have electricity, the combustion engine, airplanes, computers, and antibiotics. We've explored the outer reaches of our solar system, the surface of Mars, the ocean floor, and we've even split the atom. People, though, haven't changed one bit. All the petty jealousies, treachery, power-mongering, and aggression people practiced in the 1500s are alive and well in the modern workplace.

In fact, more than anyone else, Machiavelli has helped explain some of the contradictions around women in the workplace that have always bothered me: namely, that some of the progress is so exciting, inspiring, and undeniably amazing, but in other areas women seem stuck.

Consider this: In school, women get better grades than men in all subjects, including math and science; women graduate from high school and attend college in higher numbers than men; there are more women than men in medical school and law school; women are running for office and getting elected in unprecedented numbers. Nearly 40 percent of businesses in the United States are now started by women, and also, women are having a moment. The cultural shift brought about by the Me Too, Time's Up, Black Lives Matter, and other social and political movements are changing workplace cultures everywhere (including at NPR, where the head of the newsroom left his job in 2017 following allegations of sexual harassment).

All of this is great—real and substantial progress, hard won by generations of pioneering women. Except, in other ways, things seem to be distressingly backward:

- 80% of CEOs are men (for Fortune 500 companies, it's more than 90%).
- Corporate boards are more than 80% male.
- Women make about 80¢ for every dollar a man makes.
- Two-thirds of federal judges are male.
- 75% of elected representatives are men.
- Women start 40% of the businesses in the country, but 98% of venture capital goes to men.

What this litany of depressing statistics tells us is that although women are arriving in the workplace and breaking into new fields at an unprecedented rate, once they get there, they are not rising to the highest levels of power. They are not leading innovation. They are not making the big decisions. They are not making our laws or moving our markets or deciding our court cases or running our companies. Women are in the workplace, but they are not reaching Machiavelli's princely realms.

Why?

Everybody has their theories. Popular explanations include: Women shy away from leadership positions; women want more flexibility with their time, so they avoid the most demanding jobs; women are more nurturing and collaborative (i.e., they lack the killer instinct you need in a leader or decision-maker); women gravitate toward less lucrative fields. All of these explanations have seeds of truth in them, but I believe the real reason for the frustratingly slow progress of women in the workplace is something Machiavelli summed up quite well more than five hundred years ago:

> *Let it be noted that there is no more delicate matter to take in hand, nor more dangerous to conduct, nor more doubtful in its success, than to set up as a leader in the introduction of changes. For he who innovates will have for his enemies all those who are well off under the existing order of things, and only lukewarm supporters in those who might be better off under the new. This lukewarm temper arises partly from the fear of adversaries who have the laws on their side, and partly from the incredulity of mankind, who will never admit the merit of anything new, until they have seen it proved by the event* (Chapter VI, DTE).

If I were to translate Machiavelli's sentiments into modern English, I would say: "Changing a system is really hard and you will probably fail. The old guard will freak out because they have so much to lose, and the people who would benefit from the change will waffle because they're scared and skeptical of how much they would really benefit, even if you did manage to pull off this crazy hat trick."

Today, Niccolò Machiavelli is best-known as a ruthless power monger, devoid of ethics and compassion. The phrase most often associated with him, "The ends justify the means" (which Machiavelli never actually wrote, but probably would have heartily agreed with), has turned him into an apologist for sociopaths, tyrants, and megalo-maniacs the world over. Psychologists have even developed a category of personality disorder called Machiavellianism—part of the dreaded "Dark Triad," along with narcissism and psychopathy—character-ized by extreme duplicity, amorality, and manipulation. Conscience-less con men, that is what Machiavelli's name has come to stand for.

I think this is a gross misunderstanding of both the man and his work. *The Prince* does not condone random cruelty or tyranny or violence. It is a remarkably sober look at how people take power and how they can best hold on to it and grow it. In fact, I believe *The Prince* was not a book written out of cynicism or narcissism or power lust. I believe it was a book written out of love. Not love of people—we're basically the worst, after all—but love of a city. Machiavelli loved Florence. He *really* loved Florence. He wasn't big on warm, fuzzy-type feelings, but he actually wrote in a letter to a friend, "I love my native city more than my own soul." And Machi-avelli wrote *The Prince* to try to save his city.

Machiavelli came of age during the Italian Renaissance. It was a time of amazing progress in technology, art, philosophy, and science. Leonardo da Vinci was inventing flying machines; Michelangelo was sketching out the Sistine Chapel; Botticelli was serving up curvy pink ladies on the half shell. Italy was a cultural and commercial center of the Western World. It was also a veritable bloodbath. Italy was divided into city-states that were controlled by a motley crew of powerful families, the Catholic Church, and various foreign powers. The Italian families that could have helped Italy unite and achieve stability were instead constantly slaughtering each other and local populations in seemingly endless land grabs. "The streets were filled with the parts of men," Machiavelli recalled of a particularly grisly attack on his city that took place when he was just nine years old.

And in the middle of all the chaos was the little republic of Florence, which had shaken off the shackles of a powerful despotic family just as Machiavelli was starting his career.

Florence was free! Run by a council of elected officials. It was also a puny, relatively powerless state in the middle of a country

Machiavelli described as "torn in pieces, over-run and abandoned to destruction in every shape" (Chapter XXVI, DTE). At the peak of his career, Machiavelli was essentially the secretary of state for Florence. It was his job to represent it, protect it, and execute the orders of the Florentine council. This was not easy: Florence was unarmed, broke, and didn't have much in the way of political clout. Meanwhile, Machiavelli was trying to wheel and deal with kings and princes and popes and various petty tyrants, most of whom had endless cash and big armies that could crush Florence without breaking a sweat if they wanted to. It was Machiavelli's job to convince them that they did not want to. And to defend his little republic, Machiavelli's main weapon was his wits.

Machiavelli worked his heart out on behalf of Florence, traveling almost constantly and throwing everything he had into his work. But in the end, it wasn't enough. After fifteen years of blood, sweat, and scheming, Machiavelli saw his beloved republic fall. Florence was conquered by the rich and powerful Medici family. It was a crushing blow, but Machiavelli kept on fighting for Florence and for Italy. He wrote *The Prince* to Lorenzo de' Medici, Florence's new prince, and filled it with his best advice on how to lead and create a stable, prosperous state. Machiavelli preferred republics, but if Florence was going to have a despot, Machiavelli was going to give that despot the very best advice he could, in the hopes he would be good to Florence and maybe even unite the whole of Italy. He wrote to Lorenzo that "Italy, left as without life, waits for him who shall yet heal her wounds and put an end to the ravaging and plundering . . ." (Chapter XXVI, MPE). Machiavelli even baited the hook with a tempting picture of the love and devotion that would be lavished on Lorenzo if he took this advice: "Nor can one express the love with which he would be received . . . What door would be closed to him? . . . What Italian would refuse him homage?" (Chapter XXVI, MPE).

The more I have learned about Machiavelli and his situation at the time he wrote *The Prince*, the more I have come to think that this enticing plea to Lorenzo and *The Prince* itself is the equivalent of writing a letter to your ex's new bae, telling her how to make him happy and have the most stable and successful relationship possible with him, and even throwing in a few practical tips about dietary restrictions, turn-ons, and how he takes his coffee. You would have to *really* love your ex. Machiavelli loved Florence like that. And *The Prince* was his love letter.

And that love letter turned out to be a work of genius. *The Prince* changed the way people saw strategy leadership and human nature forever. Machiavelli's work had a clarity and a fresh intelligence that cut through Western history and the fog of politics and war like a flashlight beam. What Machiavelli offered was an unflinching and rigorous look at how people get into positions of power. And how they hold on to them.

That "how" part can be a beast, especially for women. For instance, research tells us that if a man has a cranky demeanor in a workplace, he will often be seen as a straight shooter. People will tend to trust him and see him as leadership material. If a woman has a cranky demeanor, she will be seen as difficult and bitchy and definitely *not* management material. If a man is kind and displays a sweet and helpful disposition, he will be looked upon quite favorably by colleagues and seen as good middle-management material. If a woman is kind and has a sweet demeanor, she will disappear into the wallpaper.

If this makes you angry, it should. The workplace isn't fair and it's not okay. But that is the situation we're in, so—in true Machiavellian fashion—I suggest we get the lay of the land and take it all in, identify the obstacles and advantages women have in the workplace, and look for ways forward.

What I hope to do in these pages is provide a kind of playbook for women to achieve power and prosperity in the workplace. For Machiavelli's prince, power and prosperity were measured in gold, armies, and tracts of land. But power manifests itself a little differently at the office, so I will address five of the main ways it does: money, confidence, respect, support, and title. Machiavelli used great leaders of history to inform his observations, and I will talk to some of the great women of today who are pioneers and leaders in their fields. I will also talk with working women all over the country about their experiences and what they've learned. Finally, I will look at some of the latest research about women and discrimination, negotiating, and advancement.

I will also include a few of my own workplace experiences. I, like Machiavelli, have lived a lot of this. During my fifteen years in journalism, I have stumbled into every conceivable pitfall: I've tried to hard-work my way around the glass ceiling; I've failed to negotiate; I've been overly aggressive; I've been passive-aggressive; I've cried in front of people; I've lost my temper; I've been petty; I've been two-faced; I've trusted the wrong people; I've been silent when I should have spoken up and spoken up when I should have been silent; I've been out-politicked; I've been passed over for promotions; I've been sexually harassed and called "sweetheart" and asked to fetch coffee more times than I can count. But I have also truly loved building my career. I think the workplace is glorious and I'm glad to be a part of it every day. It has been worth all the trouble and has given me so many amazing opportunities and has added so much joy and meaning to my life. And I am not an exceptional case. I am a woman in the workplace. Every single professional woman I know has run a similar gauntlet.

Of course, I can't help wondering how Machiavelli would feel about finding himself allied with a bunch of pissed-off, ambitious career women half a world away and hundreds of years in the future.

Honestly, he'd probably be psyched. He was, at his core, a practical man, and on a practical level, empowering women expands our economy and makes us all wealthier and better off. Women being shut out of the elite circles of the workforce hurts everyone. Our economy can get wealthier, stronger, more innovative, and more sustainable, and women are key. Also, Machiavelli loved attention, and he especially loved attention from women. So, Machiavelli, from a woman in a country you barely knew existed, working a job that would make no sense to you, five hundred years in the future: This one's for you.

1

Machiavelli's Playbook

"Since it is my intention to say something which will be of practical use . . . I have thought it proper to represent things as they are in real truth, rather than as they are imagined."
—Machiavelli, *The Prince* (Chapter XV)

Machiavelli wrote *The Prince* for women in the workplace. Granted, he himself might be pretty surprised to hear this—he wasn't exactly a champion of gender equality—but he writes, in the beginning of *The Prince*, that there are two kinds of princes: those who inherit their kingdoms and those who take control of a kingdom through conquest. For a prince who inherits his kingdom, Machiavelli writes, things are generally pretty cushy: the people are used to him, "his subjects will be naturally well disposed towards him," and for him to lose his position, he *really* has to screw up (Chapter II, MPE). You can think of college-educated white men as the inheriting princes of the workplace, and Machiavelli did not write *The Prince* for them.

The conquering prince, on the other hand, is in a very tricky position and "difficulties abound" (Chapter III, DTE): He just took over a new land, things are in flux, and everyone is skeptical of him—like, "Wait, who is this guy we're suddenly supposed to be taking orders from?"

It is for the conquering prince that Machiavelli wrote his most famous work. As women in the workplace, we are the conquering princes. Women have arrived in the American workplace! We are getting the degrees and we're in all the industries and we're rising through the ranks! This is good news and a real and substantial victory, but the workplace is still new territory for us. Change is incredibly hard. The patriarchy is not going quietly, and if the data is telling us anything, it's that we need to change our tactics.

As luck would have it, *The Prince* is a brilliant tactical guide for how to gain and hold power over a newly conquered land. It is not a book about war (although Machiavelli is generally very enthusiastic about war); it's a book for what to do after you win the war (the après war, if you will): You got the degree! The job! The big assignment you never thought you'd get! It's yours! Now what? How do you keep the gains? How do you grow them?

Machiavelli's Big Break

Machiavelli himself was a bit of a new prince. Nobody is quite sure how he got his first government job, but everybody agrees it was a total coup. Machiavelli was hired as a low-level diplomat when he was twenty-nine, and he was very far from a shoo-in for the position. He was not from the "right" family. His father was trained as a lawyer but had gone bankrupt, lost his license, and was reduced to trying to scratch out a living from his property. That didn't go so well: He was always in terrible debt, and Niccolò and his family grew up in near poverty. However, Machiavelli's father loved literature, history, and learning. There are even stories of him trading chunks of land for books. One thing is sure: Machiavelli Sr. spent some of the money he did have educating his son in what seems to have been a pretty over-the-top way, considering the family's situation. Niccolò Machiavelli got a full, classical education and was instilled with a deep and lifelong love of history and literature. That may have been what helped get him his job. Still, Machiavelli's spotty family history was a drag on him his entire career. Nobody worked harder than Machiavelli. He was, by all accounts, brilliant at his job, a tireless worker, and well-liked by his colleagues. But he was held back from a bunch of promotions and high-profile assignments because he simply didn't have the pedigree.

The Power Principle

Power is an interesting concept. Although it is the main focus of Machiavelli's book, he never explicitly defines it. So what is it? What is this thing Machiavelli is obsessing over?

Power doesn't exactly have the best reputation. Say the word and it conjures up images of men in expensive suits behind giant desks, screwing over investors; General Patton barking at a bunch of faceless troops that America will not tolerate a loser; the Eye of Sauron crushing little Frodo. Power has become, I think, synonymous with the ability to force people to do things. If someone is described as being power hungry or drunk on power, it is not a compliment (at least, not for most people. Maybe for Sauron).

I don't think "power" in the way we commonly think of it is what most women want: The ability to crush underlings is not a life goal for most well-adjusted people. But that does not mean women aren't interested in power. I think what women want in the workplace has a lot more to do with the original meaning of the word. Its original Anglo-French root, *poeir*, means "to be able." I think that's a very useful definition. Power means being able to do things, to have agency and be the masters of our own fates. Women in the workplace want *to be able.*

Of course, for most of recorded history, being a woman has largely been defined by *not* being able: not being able to own property, vote, smoke cigarettes, get an education, drive, practice most professions, travel alone, live alone, or participate in government. In literature and on-screen, when women weren't being locked in towers, married off to secure some political alliance, or manic-pixie-drifting through some guy's hero journey, they were home waiting for their husbands/fathers/brothers/boyfriends/baby daddies to come back. Women weren't where the action was. Women waited. Any power women had was confined to martyr-like virtue or a whisper in the ear of a man who actually did have power; see Lady Macbeth, Scheherazade, Medea, Ophelia, Cleopatra, Penelope. Even today, women tend to fit into these roles. Take the hit TV series *Game of Thrones*, which seemed, for years, to be a narrative all about strong women seizing power. The show systematically destroyed every powerful woman in the last few episodes of the show. Most offensively, Khaleesi Daenerys Targaryen—breaker of chains, mother of dragons—who, after commanding armies, traversing continents, raising actual dragons, outsmarting wizards and kings, and striding naked out of multiple burning buildings, went crazy when her boyfriend dumped her. She went so crazy, her lousy boyfriend was forced to kill her and hand the kingdom over to a white guy from a good family. These are the stories we take in all our lives. It's no wonder the world has issues with women in power.

Just look at the difference in how we use the words *prince* and *princess*. If a man is a prince, he is a model citizen, a cut above the rest, and everybody wants a piece of him. If a woman is a princess, she is difficult, entitled, demanding, and you *soooo* don't want to be in her bridal party.

What Is Standing Between Us and Power?

What is the difference between the inheriting prince and a new prince? A little bit of historical precedent and a sweet family crest, but mostly it's a story. In fact, the main obstacle between women and power is not a sexist manager or an oppressive organization or even the dreaded patriarchy. It is a story of our own worth.

The story is, quite simply, that women are less valuable than men are. Dr. Cecilia L. Ridgeway is a Stanford University sociologist and author of *Status: Why Is It Everywhere? Why Does It Matter?* She says women, by and large, are considered to be "low-status" and men—college-educated white men, specifically—are considered to be "high-status." High-status people typically "set the agenda": They talk a lot, make decisions, and have strong opinions. Low-status people follow the agenda: They listen a lot, execute orders, and make sure high-status people have the support and resources they need—they are essentially the Igors and Renfields to the high-status Dr. Frankensteins and Count Draculas.

Leaders are, by definition, high-status. So when women are in leadership positions, it often does not sit well with people. Imagine if you saw a twelve-year-old scolding her parents or the office intern started laying out his vision for the company to the CEO; those are low-status people behaving in a high-status way, and it can stir up strong emotions in people, like shock, resentment, and outrage. Those are the emotions many people feel about women in leadership roles, even if they don't want to feel that way.

But this is good news! We're not fighting anything real. We are not dealing with a lack of brains or ability or skill or work ethic. (Studies show basically everybody agrees on that.) The truth is, women already have everything they need to thrive and rise in the workplace, and the workplace will be better for it. All we have to do now is make that happen. And to do that, we need to tell a new story.

There are a bunch of things working in women's favor. First, stories change all the time. (Sixty years ago, cigarettes were good for you, marijuana was bad for you, and women didn't enjoy sex.) Also, workplaces are full of people with the best of intentions, who are ready to make changes, and who want an equal, more diverse workplace. But stories can also be formidable, because they are woven into our identities. We use stories to make sense of things, and letting go of them can make the world seem frightening and chaotic. In a way, people are fighting for their lives when they're fighting for their stories. Our stories, as David Foster Wallace pointed out, are the water we swim in.

Machiavelli Feels Your Pain

Machiavelli, incidentally, was no stranger to the awesome power of stories. In fact, when a story changed, he lost everything.

Machiavelli thrived in his job as a diplomat. For about fifteen years he was sent all over Italy and much of Western Europe to represent Florentine interests. Popes and kings knew his name; he worked on projects with Leonardo da Vinci; and he was involved in international affairs at all the highest levels. He had properties all over Tuscany, a devoted wife, six kids, and adoring friends. He was a true power player. But when he was forty-three, Machiavelli's luck ran out in a big way. The powerful Medici family seized control of Florence and, as a high-ranking member of the fallen republic, Machiavelli was stripped of his job and his money, accused of conspiracy, and thrown in jail with "shackles clawing into my ankles" and "lice so big and fat they seem like butterflies." He was tortured and interrogated for weeks, and was incredibly lucky not to have been killed. But the Medicis let him live, let him out, and ran him out of town.

It was in exile that Machiavelli wrote *The Prince*.

They say the Bedouins sang songs about water because they had no water. Niccolò Machiavelli wrote about power because, at the time he wrote *The Prince*, he had none. He had lost everything.

Machiavelli wrote *The Prince* in a tiny rural village outside Florence where his family owned a small, scruffy tavern and brothel— far from the social elites and levers of power he so loved. He spent his nights poring over ancient texts, studying the great kings and warriors of history: men who had conquered nations and created stable, prosperous kingdoms. Machiavelli confided to a close correspondent that these historical figures felt like his friends and seemed more real to him than the actual humans around him, most of whom were farmers, low-level merchants, and prostitutes. He so revered these historical figures that he would dress up in formal clothes before sitting down to do his readings, which he did alone in a small stone apartment attached to the tavern.

Machiavelli's lack of power is painfully obvious in the opening bars of *The Prince*. "Should you from the height of your greatness some time turn your eyes to these humble regions," he writes, "you will become aware how undeservedly I have to endure the keen and unremitting malignity of Fortune" (Dedication, DTE). Machiavelli wrote these words to Lorenzo de' Medici, who was, in fact, the cause of his "malignity of Fortune." *The Prince*, Machiavelli's love letter to Florence, was also a kind of cover letter. Machiavelli was hoping the book would shine so brightly, and its ideas for Florence and Italy would resonate so deeply, Lorenzo would say, *OMG, HE'S SO BRILLIANT! I DON'T CARE IF HE WORKED FOR THE OTHER SIDE, I HAVE TO HAVE THIS GUY ADVISING ME!*

The Prince was Machiavelli's *Say Anything* boom box moment to the powers that were. He writes, heartbreakingly, that the work represents the very best he has inside of him: "Though I deem the work unworthy of your greatness," he writes to Lorenzo, "yet I am bold enough to hope that your courtesy will dispose you to accept it, considering that I can offer you no better gift than . . . all that in the course of so many years, and at the cost of so many hardships and dangers, I have learned, and know" (Dedication, DTE). This is how the great and ruthless Machiavelli begins his book: begging the man who took everything from him to pity him and let him back into the fold. *The Prince*! The great treatise on power! The infamous guide to being unapologetically ruthless! And it starts out in the most submissive, pathetic way imaginable. He apologizes. He flatters. He grovels. And after all of this cringe-worthy bowing and scraping he actually delivers. In *The Prince*, Machiavelli lays out some of the boldest, most original ideas of his day. He looks at things with an honest (if slightly cynical) eye and speaks his truth—an uncomfortable and shocking truth that shook the very foundations of humanism, which Cicero had laid down centuries before. Machiavelli's observations were not noble or soaring. They were not inspiring or heartwarming. They did not make you feel good about human beings. But they were real— born of the bloody, vicious feuds Machiavelli had witnessed during his life and career and had studied from centuries past. Now *that* is a boom box moment if ever there was one.

Except that it didn't work. It seems Lorenzo never even bothered to read the book. *The Prince* did get some attention, but it was mostly shock and horror at what Machiavelli had written, culminating in a threat from the all-powerful Catholic Church to excommunicate anybody who bought the book (which, I can only imagine, was very hard on sales).

On top of being broke, exiled, and unemployable, Machiavelli was now notorious and despised. He did not get his job back. He did not return to Florence in triumph, and his city and his country were not saved by him. Machiavelli was crushed by this turn of events and wrote to his friend, "I shall continue, then, among my lousy doings, without finding a man who remembers my service or who believes that I can be good for anything."

Machiavelli went from being a power player, a patriot, and a political savant to a disgraced traitor and a villain. When a story changed, he lost everything and found himself in the same position as many women in the workplace: on the outside looking in, for reasons that had nothing to do with merit.

Machiavelli knew the powerful role stories could play in our lives all too well. So what is Machiavelli's advice when you're going up against a story that is holding you back?

Machiavelli's Lesson: Don't Blink

One of Machiavelli's main messages in *The Prince* is one of the simplest and also one of the most difficult: See the situation you're in clearly. Face reality. Don't blink.

Machiavelli thought the inability (or unwillingness) to see things as they were was one of the most common pitfalls for princes. In *The Prince* he recounts many instances of leaders and generals who refused to look at the reality of their situation and who lost battles or kingdoms as a result. His conclusion: Fully facing reality is crucial, even for the cleverest, most prepared prince, because "the times are more powerful than our brains."

It's human to want to avoid bad things and not look at something ugly. There's a reason kids lie paralyzed with terror under their comforters, convinced there is a monster under the bed, without actually ever just looking to see. Facing discrimination can feel like this: You've already put up with years of unfairness—a harder time getting hired, a harder time getting promoted, lower pay, a more critical eye on your work, harassment, disrespect in all its glorious and glittering forms—not to mention the regular challenges of a workplace: endless meetings, toxic colleagues, bad managers, layoffs, crazy politics, budget cuts, your yogurt getting stolen out of the communal fridge. And now you're supposed to focus on a big, systemic problem like discrimination? Just so you *really see it* in its full shittiness?

Yes.

To fight this monster, you need to know it. That is not easy. Most people will do almost anything to avoid looking and, for that reason, there is a major denial problem around gender discrimination in the workplace. *Me? Sexist? No way! I voted for Hillary!* The truth is, we all have gender issues. They're pretty impossible to avoid, given the culture we've grown up in. Most people don't mean to discriminate. They will tell you—and 100 percent believe—that discrimination is wrong: They would never do it and have never done it. The truth is, they almost certainly have and will again.

That denial is insidious. Institutions that claim to be meritocracies have been shown to have bigger gender discrimination problems than institutions that acknowledge having a problem. Similarly, people who think of themselves as super-woke, color-blind, equal-opportunity-for-all types tend to discriminate far more than people who acknowledge they have biases.

But this denial doesn't just come from companies or managers. You will, quite crushingly, often hear this denial from women themselves. Carly Fiorina, upon becoming the CEO of Hewlett-Packard in 1999, used the occasion to announce that her appointment was proof that gender discrimination was no longer a problem.

"I hope that we are at a point that everyone has figured out that there is not a glass ceiling," she declared at a news conference. Six years later she was pushed out of the company and largely blamed gender discrimination.

This brings us to the final place you will see denial: from yourself. Seeing discrimination is a tricky business. For one thing, it can be really hard to know if you've been a victim of gender discrimination or if things just didn't break your way. Maybe Joe *was* a little more qualified for that position. Maybe Jerry *should* be paid a little bit more. To complicate things, Joe and Jerry are usually hardworking, qualified people who are just trying to get their shot, too.

Dr. Stefanie K. Johnson studies gender discrimination and harassment at the University of Colorado Boulder's Leeds School of Business. She sees this denial all the time: "I can't tell you the number of women I interviewed who are like, 'I've never experienced sexism. Everyone loves me!' And it turns out they have been sexually harassed and passed over for jobs." This denial, says Stefanie, comes from a self-protective place: "It's actually more detrimental to your self-esteem to admit you're being discriminated against than it would be just to say, 'I wasn't good enough,'" she explains. "'I wasn't good enough' means 'I can get better!' But 'People just hate women' means 'I'm never gonna get over this.'"

Joan C. Williams, gender researcher and coauthor (with Rachel Dempsey) of *What Works for Women at Work: Four Patterns Working Women Need to Know*, was a law professor at a major university for years, and says everyone in her department thought of her as the proverbial dragon lady: "I was a bitch for twenty-five years," she says. Joan thought it was happening because she wasn't as good at office politics as her male colleagues. "Then I realized that it wasn't that I was politically maladroit; I was just encountering a lot of gender bias. Office politics are just a lot more difficult for women than they are for men." There was relief in realizing this, but there was also a lot of pain. Joan says the way she was treated in her workplace took a major toll on her and her family. "I was an angry person for a really long time," she says. "So it's really a bummer."

Joan's takeaway: "Women can totally crush it at work, so long as they're about twice as politically savvy as men." That's a lot of savvy on top of a day job. And a family. And gas bills. And getting in your ten thousand steps.

Ladies, I ask you now to face the monster—a story that is big and insidious and ugly and entrenched and powerful and destructive and annoyingly hard to kill. The reason I ask you to do this is that facing this monster is essential to slaying it.

Meet the Monster!

Individual situations can be murky, but the data shows us the glass ceiling is real. In one study (that made me want to set myself on fire, incidentally), subjects were given two (fake) résumés of applicants for a management position at a construction company. The "female" résumé had more education, and the "male" résumé had more job experience. The group was asked, before seeing the résumés, which quality was more important for the job, and determined education was more important. But guess what? After seeing the résumés, the group picked the man's résumé, saying his experience put him over the top and the woman's education just wasn't equal to it. But when the names were switched—when the man's name was on the résumé that had more education and the woman's name was on the résumé with more job experience—the man's résumé was seen as superior, citing education as the more important qualification.

In a study out of Yale University, identical résumés were topped either with a male or a female name. Study participants were asked to assess the résumés and find the best candidate for an entry-level STEM job. Not only did they think the man was more qualified for the job, they also thought he should get paid more.

When gender is taken out of the equation and people are simply judged on merit, these issues vanish. In a study by Harvard University economist Claudia Goldin, when a professional orchestra auditioned people behind a screen (so nobody knew whether the musician was a woman or a man), women were 50 percent more likely to advance in the audition process and 250 percent more likely to get the job.

Ladies, if you needed some cold, hard evidence, here it is: People's ideas of what makes someone qualified for a job, how much someone should get paid, and even how well a person knows their way around a bassoon will literally change to justify their own (certainly unconscious) biases.

So, okay, the glass ceiling is there. But how does our monster manifest? How does it show up in women's careers? There are a couple of main ways:

The Cinderella Syndrome

As long as we're talking about princes, we might as well invoke a princess. A major way the glass ceiling shows up is something I've come to think of as the Cinderella Syndrome. In the fairy tale, the good and beauteous Cinderella wants to go to the ball, but there is an obstacle in her way: namely, the evil stepmother, who does not want Cinderella to attend the ball lest she take attention away from her own two daughters. But does the stepmother say, "NO WAY, Cinderella! I'm never letting you go to the ball. I've got two ugly daughters I need to marry off, and the last thing I need is *you*, with your perfect hair and tiny feet, swanning around, making them look EVEN WORSE THAN THEY ALREADY DO!" No. The stepmother tells Cinderella, "Sure thing! Of course you can go to the ball! I'm just going to need you to clean the entryway, mop the floors, polish the silver, iron the napkins, wash all the clothes, mow the lawn, and figure out how many angels can dance on the head of a pin! And then you can 100 percent go to the ball! I'll totally even help with your hair! So fun!"

The stepmother holds out the illusion of possibility to Cinderella, and Cinderella—who, OMG, needed Machiavelli so much more than a fairy godmother—takes the stepmother at her word and dutifully starts in on the list of tasks. Meanwhile, it's all a win for the stepmother: She avoided an unpleasant conversation, blocked Cinderella from attending the ball, and has the cleanest floors in town.

Women in the workplace get put in this position all the time. Whereas men are typically promoted based on what people perceive their potential to be, women are typically promoted based on actual work they've done (usually again and again and again). This slows women down substantially in early and mid-career: Women are told they can get that promotion or raise if they just do this *one more thing.* Meanwhile, Randy and Jerry saunter on into the ball without so much as washing a dish.

Why is this? I put this question to Dr. Alice Eagly, coauthor (with Linda L. Carli) of *Through the Labyrinth: The Truth About How Women Become Leaders.* Alice says a lot of the problem is rooted in something social scientists call "confirmation bias." That is, when people experience something that confirms a pre-held idea, they tend to remember it. When they see something that goes against their preconceived ideas, they tend to forget it or ignore it.

This makes sense. If you think Jenny is a really sweet person and she is really mean to you one day, you would tend to think that Jenny is just having a bad day, not that she's actually a mean person. On the other hand, if you think Jill is a bad person who is out to get you, and one day she brings you a coffee, you are probably not going to think Jill is actually a sweet person and you just misread her. You are more likely to assume Jill wants something from you or, possibly, has spit in the coffee. That's confirmation bias.

Here is how this comes into play with gender: People have strong preconceived notions about what makes a good leader, and those qualities include being aggressive, assertive, logical, self-confident, ambitious, visionary, brave, and demanding. Leaders don't care too much what people think; they are action oriented and they are not afraid to grab the spotlight. If you look at the qualities people associate with masculinity, the crossover is almost 100 percent. An ideal man is supposed to be aggressive, ambitious, dominant, self-confident, and forceful, as well as self-reliant and individualistic. The takeaway: Being a good man and a good leader are one and the same.

Now, if you contrast leadership qualities with the qualities people associate with femininity, you see a very different picture. The qualities people associate with an ideal woman are someone who is affectionate, helpful, sympathetic, sensitive, gentle, soft-spoken, modest, and puts others first.

These are all admirable traits, but they're not exactly qualities you want in someone who is going to, say, lead troops into battle or make a life-or-death call in surgery. The implication: You can be a good leader. You can be a good woman. But you can't be both.

None of this is new. When Machiavelli laid out the best qualities a prince could have back in the 1500s, he named "greatness, courage, gravity, and fortitude." The worst qualities? "To be considered fickle, frivolous, effeminate, mean-spirited, irresolute" (Chapter XIX, MPE). That's right, being effeminate is one of the worst qualities a leader can have. You definitely don't want a ladylike leader! The horror! The horror! Oh, how the times haven't changed.

The result: When a man displays leadership qualities or does exceptional work, everyone remembers it and he gets rewarded. He has confirmed people's preconceived ideas about what a leader should look like and makes them feel good about their stories. He will, in all likelihood, rise to a leadership position quickly and with great enthusiasm on the part of everyone around him. If he stumbles in that position, people are apt to dismiss it as a one-off (like Jenny on her bad day), and he'll be given another chance or two to prove himself.

But when a woman displays leadership qualities or does exceptional work, people will often not register it, or they will see it as *good* work but not quite enough to justify a promotion. The woman will have to display these qualities or produce this amazing work over and over again. That's because the woman doesn't match the image of "leader" people have in their heads. She makes them feel uncomfortable about their stories. Think about how many coffees Jill would have to buy you before you'd assume she actually was a good person whom you had simply misjudged. Like, twenty coffees? And even that might not do it.

Of course, if the woman messes up—if she gets a shot and stumbles—she often can't recover at all. (Imagine if Jill, amid all the coffee gifting, says something mean to you in a meeting. The dozens of free coffees would immediately fade into the background and you'd think, "Same old Jill. I *knew* I couldn't trust her.")

And this leads us to the second major issue women encounter in the workplace.

The Hotbox

This is a term I got from a particularly scarring experience on my grade school T-ball team (which was, in and of itself, a scarring experience, so you can imagine). During one game, I hit the ball off the T and took off running. I got to first base and noticed the outfielders were scrambling for the ball, so I started running for second base. Then one of the outfielders got the ball and threw it to second base. I remember the second baseman's smug face as the ball smacked his mitt. But I was not on second base yet, so I turned back toward first base. As I ran, I saw the ball zip by my head and—*thwack*—the first baseman had the ball. Panting, I turned to run back to second base, when of course the first baseman threw the ball to the second baseman. This situation, I later learned, is called a hotbox: You're not technically out, but you're trapped in a losing situation. I ended up running back and forth between bases a bunch of times before finally giving up and walking, exhausted and trying not to cry, back to the bench.

The Hotbox is something that often happens to women in mid-career, when they start getting close to leadership positions or positions of power. The two "bases" in this case are femininity and leadership qualities, and many women end up caught between these two sets of expectations, running themselves ragged in a no-win situation.

Here's how it works: If a woman displays a lot of qualities people associate with femininity—is empathetic, kind, helpful, compassionate, modest, and agreeable—she will be highly thought of and well-liked, but she will not be seen as leadership material. If a woman displays "leadership" qualities—is aggressive, outspoken, assertive, demanding, and independent—she might be seen as a serious contender for leadership roles, but she will not be well-liked. People will likely think of her as difficult, abrasive, and hard to get along with. They will often feel animosity and hostility toward her.

Here's our monster: As a woman, you are in an impossible bind of expectations. If you're kind, generous, modest, and advocate for others, you will be very highly thought of and then herded, smiling supportively, into a behind-the-scenes role where you will be chronically underpaid and loaded down with thankless work. On the other hand, if you push your ideas through and ask for more and are openly ambitious, a lot of people won't like you, and although you might snag a management position or two, you probably won't ever reach a top leadership role, because top leadership roles tend to require broad support from coworkers and superiors, and who wants to promote a cranky dragon lady?

Meanwhile, men, the inheriting princes, are allowed a wide range of behaviors. Just look at some of the most iconic male CEOs: the explosive genius; the geeky, distracted type with no social skills; the calculating, cold-blooded mastermind; the slick douchebag; the affable jock who drinks a little too much at the holiday party. Women CEOs don't have these tropes. Honestly, they can't afford to. Cranky, entitled women won't get far. Explosive genius ladies will be sacked. Head-in-the-clouds women with no social skills will be shunted to a windowless office in subbasement C faster than you can say "THIS IS SO FUCKING UNFAIR!"

Machiavelli's conquering prince is in a similar double bind, although his is a bit bloodier in nature. The new prince has very likely won his kingdom through battle. Now he has to win loyalty and devotion from the people he's just conquered. Mind you, these are people whose friends and neighbors he has, in all likelihood, just slaughtered and whose barns he has probably just burned down. "The Prince cannot avoid giving offence to his new subjects . . . ," Machiavelli writes. "However . . . it is essential that in entering a new Province you should have the good will of its inhabitants (Chapter III, DTE)." In other words, to win your new kingdom, you had to do things that made the locals hate you. To keep your new kingdom, you need to get the locals to like you: Ye Olde Hotbox.

All That and Racism, Too

Being a "woman of color" means enduring all the discrimination and stereotyping white women experience on top of the discrimination and stereotyping that come with racism. The Hotbox women of color experience is particularly extreme.

Dr. Tina Opie, a workplace consultant and professor of management at Babson College, has studied workplace discrimination for decades. "Black women are the first ones to get laid off. We're the last ones to get hired. We get paid far less than white women do," she explains. "Our behavior and our appearance tend to be policed much more stringently." Before going into academia, Tina worked in banking and corporate consulting and says she constantly had her clothing, hair, and mannerisms critiqued by colleagues. "I can't even count the examples. I was told that I speak in too 'ethnic' of a way, because I use my hands to punctuate ideas," she recalls. "So I'm too 'ethnic.' That was the word they used."

Dr. Isabel Escobar is a professor of chemical engineering at the University of Kentucky. She says as a Latina, her emotional reactions get far more scrutiny than those of her white colleagues. Isabel is deeply committed to her work and says that sometimes manifests itself emotionally. "If I am beside myself with anger and frustration, I will cry. It's true," she says, laughing. "I am fully in control of what I'm saying and my emotions, but the tears just come." When this happened at a previous workplace, Isabel says she was infantilized by colleagues: "Like 'Calm down, Isabel. Let's take a deep breath.' It was parental. Like 'Okay, sweetheart, would you like some water?' " Isabel says it was infuriating. She was just feeling frustrated and a couple of tears had rolled down her face, and the narrative had suddenly become that she was "the hot-blooded Latina."

Women of color will also get the message that they don't belong in certain jobs or professions. Often these messages aren't intentional, but they are constant. Lisa Gelobter is the CEO of tEQuitable, a software company that helps businesses address harassment and discrimination. She is a Black woman who has worked in tech for decades. Still, Lisa says she can't even count the number of times she has been mistaken for someone's personal assistant and asked to order lunch.

Lisa recalls one time in particular, a man from another company was visiting her workplace and asked her, "Oh, do you support Digital?"—thinking she was an assistant for someone on the digital team. "At the time I ran Digital," Lisa says.

LGBTQ

Lesbian, gay, bisexual, transgender, queer, and nonbinary workers have an extra-tough time in the workplace. Problems with bullying and harassment—particularly sexual harassment—are extremely common. LGBTQ workers have a harder time getting hired, are often held back from promotions, and receive lower pay than their male and straight cis coworkers. Unemployment rates for LGBTQ workers are consistently higher than they are for the overall population. As a result, nearly half of bisexual and transgender women live below the poverty line.

Sharita Gruberg is the senior director of LGBTQ research at the Center for American Progress. She says data about the LGBTQ community in the workplace is pretty sobering. More than a third of LGBTQ workers say they have experienced discrimination at work. "There was one woman working in an elder care setting who was really being harassed by her coworkers," Sharita recalls. "She had her car keyed; she had her tires flattened." Eventually the woman was fired and was informed, in writing, that she was being let go because she was gay. The woman had no legal recourse because what the company had done was not technically illegal in her state at the time. "It was unbelievable," says Sharita.

The Results

The Cinderella Syndrome and the Hotbox combine to create what researchers call an "accumulation of disadvantage"—a slightly lower starting salary here, a slower promotion there—and after ten years of being in the workforce, women are in a significantly different place professionally and financially than the men they started out alongside.

Consider this: Young, single women in urban areas out-earn their male counterparts, but by mid-career they've been left in the statistical dust. So much so that by the time they retire, they have less than a third of the savings men do and they're much more likely to be living below the poverty line.

Machiavelli's Lesson: Embrace the Struggle

So the monster has been looked over in all its horrifying detail: You are paid less, promoted more slowly, and harassed. You also have a more critical eye cast on your work, appearance, speech, and emotions. What now? Other than sinking into a pit of despair, where do you go from here?

To the top! And my favorite fighting words come from Machiavelli himself. Machiavelli observed that princes who had to struggle for their kingdoms actually did better in the long run than the princes who had everything handed to them. "They who . . . acquire with difficulty . . . keep with ease," he writes (Chapter VI, DTE). Machiavelli noted that inheriting princes often lost their kingdoms because they didn't know what to do when the going got tough: "The prince who relies entirely on fortune is lost when it changes (Chapter XXV, MPE)." Machiavelli's lesson: Your hardships are setting you up for success—not only to get what you want, but to keep it. "Princes become great," he writes, "by vanquishing difficulties and opposition" (Chapter XX, DTE).

Machiavelli's Moment of Zen

No, you're not crazy. It's real. Discrimination in the workplace is shockingly entrenched and it holds women back in all kinds of ways. It is easy to become discouraged, depressed, and enraged when you experience discrimination and read the depressing statistics about it. That is why people don't want to face this monster in the first place. But take heart! Inside all of that darkness is a gift: That struggle is making you strong. That might sound trite or saccharine, but Machiavelli was neither of those things, and he felt so strongly about the value of hardship, he has a rare Zen moment in *The Prince* of the "things happen *for* me, not *to* me" variety. "Fortune," he writes, "especially when she desires to make a new prince great . . . causes enemies to arise and form designs against him, in order that he may have the opportunity of overcoming them . . ." (Chapter XX, MPE). That's an extraordinary thing to say, especially coming from a man who had just lost his job and his good name, and had been jailed and tortured. Machiavelli's conclusion: Great leaders become great because of hardship and struggle.

2

Money

Adele Lim: The Value of Knowing Your Worth

"Where the willingness is great, the difficulties cannot be great . . ."

—Machiavelli, *The Prince* (Chapter XXVI, MPE)

One of the main ways power is reflected in the workplace is pay. Pay is also one of the clearest, most concrete ways we see discrimination against women in the workplace. The silver lining here is that, unlike with many forms of discrimination, you can actually measure it. Economists call it the "gender pay gap"; really, though, that's just a fancy name for women earning less money than men for the same work. Women earn roughly 80 cents for every dollar a man makes. For African American women, it's about 60 cents on the dollar. Native American and Hispanic women earn about 55 cents for every dollar a man earns.

The pay gap closed steadily between 1980 and 2000, as more women entered the workforce and caught up with men in terms of education and experience. But about twenty years ago the pay gap stopped shrinking. More and more women got degrees and entered the workforce, but the pay gap didn't really budge.

Money is nothing more than an abstraction, an agreed-upon fiction that we all use to express the value of something. This is what makes money a particularly emotional subject. If money is an expression of value and women are paid less than men, it means women are valued less than men in the workplace: Their time and efforts and ideas and output are worth less because they came from a woman instead of a man. If Black women, Native American women, and Hispanic women earn less than white women, it means our society values the work, time, and efforts of these women less than those of white women. The next time you're getting a coffee, think about the fact that your white male barista is earning roughly twice the salary of the Latina standing next to him.

In fact, the gender pay gap was my first introduction to discrimination in the workplace. The first job I got in public radio was as an entry-level producer. It involved working the graveyard shift and pulling down a cool $35,000 a year. My twenty-six-year-old self was over the moon. Thirty-five thousand dollars felt like a fortune. But, most important, I was in! I had a job in radio! I was going to be a journalist! Not only that, but two of my good friends, whom I will call Josh and Ellen, had also just been hired by the same place. We were all very excited and went out to brunch to celebrate. We were toasting our new jobs when Josh mentioned how low the pay was. Ellen groaned in agreement. We'd all tried to negotiate for higher salaries and we'd all failed. We were laughing and griping about work, and I was drinking a cocktail at brunch. This was hard-core adulting. It felt like a dream.

"I mean, listen, it's just an entry-level job, but $45,000 a year? That's barely enough to live on!" said Josh.

I felt my stomach drop. "You're getting $45,000?"

"Yeah . . . Aren't you?" he asked.

"No." There was a long pause.

"But we all have the same job!" Josh sounded panicked. "We have the same experience. It's the same job!" Ellen's eyes filled with tears. I put my hand on her arm.

"I'm making $35,000," I said.

"I'm making $32,000," she said.

Josh was a white man, I was a white woman, and Ellen was a

woman of color. Our salaries were almost perfectly aligned with national statistics. The rest of the brunch was awful. A job and a salary that had felt like a dream just a minute before now felt like a slap in the face.

Women Don't Ask!

I once had a male colleague tell me very matter-of-factly that the reason women got paid less was that they accepted lower pay. I remember consciously suppressing the urge to rip his arm off and beat him with it. Really, though, he was just parroting the thing people often think about the gender pay gap: It's our own fault.

Women don't ask.

This is probably the explanation I hear most often when a conversation about gender and pay comes up. The really annoying part is, it's true. One famous study from 2002 found that only 7 percent of women negotiated their starting salaries, while 57 percent of men did. The kicker: One in five women reported that they had never negotiated their pay at all. Ever.

All of this seems pretty damning. We're wimping out! We're not asking for what we deserve, so we're not getting it. There's truth in this, but the reasons behind it are complicated. In fact, Dr. Linda Babcock, the Carnegie Mellon University economist who did that famous study and later wrote (with Sara Laschever) a book on the subject, *Women Don't Ask: The High Cost of Avoiding Negotiation— and Positive Strategies for Change*, says she has been truly dismayed that her careful, nuanced research has been used to essentially blame women for the gender pay gap.

Shortly after her book came out, one of Linda's students called to tell her that the ultraconservative radio personality Rush Limbaugh was talking about her research on his show. "He was saying, 'Now we know why women don't get paid as much as men and it's because it's all their fault,'" Linda recalls. "And, basically, I wanted to put my head into an oven." Had Rush read a bit farther, he *might* have realized there was a little more to it. In fact, Linda says, in some cases, women choosing *not* to negotiate their salaries is the savvy, Machiavellian move.

I know this might sound like feminist sacrilege—how could not advocating for yourself or speaking up for your worth possibly be a Machiavellian move?—but it's the truth. And I think it's important to spend some time on this because I have spoken to so many women over the years (and have been one of those women) who were ashamed that they didn't negotiate or didn't negotiate hard enough, or who discovered they were paid less than a male colleague and blamed themselves. But a lot of times, when women don't make the ask or back down in a negotiation, it's because they think if they push for more, bad things could happen. And they are not wrong.

Here's the painful truth: When it comes to asking for more money, the Machiavellian woman sees a situation where the downside is certain and the upside is iffy. So she doesn't ask.

Why Women Don't Ask

The reasons women don't ask are complicated and, of course, vary from person to person. But exploring them is key to understanding the gender pay gap and, ultimately, to closing it. I've identified five of the major obstacles women encounter around salary and salary negotiation. So let's meet the money monster!

1. Women Are Happy with Less

As women, most of us already know we're being paid less because of our gender. *So why aren't we demanding more?* Where is the outrage? Where are the demands for company salary reviews? Where are the torches? The pitchforks? The flaming Epiladies?

Women aren't as angry as they should be about lower pay. In fact, in a lot of cases, women aren't angry at all. Most women feel they are fairly compensated in their jobs in spite of a mountain range of evidence to the contrary. Here's the problem: When it comes to pay, women are too damned grateful.

This is a weird thing to address, because an attitude of gratitude has been directly linked to happiness in about a billion studies, and that is certainly worth more than a higher salary. Do I want to make everyone feel terrible and tormented just so they can earn a little more? NO! No. Of course not. But . . . also, kind of, yes.

The reason: The gratitude is coming from the wrong place. Women have lower expectations about their salaries than men do, so even when a man gets more money, he will tend to feel worse about his compensation than a woman who is getting paid less. Remember, I was thrilled to be earning $35,000 a year and my male colleague was upset about earning $45,000 for the same job. The reason for this seems to be that women are grateful to be in the workforce at all—like we're still playing dress-up and kind of can't believe we're actually getting paid to do work. The result being, when it comes to salary, women tend to focus on what they need instead of what their work is actually worth. Men tend to focus on—and be far more aware of—the market value of their skills. Because the woman expects less, she's happy with less.

2. Negotiation Is Painful

At its heart, negotiation is a kind of conflict, and women are raised to avoid conflict—especially conflict with men. Men are raised to embrace it.

Historically, women have relied on men for their livelihoods and have suffered greatly when their relationships with men suffered. Being agreeable, pleasing, and attractive and getting along with others (especially men) has historically been a life-or-death matter for women—a survival skill on a par with starting a fire or spearing a mastodon. The aversion to conflict with men is baked into our psyches. When women negotiate, it can feel dire, like your very life is at stake.

As a result, women report feeling more than twice the level of anxiety men do around negotiating and they will go to great lengths to avoid it. In one study, women were asked about negotiating the price of a car, and they said, on average, they would be willing to pay around $1,300 more for the car just to not have to negotiate. That was more than twice as much as what men were willing to pay to avoid negotiating.

3. Safety in Lower Numbers

Being paid less can make women feel safe. A woman, whom I'll call Liza, has worked in academia for years and says she actually prefers to keep her pay a bit on the low side. "I don't want to be fired because I'm earning too much," she told me. "We've all seen that happen. You're not going to stick around if you're expensive and times get tight."

But getting paid less does not protect you. In fact, it can make you vulnerable. People are shockingly basic when it comes to pay. They will often think that if someone (or something) is more expensive, it's superior. If you are underpaid, it could affect the value your employer places on your work and could even hurt your chances of getting a new job, because the potential employer might assume your current employer doesn't value you or your work very highly. This belief is powerful: Studies have shown that when medicine is more expensive, it ends up being more effective at treating an illness than the exact same medicine at a lower price. Why? Because the high price leads the people taking the medicine to *believe* it's more effective. That belief makes it real.

The same holds true with work. Youngja Yoo ran a successful flower shop in Los Angeles for years. It's a tough business that relies on regular orders (like hotels needing daily arrangements for their lobbies) and big events (like weddings). When Youngja first opened her shop, she says, a bunch of prospective customers approached her offering their regular business but demanding a big discount: "They thought, 'She has a new business, she needs customers.' They were right. I did need customers!" Still, Youngja decided not to offer a discount for her flowers. Turning down that business was scary, but ultimately it paid off. Eventually, many of those people came back to Youngja agreeing to pay full price. Why? They had gone with someone else and weren't happy with the results, and they assumed that because Youngja wouldn't give a discount, her work and her flowers must be top-quality. "They saw that *I* valued my work," explains Youngja. "So they thought, 'Her work must be very good; she won't disappoint us.' I got a lot of customers that way."

4. It Hurts to Ask

Here's the truth: People don't like it when a woman asks for more, and the woman will often be punished for it. Research has found that women who ask for more money after being offered a job are automatically considered less desirable to work with. And it does not seem to matter how they ask: Swashbuckling and aggressive, matter-of-fact, couched in apologies—it all leaves a bad taste in people's mouths. Add to that the fact that women walk into an interview far less likely to get the job than a male applicant, and you have a very compelling case for smiling and taking what they give you.

Liza, the woman who works in academia, does a lot of hiring in her job, and she has actually found herself feeling resentful when women ask for more money. She has been very distressed by her response because she has always made it a point to promote women and people of color in the workplace. Still, she says, when women have negotiated their pay with her, she has felt a negative reaction: "I got judgy about them. I thought, 'Wow that was kind of pushy . . . we pay pretty well.' And then I really question, 'Am I a self-hating woman? Am I being unfair?'" It's definitely not just Liza; it's our culture. Women lose points for asking. Men don't.

The reason: People like to see a man asking for more. The man might not get more money—even men are only successful in nego-tiation about 20 percent of the time—but he'll typically walk away with the respect of the person he asked. "We see a man being very daring and forceful, and we see that as a positive thing," says Dr. Linda Babcock, who, in addition to studying gender, has also stud-ied negotiation for thirty years. "For a woman, she can be seen quite negatively: She's aggressive. She's a bitch. It doesn't seem as reason-able for her to ask." As a result, people don't like a woman who asks for more, and they are also less likely to give her what she's asking for.

If a woman bucks the odds and *does* get what she's asking for, it's not necessarily a total victory, either. There's often lingering resentment or hostility toward her. A small monetary win can do real damage to a crucial relationship with someone who has a lot of control over your job. "You are seen as not a team player, or difficult," Linda explains. "It can have dire consequences for your career."

Liza has lived this. She used to do a lot of contract work for a large company. She had a strong track record with them and hadn't gotten a raise in years. Money started getting tight for her, so she asked the company for a higher rate—citing her years of work and the fact that her rate hadn't been adjusted in ages. The company agreed, but Liza experienced a lot of blowback: "I was reminded constantly of how expensive I was," she says. "I really wasn't even making that much. I was making way less than other people who worked there." Asking for this raise had worked, but it had also given Liza the reputation of being overpaid and high-maintenance. It added a lot of tension and hostility to her working relationship with that company. Since then, Liza has shied away from asking for raises—she's conscious of the resentment and animosity it can cause.

5. Women and Money: It's Complicated!

Women are typically taught, in all kinds of subtle and not-so-subtle ways, that money is not their realm. Many women—even young women I know—are not comfortable handling money or talking about money, and many heterosexual couples still put the man in charge of family finances. I myself, in spite of having reported on business and money for more than a decade, nearly had a panic attack in my accountant's office when I went to visit him with a complicated tax question. My accountant is one of the sweetest, calmest men alive, and still, it was terrible: My hands were shaking and I kept losing things in my purse.

Part of the reason for this is just my own personal crap, but some of it is cultural. Women dealing with money is seen as . . . a bit unseemly.

Even talking about money is dangerous terrain for women. Dr. Linda Babcock points out that supermodel Linda Evangelista was raked over the coals in 1990 after she made her legendary comment that she didn't get out of bed for less than $10,000 a day. In an interview a decade later, she said, "I feel like those words are going to be engraved on my tombstone . . . I apologized for it . . . I said it was a joke . . . Would I hope that I would never say something like that ever again? Yes."

The same year Linda made her infamous remark, *Playboy* magazine did a profile of Donald Trump in which he bragged endlessly about his wealth. "I paid twenty-nine million dollars for the Khashoggi yacht," he told the reporter. "Two years later, I'll be selling it for more than one hundred million dollars and getting a bigger one." Not only did Trump's comment get zero backlash, we eventually elected him president. If a man brags about money, it's swagger and bravado and makes him look successful. If a woman does it, she's an arrogant gold digger and she spends the next decade apologizing for it.

Women also appear far less often in the media talking about money. At NPR, we did an internal study to see how often women were tapped as experts in business and finance stories: The number was around 20 percent (the numbers were far worse for sources of color). At my show, *The Indicator* from *Planet Money*, we were horrified. (Me especially: I WAS LITERALLY WRITING A BOOK ABOUT THIS! HOW COULD I BE LETTING THIS HAPPEN? I felt so ashamed.) But in some ways, it's understandable. About 75 percent of economists are men, and the stats in banking and finance are not much better.

Machiavelli on How to Get That Bread

So this is all super discouraging. Is it even worth it to negotiate your salary? Yes, yes, yes, yes, yes, yes. YES. YESSSSSSSSSSSSSSS. Also, yes. First of all, you deserve it. If you are a lady on Earth and you work for a company run by earthlings, you are almost certainly underpaid. And the best thing you can do for yourself and for womankind is to fight to be paid as much as possible.

Also, you need the money. Women retire with a fraction of the retirement savings men have and they live significantly longer. As a result, a huge number of women live in poverty after they retire. And even if retirement seems very far off in the mists for you, keep in mind that money can impact your life in all kinds of ways. One effect of women earning less is they are more likely to stay in toxic jobs and relationships, because they feel like they can't afford to go. Money can provide freedom, stability, and security, and women aren't getting enough of those things. Ask. For. More.

Also, I think salary is tied up in feelings of worth that many women (and humans) struggle with, and for that reason alone—even if the whole thing explodes in your face like a misogynistic grenade—I would recommend that you negotiate instead. You should speak up for yourself and fight for your worth and push out of your comfort zone and stand up to the Man and to all the messed-up messaging we've all received since conception that somehow our time and efforts and ideas are worth less because of our gender.

But What if I'm Terrible at This?

Most people I know do not like negotiating and insist they're terrible at it. If you are one of these people, know that negotiating is a skill that can be practiced and perfected. When I asked negotiation expert Dr. Linda Babcock for her best advice for people who were truly hopeless at negotiating, she rejected the premise of my question outright: "That's ridiculous. I've taught negotiation for thirty years. Everyone can become a great negotiator. I truly believe that."

For the record, I am *not* a good negotiator: I don't like negotiating. I would actually rather get a cavity filled. I don't have a poker face; I fixate on little things; and I tend to make everything personal. And most of the time when I have negotiated, I have gotten very little for my pains. Looking back, part of the problem was that

I was preparing in the wrong way. I read a bunch of negotiation tips that had been written for men and they . . . did not work for me.

Case in point: starting a negotiation with an ultimatum; for example, "For a job like this, I can't take less than $80,000." This, in fact, is a tactic that can be effective for men, but it totally backfired for me. I had an employer threaten to take a job offer away when I tried this.

Another common negotiating tip: Talk yourself up! Talk about your accomplishments and make a case for why you should get this job/promotion/raise (i.e., *brag* like your house is on fire!). I dutifully tried this, too. Result: My manager said, "Wow. You definitely think a lot of yourself." I nearly burst into tears and never got around to asking for a raise.

What Works for Women

Here's my advice: Ask for more! But ask like a woman. Successfully asking for more money and not getting punished for it requires a very particular approach.

Caveat: Some of these tips may seem . . . not awesome. Pandery. Cringey. Aren't-we-past-this–y? Stone Agey. "Really it is," says gender researcher Joan C. Williams. "There's no blinking here. But my reaction always is, 'You asked me what works for women at work. What *should* work for women at work is a different thing. But being pure at the cost of tremendous personal, emotional, and career sacrifice . . . I'm not interested in that advice."

It's probably not going to come as a great surprise that Machiavelli was a big advocate for compromising to get what you want: "The manner in which we live, and that in which we ought to live, are things so wide asunder," he writes. "It is essential, therefore, for a Prince who desires to maintain his position, to have learned how to be other than good . . ." (Chapter XV, DTE). To be honest, I don't like writing these words. Part of me is proud that I'm a bad negotiator and I don't want to be "other than good" or do things like smile and laugh more in a negotiation in order to be more appealing to some stuffed shirt just so he will pay me what he's already paying Sick Day Joe, who has a fraction of my experience and never shows up to work. Still, in the end, I agree with Joan Williams: Getting paid less than you should, feeling trapped in a job or relationship, or pinching pennies in retirement are not badges of honor I can get behind.

In chapter 10 of this book, I have written a step-by-step guide to negotiating, with all the pitfalls women tend to experience, as well as some pro tips for getting around them. For now, I'll cover three of the main pillars of negotiating while female: Arm Yourself; It's Not (Just) About the Money; and Smile like You Mean It. (Yeah, I know.)

My main piece of advice going in is not to take any of this personally—that will hold you back. If you find out you're getting paid less than your male colleague or aren't getting promoted as fast as you should be, do not take it as a sign that your work isn't as good or that your manager thinks you're a sucker or a pushover. This is a huge, entrenched, systemic problem. The fact it has happened to you is normal: Venus Williams, Jennifer Lawrence, Meryl Streep, Emma Stone, Natalie Portman, Oprah Winfrey—all of these women have been paid less than the men they were working alongside. If you are a victim of the gender pay gap, you are in vast and truly wonderful company. Take comfort in that.

Machiavelli's Lesson: Arm Yourself

One of the main messages Machiavelli gives the new prince: Arm yourself. Machiavelli spent years preaching this to the Council of Florence, which had no army and was constantly at risk of being conquered by the many surrounding forces that did. "The main foundations of all States," he writes, "are good laws and good arms" (Chapter XII, DTE). Machiavelli felt so passionately about this issue that, at one point, he actually went from town to town himself, raising a little army for Florence.

In the context of a negotiation, information is your weapon. Before you go in to ask for more money, you want to arm yourself with information. Lots of information. As much information as you can legally get. Women do much better in negotiations when they have information. Dr. Linda Babcock says that's the main thing she's learned in thirty years of teaching negotiation: "Most of what determines the negotiation's success happens before you even open your mouth."

Having information does a couple of things. First, it gives you parameters: What is the salary range for this position? What do the other people who do this job get paid? How much experience do you have relative to the other people who have or have had this job? This information is critical, because it moves the negotiation away from the nebulous, emotional, and personal (where discrimination thrives) and toward the factual, rational, and concrete. Also, even if you don't trot out every fact you know, your demeanor will be different when you have the facts on your side and the negotiation is likely to be more successful.

Case in point: One woman I spoke with for the book, whom I will call Helena, was offered a job she was really excited about. There was one problem: the salary. She was offered about $80,000, which was less than she was making at the job she had. She also had the impression that the position in question generally paid a lot more—around $110,000. Helena hesitated to ask for so much more, though, because when the employer had made the initial offer, it had come with the caveat that the low salary was all the company could pay, and when Helena mentioned the amount she wanted, it was dismissed outright. Helena thought it over and decided she would be willing to take the lower salary because she was so excited about the job. But this scared her. She knew if she did accept the lower salary, she would be putting herself into a difficult financial situation (she had a mortgage and was supporting herself) and that she would be upset with herself and with her future employer before she'd even started her job.

So Helena started doing her homework. She called around to people she knew in the field and asked for the salary range for that particular position. She learned that, indeed, $110,000 was entirely in line with the industry standard and $80,000 was quite low. So she called the prospective employer and said, "I'd like to ask for a salary of $110,000. I'm happy to tell you how I got there." But, to her surprise, the employer didn't push back this time or even ask Helena how she'd gotten there. He said he needed to talk to his colleagues and then called back shortly after to say she could have the amount she wanted. He even threw in an apology, saying there had been a misunderstanding about the salary and he didn't want her to feel like she'd been lowballed. She got a $30,000 pay bump *and* an apology. Behold the power of homework.

Machiavelli's Lesson: It's Not (Just) About the Money

Money can be one of the hardest things to negotiate because it can seem like a zero-sum game: A company has only so much money to spend, and if they pay you more of it, they have less of it. So one thing that's helpful in negotiation is to think of other things you want in addition to money. This is a negotiation tactic known as logrolling: You bring a bunch of different elements into a negotiation, which broadens the conversation and helps you get more. Sure, you want more money, but what else do you want? A different title? A chance to get on (or off) a particular project? The ability to do freelance work outside the company? More vacation time? Is there a conference you want to attend? Training you'd like to get? A onetime bonus (often easier to get than a permanent raise)? All of these things cost money—they are all tantamount to a raise—but employers will sometimes be more willing to pony up this kind of thing. If a negotiation is stalling, this gives you options.

Negotiation expert Linda Babcock recommends thinking of ten different things you want and introducing those as options during critical moments in a negotiation: "People often make the mistake of fixating on one thing. 'Here is how it *has* to be. I want it this one way.'" Linda says other things, like a promotion, an assistant, or Fridays working from home might be worth a lot to you and might be easier for your boss to provide right away.

Machiavelli's Lesson: Smile Like You Mean It

A good woman is kind, collaborative, compassionate, modest, and grateful. She smiles a lot. That is what the data tells us, anyway. These beliefs are annoying and destructive, but in the spirit of "other than good," you can use them to your advantage. As a woman going into a negotiation, it helps to have an attitude of gratitude.

I KNOW! I was just saying how women are too grateful. But this is *strategic* gratitude: Women don't tend to get what they want in a combative or competitive atmosphere. (Men, on the other hand, often will.) By opening with gratitude, you are setting a positive, collaborative tone for this meeting. Find something you are genuinely excited about and grateful for in your job or in a prospective job. Express that first and then pivot to what you want. You LOVE this job! You LOVE this company! You are *so excited* for your future here! You are *so inspired* by the work the company does! You want to contribute in ever greater ways! But in order to work at your highest level, you will need to get paid in a way that reflects the work you're doing.

I'm telling you, it's extremely annoying to even write this, but we are talking about Machiavelli, who wasn't interested in what felt good or even what was morally right. He was interested in what worked. Positivity works. Gratitude works. Research shows us that—get ready for it—your negotiation will go better if you are friendly and smile and emphasize common interests and your personal relationship. Essentially, what you're trying to do here is reset the typical negotiation dynamic of the company versus you and, instead, create a collaborative, win-win mentality.

Linda Babcock says a good tool to use is something that is actually the result of centuries of destructive cultural conditioning. "As women, we tend to be more accommodating," she says. "We're good at figuring out what people want. That's a really important part of negotiation: figuring out how the other side sees things."

Think about what your manager and your company want and figure out how giving you more money (or whatever you're asking for) will help *them* get what they want. Do they want you to work longer hours? Do they want to think of themselves as a place that pays women equally? Do they want to increase sales? Do they want more clients? More publicity? More output? More diversity? Can you help make that happen? When negotiating while female, it's all about "we."

As Linda puts it, "What's going to make your employer *want* you to earn more? Something like 'I really want to advance in this company. I'd love to talk with you about how I can do that.'" You're not asking for a raise; you're asking your employer to plan an exciting and mutually beneficial future with you (which just *happens* to involve you getting paid more)! Frame everything you ask for in terms of *everyone* getting what they want.

Silver lining: Studies have shown that when people negotiate in this way, they are able to "enlarge the pie"; in other words, they come to agreements that benefit everyone. In this way a woman's disadvantage in negotiating becomes a kind of superpower. By reframing a negotiation as working toward a common good instead of creating some kind of high noon situation, you direct your power in a way that benefits everyone.

ADELE LIM:
The Value of Knowing Your Worth

There aren't a lot of blockbuster movies these days—and there *really* aren't a lot of blockbuster movies that don't involve a superhero or a lot of explosions—but *Crazy Rich Asians* was one of them. Not only were there no superheroes (unless you count Michelle Yeoh), but the film also featured an almost entirely Asian cast—pretty much unheard-of in Hollywood.

The screenplay for *Crazy Rich Asians* was cowritten by Adele Lim. Adele was a TV writer who had busted her butt (and not slept) for nearly two decades to reach the highest levels of the extremely male and extremely white world of television writing. *Crazy Rich Asians* was the culmination of all those years and all that work. She says the incredible success of the film and all the acclaim were totally overwhelming—like a dream. But she turned down an offer to write the sequel. The reason? Money. The salary Warner Bros. offered Adele was one-eighth of what they offered her white male cowriter. Adele walked away.

Adele grew up in Malaysia and, even as a young girl, loved telling stories. She came to the United States for college and drove out to LA after graduation to try to break into Hollywood. Adele got a job as a writer's assistant and loved it, but one of the first things she noticed was that "writers' rooms" in television were very male and very white. There would typically be one spot set aside for a writer of color—known as the "diversity slot." Typically, these positions were just a one-year rotation and there was special funding set aside for them. All of that was great. The trouble was, the people who cycled through those spots almost never got promoted and generally didn't stick around.

Adele's Lesson: Take the *In* You Get

As an assistant, Adele soaked up every bit of knowledge she could and practiced writing scripts and coming up with ideas. Eventually, she got an agent and a manager, and referrals from colleagues. Through this and her writing samples, Adele eventually got her first writing job, on a cop show. She was over the moon until she learned it was one of the "minority" spots. "I said to my manager, 'I don't want to be the minority writer. I want to be a *writer* writer.' My manager was very smart. He sat me down and said, 'Listen, all these other writers have ins you are never going to have: You didn't go to their schools. You're not going to be able to shoot the shit about sports or strip clubs. You take whatever in you get. Once you're there, then you can prove yourself.'" Adele took the job. It paid off. Over the next fifteen years, Adele worked on shows like *One Tree Hill*, *Life on Mars*, *Private Practice*, *Missing*, *Life Unexpected*, and *Reign*. She was at the top of the profession.

That was when Jon M. Chu came to her about *Crazy Rich Asians*. It had been a bestselling book and Jon was part of a team that was turning it into a movie. They had a screenplay written by an established screenwriter, but Jon thought Adele could bring some authenticity and a female point of view to the script. Adele agreed to look at it. "Right away, I was like, 'Oh my God, yes. I'm your person for this 100 percent,'" she says. "In one of the opening scenes, Michelle Yeoh's character is at Bible class. And my mother is 100 percent in those Bible classes with other church ladies, wearing their jewelry and their handbags, and they're talking about Jesus, but it's also an excuse to talk about your sons, your daughters, who's doing what in school, who's getting pregnant, and 'How do we fix our children's lives?'"

Adele says the pay wasn't much, because she was a late addition, but she jumped on board. She was excited about the project and about seeing Asians represented in a big-budget Hollywood film. "In all my years in television, I never had a chance to write for a lead character who looked like me," says Adele. "What I wrote was a love letter to the world I grew up in." The script was a hit. A bunch of studios wanted it. Warner Bros. eventually got the movie, and Adele was ecstatic.

Crazy Rich Asians earned more than $230 million, and critics and audiences all over the world loved it. The media declared the romantic comedy was back! Adele says the whole experience was exhilarating and beyond anything she could have imagined. Most important for her, she was frequently approached by fans who said seeing an all-Asian cast in a big-budget Hollywood movie had been incredibly meaningful. "There's a scene in the movie where the main characters have just arrived in Singapore and they're driving in a Jeep down the highway," says Adele. "This guy told me he started crying at that scene, because it was a scene just of two Asian couples doing an everyday thing and you never see that on-screen. Seeing yourself on-screen just being a regular person—not being, you know, some sort of weird dragon lady dominatrix or the nerd best friend—it's powerful. The movie is about you. You're the hero of the story."

Adele's Lesson: Don't Settle for Less

In the wake of all the success, press, and accolades, Warner Bros. wanted to lock down the same dream team to write *Crazy Rich*

Asians 2 and *3*. Adele was thrilled. And then she got the offer: $110,000. The male writer, she found out, had been offered $800,000. At first Adele thought it was a typo: "I burst out laughing, and my agents assured me, 'No, no, no, it's not a mistake.'" Adele told Warner Bros. she would need equal pay. Warner Bros. refused, citing her lack of experience writing movie scripts—never mind the nearly two decades of television script writing she'd done and the fact she had just written a $230 million hit for them. Warner Bros. wouldn't budge. Adele walked away.

"It was heartbreaking," she recalls. "I loved the movie. I loved Jon. I loved the crew. I loved everything it did for the community." But Adele was sure in her decision. She knew what her contribution had been and she wouldn't accept anything less than equal pay. "There's this idea in Hollywood that 'Oh, well, maybe they brought her on for optics, but the person who was really doing the work was the tried-and-true white-guy writer.' I couldn't stand the idea of people thinking that about me."

Some friends and colleagues warned Adele that this could hurt her career—that she might be labeled as difficult or a diva. Her mother worried about this, too, and encouraged Adele to take the job. After all, *Crazy Rich Asians* was a huge, groundbreaking hit, and being a part of something like that can be a once-in-a-lifetime thing. But Adele stuck to her guns.

I asked Adele if she regretted walking away. "No," she said without hesitation. "Not for a hot second. It would have absolutely eaten at me. Also, I have a daughter, and I would never want her to stick it out in a situation where she was being valued less than a guy."

When news of the deal and of Adele's decision to leave the megahit franchise got out, the press went nuts and Adele heard from women all over the world, thanking her for not accepting less. "Women from all industries, basically talking about being in the same situation, where you're constantly made to feel that you're lucky to be at the table and you should just take what you get."

Adele's career does not seem to have suffered. She was snapped up by Disney to write the animated film *Raya and the Last Dragon*, and she sold a script to Lionsgate and was brought on to direct the film. Even her mom came around: "She called up one day and said, 'I'm so glad you did it.' She said there were so many times when she had to go through that in her life and felt like there was no choice. She had to go along with it. This really made her feel like 'You can stand up and speak up for yourself.'"

Knowing Your Worth

Money is an expression of value. Getting paid what you're worth is about knowing and owning the value of your work and time. That isn't easy: You're up against a lot of stories about why you should accept less and why your work is worth less, and you will likely encounter resistance. But demanding that your value be acknowledged in the workplace is one of the most important steps to gaining power and success (and sanity) in your professional life. Making that happen is a process—a process that takes time, effort, courage, and homework. But realizing your worth and fighting for it is one of the most powerful and impactful things you can do for your career and for yourself.

I wish I could say my first job was the last time salary disparities were an issue for me. It most definitely wasn't. Years later, I would find myself sobbing in a bathroom stall after learning I was being paid a quarter less than a male colleague who had fewer years of experience.

From that stall, I called a dear friend and told him what was happening. "I'm just so embarrassed," I whispered between rattling breaths. My friend then told me something his mother had said to him once, when he was in a similar situation. "The pain you feel now is good. It's you waking up to your own worth." I have never forgotten that. Every time I feel the sting of discrimination or talk with someone else who is going through it, I think about that. Facing this monster is hard and painful. But not facing it is worse. Feel the pain. Make a plan. And then go back and ask for what you're worth.

3

Confidence

Vivienne Ming: Transformation and the Power of Purpose

"Every one sees what you seem, but few know what you are."
—Machiavelli, *The Prince* (Chapter XVIII, DTE)

When I think about confidence in the workplace, I always think of an episode of *The Office* I saw years ago. In it, a hiring committee is interviewing people for the position of manager for the Scranton, Pennsylvania, branch of paper company Dunder Mifflin. One of the candidates is a man named Robert California (the amazing James Spader). Robert has no experience in the paper industry. In fact, he knows nothing at all about paper or the company. All of his work experience seems to involve selling deep-sea drilling equipment. One member of the hiring committee asks Robert how he plans to manage a paper company when he knows nothing about the business or the product. "You don't work in sales, do you?" Robert asks, leaning back in his chair. "I sit across from a man, I see his face, I see his eyes. Now, does it matter if he wants a hundred dollars of paper or a hundred million dollars of deep-sea drilling equipment? Don't be a fool. He wants respect. He wants love. He wants to be younger. He wants to be attractive." Robert pauses. "There is no such thing as a product. Don't ever think there is. There is only sex. Everything is sex." The men on the hiring committee are stunned. One of them blurts out that Robert is probably *overqualified* for the job; another says he thinks Robert might be a genius. Robert

California walks into the interview with no relevant experience or credentials and demonstrates no knowledge of the business or the job in question. What he does demonstrate? *A lot* of confidence. "I will get offered the job," he asserts after leaving the interview. And he does. Granted, this is TV, but I've thought about that episode many times, because what it has to say is, I think, very profound.

Confidence. It can feel elusive and ephemeral, but its impact is undeniable. Studies show confidence has a much bigger impact on a person's career than almost anything else—including (depressingly) competence. Confidence impacts the career you choose, how far you go in your career, how much money you make, and how happy you are in your job. It also determines how likely you are to take opportunities that come your way. Less confident people are less likely to take risks or try something new. If you're feeling stuck, a lack of confidence is very likely part of the reason. Not shockingly, women struggle in this department. Studies have shown that, on average, women are about half as confident as men are.

Cold, Hard Confidence

The consequences of a lack of confidence show up in all kinds of ways, including how we value ourselves and our work. In study after study, men place a higher dollar value on their work than women do. In one study, men and women were presented with a task and then asked to pay themselves what they felt they deserved. The men paid themselves 63 percent more, on average, than the women did and were significantly less productive.

Confidence, of course, doesn't just affect salary. It also plays a big role in promotions. Several years ago, Google noticed women were rising through the ranks much more slowly than their male counterparts. Natalie Johnson was part of a team tasked with understanding what was going on. The team started looking into how people got promoted at Google, and it turned out the company had a system in place that required employees to nominate themselves for a promotion before a manager would consider it. Women were far slower to nominate themselves than men were. "The self-nomination process was benefiting men," Natalie recalls. That squares with an oft-cited study from Hewlett-Packard, in which the company noticed men would nominate themselves for a promotion when they had 60 percent of the required skills for the position they were aiming for. Women didn't tend to nominate themselves until they had 100 percent of the required skills. Think about how much sooner you have 60 percent of required skills for a job versus 100 percent. Think about how fast that would compound over the course of a career.

And it's not just that confident people nominate themselves before all the rest of us insecure schlubs. They are also more likely to get promoted by others because we admire confident people more. Dr. Cameron Anderson, a researcher at the University of California, Berkeley, has done extensive research on the phenomenon of confidence and has found that people respond very positively to those who appear confident and tend to award them high status in groups (i.e., leadership roles).

Of course, confidence, or a lack of it, doesn't come from nowhere. It comes from decades of reinforcement and cultural messaging. Men are encouraged to be confident and cocky and are assured of their value in the workplace and the world. Women, on the other hand, are encouraged to be modest and self-deprecating and to question themselves. They are given the message that their value depends on things like youth, beauty, sweetness, hotness, the ability to walk in extremely uncomfortable shoes, and a bunch of other things that can leave a lady feeling anxious and insecure and most definitely not ready to sell somebody $100 million worth of deep-sea drilling equipment.

Machiavelli's Lesson: Crazy Confident

Machiavelli understood how crucial confidence is for a prince. In fact, one of his very favorite generals was kind of a model of un-earned confidence: Cesare Borgia. Cesare was a formidable general at the time Machiavelli was representing Florence. Cesare's father was the pope. (Yes, popes aren't technically supposed to have children—or pregnant teenage mistresses who are married to other men living in the Vatican—but these were unusual times.) Cesare used his family fortune and connections to assemble an army and launch a campaign to seize as much Italian territory as he could. He was shockingly successful at mobilizing and motivating his troops. He used them to carve out his own little state in northern Italy. It was a bloody affair, and Cesare needed friends and allies. He wanted support from Florence, which shared a border with Cesare's new territory, and he called a meeting with the republic. Florence sent Machiavelli and a fellow diplomat to meet with him.

Cesare seems to have had quite a flair for the dramatic: He arranged the meeting at night, and met Machiavelli and his colleague in a torchlit room and had the door locked behind them. He told the men he wanted to be a friend of Florence, but if Florence wouldn't be his friend, he would crush it. Then he demanded that Florence pay him an enormous sum of money. (Perhaps that was his idea of friendship?) It was brutish, unnecessarily aggro, and, honestly, a little weird. Most people probably would have been scared, shocked, or put off. Machiavelli was enchanted. "This lord is truly splendid and magnificent," he gushed in a letter shortly after the meeting. What was it that Machiavelli loved about Cesare? His confidence: "This makes him victorious and formidable."

And all of that is great for Cesare, but what if you're fresh out of torches and armies your dad bought for you? What do you do if you're not confident? It's not like people don't *want* to have confidence. The trouble is, wanting confidence doesn't make you confident. In fact, it probably makes you seem less confident, and the whole thing makes me feel a little bit like I did in junior high, when I was trying *so hard* to be cool and it was, ironically and tragically, all the trying that made me so desperately *uncool*.

If I'm very bad in this life, I will probably be sent back to junior high to spend all of eternity trying to figure out how to be cool. But (perhaps unlike with coolness) research shows you actually can homework your way to confidence—at least to a certain extent.

Machiavelli's Lesson: Fake It Till You Make It

While fake confidence isn't as effective as the real thing, Dr. Cameron Anderson has found that it's still very effective. If two people perform at the same skill level, the one who seems more confident will end up seeming more competent. Remember this when you are scared to speak up in a meeting, present a new idea, or ask for a raise. Pretending to be confident will get you pretty far.

So how do you do this? How do you fake confidence? There are a few key things you can do to come off as, and eventually become, more confident.

Machiavelli's Lesson: Just Do It

In many ways, Cesare Borgia's dream of creating his own little state from scratch was insane. He wasn't a prince or a general or a warrior. He was a priest by profession. He was supposed to be praying and fasting and contemplating the ephemerality of the mortal coil, not raising armies, slaughtering peasants, and seizing territory. Also, there were vicious rumors about Cesare and his family, including that he had killed his own brother and was sleeping with his sister. That is the kind of thing that could be very hard on a fellow's self-esteem. What's more, Cesare was sick. He had syphilis and would sometimes break out in terrible sores all over his face, forcing him to wear a black leather mask he'd had custom-made. Syphilis was fatal at the time and it was a slow, terrible death. Victims would gradually go deaf and insane and lose control over their bodies. For many people, this would have been terrifying, and they *would* have spent all their time praying and fasting and contemplating the ephemerality of the mortal coil. Not Cesare. Cesare was confident. Very confident. Crazy confident. He got it into his head to make Cesare-land, bought himself an army, and started marching it around Italy. His aggression, erratic arrogance, and shrewdness proved very effective with his troops and world leaders. Cesare had the pope's (his dad's) support and money, and the guy just made it happen.

Confident people act. People who lack confidence waffle. That is part of why a lack of confidence can do real and lasting damage to a career: It leads to inaction. In their book *The Confidence Code: The Science and Art of Self-Assurance—What Women Should Know*, authors Claire Shipman and Katty Kay define *confidence* as "the stuff that turns thoughts into actions." People who struggle with confidence will often spin their wheels in a bad situation, trying to get everything lined up perfectly before they ask for more or try to make a change. They fall into the perfectionism trap.

The Perfectionism Pitfall

Women experience a lot of issues around perfectionism in the workplace, and it makes sense: Perfectionism is about control. If you perceive yourself to be in an unfair system, the one thing you can control is the work you do. A lot of women get stuck obsessing over making something so amazingly good that it cannot be denied. Dr. Tina Opie experienced this when she was earning her PhD and trying to get her research published. She had become frustrated because her work kept getting turned down by journals, while papers from white male colleagues that were not as thoroughly researched got published. Tina decided to double down and put even *more* research and rigor into her work. It didn't help. Then a mentor offered her some advice. "She said, 'Listen, I know you're trying to write in this very codified way, but I need you to write like these arrogant white boys,'" Tina recalls. Her mentor told her, "You have five citations in every sentence, which makes it very difficult to focus on your main point. Some of these white men, they are submitting stuff that's not half as well researched. But you're getting rejected because you're trying too hard to prove that you're competent." Tina realized her writing didn't need more research and rigor; it needed more confidence. "Beyoncé channels Sasha Fierce. So I started channeling Billy the White Man," Tina says, laughing. "All of a sudden my work started getting published."

Perfectionism is a destructive, paralyzing mentality that will sap all your energy. The workplace isn't logical. *People* aren't logical.

That is part of why confidence is so powerful in the first place. If you ever doubt this, just remember the story of Cesare Borgia.

If the consequence of a lack of confidence is inaction, one way to start being more confident is to start taking more action: Ask for the raise, speak up at the meeting, push for more resources. Think: *What would Cesare Borgia do?*—and then do that. (Well, maybe not *that*, but you get the idea.)

You want a raise or a promotion or a new job?

Ask.

It might be horrifically uncomfortable, and you might not be able to sleep for a few nights beforehand, but the point is that you are in there, fighting the good fight and pushing against everything that has caused millions of women the world over to shy away from asking for more.

Ask. Ask now.

Claire Wasserman is a salary coach and author of *Ladies Get Paid: The Ultimate Guide to Breaking Barriers, Owning Your Worth, and Taking Command of Your Career.* She has worked with thousands of women on asking for more at work. Claire says waiting is probably the biggest pitfall she sees: "I see a lot of women just waiting until the 'right moment' and putting so much pressure on themselves." Claire recommends thinking of a negotiation as the first step in an ongoing conversation. In other words, this isn't a onetime ask. This is part of an evolving relationship between you and this company. It's like flossing: Do it frequently and it will be easier and infinitely less painful (and less bloody) than it will be if you make it an annual event.

Machiavelli banged this point again and again in *The Prince*, mostly because he was so frustrated with the Florentine council's constant waffling. Unlike the swashbuckling Cesare, the Council of Florence never wanted to make difficult decisions or offend anyone or choose sides in the countless skirmishes and battles going on around them. But waffling was not a safe approach. It was, in fact, partially due to that very waffling that Florence lost its republican government and ended up back in the hands of a powerful ruling family. As a result of these experiences, Machiavelli felt passionately that, when in doubt, it was always better to act. "I know that many say a policy of neutrality is the safest option," he wrote in a letter to a friend. "I believe to the contrary that neutrality is an exceedingly dangerous path." And for a prince, Machiavelli declares that waffling will lead "in most instances to their destruction" (Chapter XXI, DTE).

Machiavelli's Lesson: Shoot for the Stars

Confident people expect a lot for themselves. So if you want to be more confident, look at your own aspirations and expectations and ratchet them up. Machiavelli's advice to the conquering prince was to set expectations far above what he actually wanted, "like the skilful archer, who . . . takes aim much above the destined mark . . ." (Chapter VI, DTE).

Salary coach Claire Wasserman says aiming high can pay off in a big way. "A woman came to me and said she had recently discovered that she was being paid less than her male colleague, but for her it wasn't so much discrimination as it was that her male counterpart felt comfortable throwing out large numbers she wouldn't even fathom she could ask for." Claire says confidence is an incredibly powerful tool in negotiation. In fact, she says, the magic ingredient in any negotiation is truly believing you deserve what you are asking for.

The Easy Ask. Janet Babin is a longtime public radio/podcast reporter and producer. For most of her career, she was an employee; she'd never managed anyone or dealt with budgets. But she got a job helping launch a podcast and found herself running a team, managing a budget, and in charge of hiring for a couple of positions. Her top choice for one job was a man and for the second job was a woman. Janet had a range she could pay each worker. For the woman's job, the range was $50,000 to $58,000. She offered the woman $50,000 and the woman took it right away: "She jumped at it. She didn't try to negotiate." Janet was very excited about the woman and would have given her more if she'd asked. But she didn't. "I felt kind of bad, but that was also more money I could spend on other things." Because this young woman didn't ask, she left $8,000 on the table.

When Janet made an offer to the man, she had a much different experience. The man's position was more senior, and Janet offered him $65,000 out of an available budget of $72,000. "He called back right away and said he was really excited about the offer but that he would need $70,000." What struck Janet was not just that he asked but how relaxed the whole exchange was: "He just sounded so confident and upbeat. When I've asked for raises, it always feels stressful and I'm up all night justifying why I need the money and what I'm going to say, and it feels very adversarial. But he was so agreeable and it felt so pleasant and normal." Janet gave him the extra money and the young man left only $2,000 on the table. Janet says she learned something from that experience: "The next time I ask for a raise, I'm not going to explain why I need the money or apologize. I'm just going to ask. It doesn't have to be this stressful thing."

So, to effectively fake it, think about what you'd ask for if you didn't have to negotiate. What do you deserve? If the world were fair and the streams ran clear and justice reigned, what would you be getting paid right now? Add 10 percent. Ask for that.

If you're having trouble finding a number, there's a great trick you can try. It comes from a study Dr. Linda Babcock and her colleague Dr. Julia Bear did: They found that when women prepared for a negotiation as if they were negotiating on behalf of someone else, they tended to ask for a lot more and it also greatly improved the outcome. So think about your colleague and what you think *she* or *he* should get paid and ask for that.

You may not get nearly what you want or nearly what you would get if you were a crazy white man with an army your dad bought, but don't *you* contribute to the problem by asking for less than you deserve.

Machiavelli's Lesson: Baby Steps

Dr. Cameron Anderson says he has learned that confidence is like a muscle: It's something you can practice and build up over time.

Cameron recommends starting small. "Look for smaller achievements first," he says. "Then move to increasingly larger challenges so that you leverage the virtuous cycle." Ask someone to help you carry something; ask the barista to fill your coffee all the way up; ask your boss for an extra day to finish a project. All of these things will help you work your confidence muscle.

This also holds true if you are facing a task that seems daunting. "Focus on the elements of a task that are familiar to you, rather than the elements that are different and novel," Cameron advises. "People who approach new tasks with confidence say to themselves, 'This isn't totally foreign—these parts are just like what I used to do.'" Confident people see that things are possible. In the end, this approach makes confident people more likely to succeed because they believe they will. They are more resilient when they fail, which makes them more likely to try again and, eventually, succeed.

Machiavelli's Lesson: Birds of a Confident Feather

Finally, if you want to build your confidence, Dr. Cameron Anderson recommends finding a positive, can-do tribe. "Surround yourself with people who believe in you," he advises, "and people who provide you with models so you can emulate their behavior." This is important for a lot of reasons. Spending time with people who feel defeated and held back in their lives will have adverse effects on you. Not only is that attitude contagious, but also these friends are not likely to encourage you to reach for the stars, because reaching for the stars is not what they do.

The Confidence Conundrum

You might very well encounter some pushback when you start to assert yourself and act more confident. Your manager/coworkers/ friends/partner/family might not love that you are suddenly asking for more, speaking up more, and wanting more for yourself. Even people who love you and support you might want things to stay the way they are and might also be scared that these changes will threaten your relationship with them.

Know that pushback is normal. Becoming a more confident person is a powerful transformation, and transformation is one of the most difficult and rewarding things we can do in our lives. Not everybody is going to like it.

Also, women walk a tricky line when it comes to confidence: There can be a backlash issue. The confidence that works so well for Robert California might come off as insufferable arrogance from Roberta California. Gender researcher Dr. Linda Babcock was able to prove this with an ingenious study in which she videotaped male and female actors advocating for themselves. The actors read identical scripts, and then a group of people watched the videos and gave their impressions of each actor. "People thought the man was great," Linda says. "'We really want to work with him! He's really likable.'" But a woman reading the same exact script got a very different reaction: "The woman was too demanding and they didn't want to work with her."

One way around this is to pair confidence with modesty. Don't brag or boast, even if the men around you are doing it to great effect. Gender researcher Joan C. Williams tried this tactic in her workplace. She says her own confidence became a problem with her male colleagues when she was working in academic law. Joan realized there was a culture of bragging in her department and she stopped taking part in it. "I became much more modest," she notes. "I just figured, 'My reputation speaks for itself.'" It helped. Joan kept the confidence but modified the way she expressed it. I will talk later in the book (see chapter 5) about how to express confidence and assert yourself in ways that help minimize backlash. But even with the best advice, it can be a tricky line to walk.

How Far Is Too Far?

There is, of course, the danger of overconfidence. Machiavelli's mancrush Cesare Borgia eventually suffered from this; the very thing that brought Cesare so much success proved to be his downfall. When

Cesare's dad was pope and he was in relatively good health, Cesare could back his confidence up with money and armies and clever strategies. But things changed for Cesare: His father died and the new pope hated him. Cesare didn't have the political backing he once did. He was also very sick and physically less able to lead his troops. But instead of changing his tactics to fit his new circumstances, Cesare continued on the aggressive, hyperconfident path he'd used in the past. It backfired. The new pope overpowered him, took his land and money, and threw Cesare in jail. Truly, the guy went down hard. He was hunted down and killed—stabbed dozens of times—his clothes were stripped away, and his naked body was left out in the open with only a little piece of tile covering his genitals.

To make sure you're not walking the treacherous, tiled path of Cesare, check in with yourself and try to be honest about your work and what you're asking for. Check in with supportive (honest) friends. And if you're not sure, err on the side of overconfidence. Considering all the messaging you have taken in your whole life, chances are you are vastly underestimating your own worth.

VIVIENNE MING:
Transformation and the Power of Purpose

There is probably no one who embodies the power of transformation and confidence better than Dr. Vivienne Ming. Vivienne is a theoretical neuroscientist and the founder and head of Socos Labs, a philanthropic research company that uses machine learning to solve some of the world's most intractable problems. She describes herself as House, the doctor from TV, except "slightly less cranky." Vivienne is also a world-renowned speaker who has inspired people from all walks of life to find their own personal confidence and change their lives.

Vivienne can speak on this topic with great authority, because for a long time she had no confidence at all. In fact, a lack of confidence almost cost Vivienne her life. Vivienne transitioned genders, but before that, when she was in her twenties, she underwent a terrible depression. At the time Vivienne was a young man in college who was struggling with feelings of unworthiness and failure. She got to the point where she couldn't even get out of bed. Vivienne dropped out of college, moved into her car, and went into a terrible spiral. Things got so bad, she decided she couldn't go on. She got a little money together and bought a gun: "I spent a very long night trying to figure out why I should be alive," she recalls. "I thought, 'I've only been a disappointment to myself and everyone else in my life. I've never really been happy.'"

During a long internal search that night, Vivienne found something inside herself: a purpose. She did not believe she could ever be happy herself but thought maybe she could use her life to make the world better. "So my purpose, if I were to articulate it . . . is to live a life that makes other people's lives better." Vivienne thought the key to making the world a better place was through work. She decided that night that she would reenroll in school and channel everything inside her into doing the kind of work that would help people. In that way her life would have value.

That sense of purpose gave Vivienne incredible confidence. She was still horribly depressed, but she suddenly had energy and a drive and that fueled her. "I sat up front in every single class and I thought to myself, 'How can I use this?'"

Vivienne says she didn't necessarily believe in herself, but she believed in her purpose and that gave her the confidence to take drastic and sweeping action in her life. This purpose became a kind of superpower that pushed her to the top of her class and led her to find her life partner and create a loving relationship. It gave her the courage to transition genders and the chutzpah to start her own company. It was that sense of purpose that sparked in Vivienne the desire to start a family; she now has two kids she adores. That sense of purpose still informs everything she does.

Vivienne's Lesson: Learned Courage

Vivienne has also made a scientific study of confidence and courage. She believes, contrary to what we typically think, courage can be learned. "Courage isn't something you just have. It isn't something you are. It's something you practice and that practice is brutally hard," she says. "I think most of my life is about structuring it to be as easy as possible to be as courageous as possible, because I'm not that good at it." As an example, Vivienne says she structured her company to make it easier to try risky things or take on projects that might be really important but are not necessarily profitable, like diabetes research and education in low-income schools—both issues that Socos Labs has tackled.

Vivienne still struggles with confidence, but she has learned to avoid situations that might trigger her inner critic and take her confidence away: "I will never read about myself. I've never watched myself onstage. If I ever, *ever* made the mistake of believing my own press, it would be a disaster for what I do. My life is wonderful. What more could I possibly need?"

Vivienne's Lesson: Finding Your Purpose

But what if you don't know what your purpose is? Vivienne says there's a powerful exercise you can do to help you find your purpose. "Imagine everything you would want to be true about you when you're sixty-five," she says. Just knowing what you want makes it more likely to happen, because you're starting to know your purpose. "Purpose is unique in having a strong relationship with happiness. Everything you would want to be true about you is more likely to be true if you have a strong sense of purpose."

I like this advice because it points you back to yourself—to your own measures of success. In the workplace, it can be very easy to get caught up in the things other people use to measure success: a certain office, a certain project, a certain title. (If I could even talk about the hundreds of sleepless nights I spent obsessing over being "Senior Reporter" instead of "Reporter II," I could write a whole other book.) There's nothing wrong with wanting those things and pushing for them, but do beware the dreaded "groupthink." What do *you* want? What do *you* value? What is *your* little kingdom in northern Italy? Have the confidence to trust your own goals and dreams. You don't want to find yourself halfway up a ladder you never really wanted to climb just because someone else thought it seemed like a great ladder.

True Believer

The lesson of workplace confidence is having faith in yourself. You should be your biggest booster, sitting up front, jumping up and down, waving the foam finger for YOU! YOU! YOU! You definitely should not be the one creating limitations for yourself, telling yourself why things aren't possible or why you don't deserve them. Believe in yourself and your abilities; ask for what you want and believe it's possible. And if you find yourself intimidated by more confident colleagues or a critical manager or a job that seems beyond your skills, remember that confidence can actually create competence. That is the magical secret of Robert California. That is what he knew when he walked into that job interview. That and, of course, that everything is sex.

4

Respect

Sallie Krawcheck: She-Wolf of Wall Street

"Here comes in the question whether it is better to be loved rather than feared, or feared rather than loved. . . . We should wish to be both; but . . . if we must choose between them, it is far safer to be feared than loved."

—Machiavelli, *The Prince* (Chapter XVII, DTE)

Respect. It can be a difficult thing to quantify, but you certainly feel it when it's not there. Any woman who has been called "sweetheart" (I have!) or had her outfit critiqued in a meeting (I have!) or who has been interrupted and talked over (Ruth Bader Ginsburg was!) knows what I mean. Women are disrespected in the workplace in big and small ways. The reason: The workplace is seen as male turf and women are outsiders—easy pickings in that space.

Justice, Interrupted

If you are a woman and you have been in a meeting, you have probably been interrupted. But take heart! You are in pretty stellar company: namely, the women who serve on the Supreme Court of the United States. A study of Supreme Court transcripts found that male justices interrupted female justices three times more often than they interrupted other male justices. The problem has actually gotten worse in recent years.

And it's not just justices doing the interrupting. The lawyers arguing cases before the Supreme Court also interrupted female justices more often even though they are explicitly forbidden from interrupting the justices (not to mention that it seems like a *really* bad idea). The study cites many examples, but here is a particularly striking one: Kenneth Steven Geller was the lawyer arguing the case, and Ruth Bader Ginsburg was . . . Ruth Bader F**king Ginsburg:

> **Ruth Bader Ginsburg:** But when you take what the President undertook, which was just to use best efforts, that doesn't sound like—
> **Kenneth Steven Geller:** —Under the Supremacy—
> **Ruth Bader Ginsburg:** —this Court would have much to—
> **Kenneth Steven Geller:** —Justice Ginsburg, I think it's the operation of the Supremacy Clause.

It would appear Kenneth Steven Geller interrupts RBG twice to mansplain the Supremacy Clause. And this happened to *Ruth Bader Ginsburg*. What if you are just Erika in Accounting? How can you ever expect anyone to listen to what you have to say when THE NOTORIOUS RBG WAS GETTING INTERRUPTED BY SOME LAWYER WHO NEEDED HER VOTE?

Most of us are not getting interrupted in places anywhere near as glorious as the Supreme Court, but most of us are getting interrupted. Consider this: When men are in meetings with just men, they do not tend to interrupt each other. When men are in a mixed-gender group, though, they will typically talk over women, interrupt them, and dismiss their ideas. And before you get too judgy about the fellows, it turns out even *women* interrupt women more often than they interrupt men. Mind you, this isn't happening because women are talking more; women actually speak less in meetings, on average, than men do. This held true in the Supreme Court study. Although female justices were interrupted far more often, they spoke less than the male justices and tended to use fewer words when they did speak.

What's going on? Dr. Cecilia L. Ridgeway, the Stanford University sociologist, says the answer goes back to status: Women's ideas and contributions are seen as less valuable, so when they do talk, it's perceived to be a non-ideal use of everyone's time. (Sort of like when Jar Jar Binks is on camera in *Star Wars*: Even a little bit feels like too much.)

Cecilia says people in "low-status" positions are not supposed to talk. They are supposed to listen while "high-status" people talk. So when a woman speaks up, she can be seen as violating her rank in a way that evokes hostility. Interrupting is simply a microaggression—a subtle (and often unconscious) reaction to someone who is "overstepping"—a way to put a woman in her place.

If You Can't Stand the "He-peat" . . .

Another thing that famously happens to women is the dreaded "he-peat." Astronomer Nicole Gugliucci coined the term "for when a woman suggests an idea and it's ignored, but then a guy says the same thing and everyone loves it." Dr. Şebnem Kalemli-Özcan, an economist at the University of Maryland, says when she first noticed this, she thought it was her own fault. Şebnem grew up in Turkey and speaks (perfect) English with an accent. When she would ask questions or comment on a colleague's paper in a group setting or at a conference, she was often dismissed or ignored entirely: "And then the same question is asked by a male colleague ten minutes down the road and everyone is like, 'Oh. That's so smart. This is such a great question!' At first, I'm thinking, 'Maybe it's my English; you know, people are just not understanding me.'" But then Şebnem noticed this was happening to her accentless female colleagues as well, and she realized her accent wasn't the problem. Her gender was.

Talk like a Woman

A couple of years ago a bit of news caught my attention. It came from an amazingly natural experiment that unfolded in a little career services start-up in Philadelphia. Martin Schneider and Nicole Hallberg worked for a company that wrote résumés, LinkedIn profiles, and other professional materials for clients. Almost all their communication was via email, and Martin and Nicole shared a work account. Martin was emailing with a client one day, "and he is just being IMPOSSIBLE. Rude, dismissive, ignoring my questions. Telling me his methods were the industry standards (they weren't) and I couldn't understand the terms he used (I could)." And then Martin noticed something: "Thanks to our shared in-box, I'd been signing all communications 'Nicole.'" He emailed the client, letting him know of the mix-up. "IMMEDIATE IMPROVEMENT. Positive reception, thanking me for suggestions, responds promptly, saying 'Great questions!' Became a model client."

As a result of this mix-up, Nicole and Martin decided to run an experiment and switch email accounts for a couple of weeks to see what kind of experience they would have.

There were a few differences that became immediately clear to Nicole. For one thing, people showed her a lot more respect: "It was a shift . . . to like, 'Hey, we're equal. We're both professionals trying to get this project done.'" Nicole also noticed she became more relaxed as a result of this newfound collegiality and naturally began communicating more the way she'd noticed men communicate: more matter-of-fact, less apologetic, with far fewer words and far less explaining herself. She says, "It felt so freeing. I think you don't realize how much anxiety you carry with you every day, because it's just a baseline."

Martin's experience was less freeing. "I was in hell," he wrote. "Everything I asked or suggested was questioned. Clients I could do in my sleep were condescending. One asked if I was single."

This didn't just affect morale; it also had a big impact on Martin's and Nicole's work. Before the experiment, Nicole's productivity had been significantly lower than Martin's, something that was a persistent source of stress for her. But when the email accounts were switched, Nicole's output skyrocketed and Martin's plummeted. "I realized the reason she took longer," Martin said, "is by the time she could get clients to accept that she knew what she was doing, I could get halfway through another client. I wasn't any better at the job than she was; I just had this invisible advantage."

Nicole says she almost started crying when Martin told her that. She had been so hard on herself about her speed with clients, and the idea that it wasn't her fault was an enormous relief. At the same time, it made her incredibly sad because she saw how destructive this discrimination had been to her work and her self-image. "I realized I had to fight, fight, fight before I even got to the work. I had to prove to them that I knew what I was doing, and that slowed me down so much."

Machiavelli's Lesson: Talking Back

Getting talked over, ignored, disrespected, or having your ideas stolen puts you in the middle of a classic female Hotbox conundrum: On the one hand, if you righteously cry out, "I'm glad you are *so freaking in love* with Joe's idea, because ten minutes ago, when I HAD THAT EXACT SAME IDEA, you all didn't seem to think it was so great!" people will think you're a crazy dragon lady and they won't listen to you anyway. On the other hand, if you sink back into your chair, smiling sweetly while Joe bathes in the accolades for *his* great idea, people will assume you're a doormat. Also, you will probably die a little bit inside and that's never good.

The first thing to remember is, this is not your fault! You haven't done anything wrong. "What's important is not to feel guilty for not handling challenging situations perfectly," advises Arianna Huffington, who says she has been in this situation countless times in her legendary career. "Inclusiveness is a universal value that benefits everybody. And when it's challenged, men should also be responsible for defending it." Still, the reality is, a lot of times the men in the room won't defend it, and you will have to figure out a way to deal with this situation yourself or it will keep happening.

Machiavelli addresses this particular bind many times in *The Prince*. Remember, it's crucial that the new prince be loved by his people—"otherwise he has no security in adversity" (Chapter IX,

MPE), but the prince also needs the people to fear his wrath, follow his laws, and, of course, pay his taxes. In moments when a prince has to choose between doormat and dragon lady, Machiavelli comes down squarely on the side of aggro-bitch, because "men are less careful how they offend him who makes himself loved than him who makes himself feared." Machiavelli does emphasize that you should avoid lashing out at people in these situations or creating unnecessary animosity. You want to "inspire fear" but also "escape hate" (Chapter XVII, DTE). You want to be a leader? You want to thrive in your workplace? You don't want stupid Joe getting credit for your ideas? Suit up. It's time to get your aggro-bitch on. Well . . . a subtle, Machiavellian aggro-bitch.

Machiavelli's Lesson: The Humble Add

One effective subtle aggro-bitch approach? The Humble Add. Dr. Cecilia L. Ridgeway stumbled on this solution when she was starting out in academia and found herself getting interrupted and having her ideas stolen all the time. She tried straight-up calling out the men in question, but it didn't work for her. "That was not a good strategy," she says with a laugh. "That was *not* good." So Cecilia started exploring how to claim credit for her ideas in a way that would work for her.

Here is how the Humble Add works: Let's say you offer up an idea and Steve he-peats it, and everyone starts freaking out about how brilliant Steve has done it again! Try saying something to add to your original idea and slip in that it was your idea. For instance, "I love this idea, Steve. I was thinking this over last night and I got worried because I wasn't sure what to do if X happened. What you're saying is the perfect solution!" If that sounds awkward, cringey, and hard to pull off, it is! "It's a very messy, messy business," says Cecilia. Still, she says, it's better than doing nothing.

Machiavelli's Lesson: Reading the Room

Overtalk and he-peating are pretty universal experiences, but the specific circumstances of your workplace can offer solutions. Adele

Lim, screenwriter of *Crazy Rich Asians*, struggled a lot to be heard when she first started working on a team of TV writers. Senior male writers would often talk over her and other female or junior writers. "You'd be right in the middle of a pitch to your bosses and some guy would just steamroll you," she recalls. Adele says the culture of disrespect and discrimination in many writers' rooms was shocking and way over the line. But it is also an incredibly competitive industry, and when Adele was starting out, she had to find ways to navigate the situation in order to survive. The first thing she learned to do was immediately speak up. "I would snap back," she says. "Like, 'Hey, I was talking. I was in the middle of the pitch.'" She says this didn't necessarily stop the overtalk from happening, but it was effective in the moment: "It would check them."

Another workaround Adele found was observing the moments when the interrupting and ignoring were happening. She realized part of the issue was the fear and pressure people felt at having to come up with new ideas and stories all the time. There was an enormous amount of insecurity and stress that was leading people to lash out in ways micro and not-so-micro. "The show runners are not always these über-confident people who know exactly what they want," says Adele. "Sometimes they're looking at the room, thinking, 'I hope someone smart gives me a North Star for this episode, because I don't have it.'" She noticed that in this stressful atmosphere there were a few trusted writers who were treated with respect and listened to because they were seen as people who could help and offer solutions. So part of addressing the overtalk issue, for Adele, was becoming a person who could offer a solution to the stress and panic her bosses and colleagues were feeling. She started coming up with story ideas—dozens of them, every day. Eventually the show runners and other writers started counting on her endless fountain of ideas, turning to her for help, and listening to her when she spoke. Adele stresses the problem didn't go away and the situation was never "okay." But her Machiavellian solution helped her navigate and improve the situation.

If you are getting interrupted or he-peated, take some time to assess what's going on underneath the bad behavior. In *The Prince*, Machiavelli observes that "men injure either from fear or hatred" (Chapter VII, MPE). So either this person doesn't like you specifically (did you get a promotion he wanted or take the last bag of Hot Cheetos out of the vending machine?) or he is afraid. So observe: Is this interrupter/idea-stealer feeling insecure? Is he afraid you will outshine him? Is he just stressed and you are the one he feels he can get away with pushing around? Notice if this person interrupts everyone, interrupts only women, interrupts select people, or interrupts only you. See how others react and what effect those reactions have. This can give you a good road map to dealing with the problem.

Machiavelli's Lesson: That's What She Said

Another weapon you can deploy to stop the overtalk and the hepeating is something called amplification. That is what Dr. Tina Opie started doing with a group of female colleagues. Tina is a Black woman and points out that women of color have a particularly hard time being listened to in meetings. In fact, studies have found that Black women's statements are forgotten or misremembered significantly more often than those of white women. Tina learned the amplification strategy from an article in the *Washington Post* about women in the Obama administration. Their ideas weren't gaining momentum in the ultra-cutthroat White House, so they teamed up to create a solution: One woman would make a point in a meeting and, immediately, another woman would repeat the idea and commend it. A third woman would chime in and move the idea forward, and voilà: The original idea gets said, repeated, supported, and amplified. "It works," Tina says. "It's *amazing* how well it works."

The Erin Brockovich Exception

Part of why amplification works so well is something I'll call the Erin Brockovich Exception, after the activist and advocate Erin Brockovich. Erin is famously salty and aggressive, but is also admired and beloved for taking on big corporations that harmed people who didn't have much power. Here's the thing: As a culture, we don't like feisty, pushy women—*but* we do like them if they're being feisty and pushy on behalf of someone else. "We don't push back against women who are negotiating assertively for somebody else," says gender researcher Linda Babcock, "because that's entirely consistent with women's role." It's the Erin Brockovich Exception and it's one of the most powerful escape hatches from the Hotbox. We're perfectly happy for a woman to be pushy, feisty, grabby, and loud, as long as she's not doing it for herself.

Not only will the Erin Brockovich exception give you a gender discrimination hall pass, it is also a very powerful way to start establishing yourself as a leader. If another woman is getting talked over or he-peated, jump in and back her up. This advice comes straight from our man, Machiavelli. One of his main pieces of advice in a situation where you don't have a lot of power, is to stick up for other people who also don't have much power. "The prince," he writes, "ought to make himself the head and defender of his less powerful neighbors, and to weaken the more powerful amongst them . . ." (Chapter III, MPE). The reason? Not only are you weakening the powers that be and creating a potential opening for yourself, but also the people you speak up for will be loyal to you and will fight for you and your ideas in the future. As Machiavelli puts it, "By arming them, those arms become yours . . ." (Chapter XX, MPE).

Machiavelli is careful to stipulate that you should not speak up on behalf of people who have *more* power than you do. Don't jump in if the boss gets interrupted by hapless Dave. The benefits of smacking down hapless Dave are minimal, and you risk being seen as a suck-up and a bully. Let the boss deal with Dave herself.

The Girl Talk Hotbox

Oh! Hey! :) I just wanted to say one more thing really fast. I mean, it's not just the way that people talk to women that's different. I guess women will talk differently sometimes, too? Like, in the office?

The technical term for all the extra words and qualifiers and smiley faces and apologies women tend to use when communicating is *softeners.* Dr. Cecilia L. Ridgeway says softeners are a way for people to acknowledge their low status while still speaking up in a group or introducing an idea, both of which are high-status activities: "Essentially to say, 'It's safe to listen to me because I'm not going to poke you with my spear.'"

Softeners get a lot of flak, but the interesting thing about softeners is they work. Studies have shown that when women use softeners, it actually increases their influence with men. (So the next time you hear a man complaining about uptalk or making fun of the cutesy emoji a female colleague put in an email, know that he's way more likely to pay attention to what is said in that email exactly because of the winky face and waving hand.)

So if you find yourself apologizing for no reason, or ending a sentence in a question, or concluding a professional email with "Thank you!," don't beat yourself up. You are doing this because, subconsciously, you know it's effective.

Of course, using softeners comes at a price. "People are more likely to listen to you," says Dr. Cecilia L. Ridgeway, "but it can undermine your message." People are less inclined to take your softened ideas seriously, even if they do listen to them.

Of course, if you *don't* use softeners, you pay the price as well. Carlee Barackman experienced this firsthand. She worked at a tech company in Detroit on a team of mostly men and she communicated like they did: "Efficiently and directly, which means I cut out extra adjectives and some extra exclamation points." But the company CEO pulled her aside and accused her of being too brusque in her emails. A few weeks later Carlee replied to an email with an "Okay, thanks" and the CEO sent her a note about it. "He asked that I include something to lighten it up, such as an exclamation point, so that the recipient knew I was happy about the work done." Shortly after that, Carlee noticed some emails her male colleagues were sending that were written in a style that was nearly identical to the one the CEO had called her out on. Those emails didn't seem to be a problem—at least, not when they came from a man.

"I remember sitting down at my desk and having no idea who

to ask about how to email 'like a woman,'" she says. "Is emailing 'like a woman' even a thing? . . . I felt stuck. I was worried that, by adding extra fluff to an email, I would appear unprofessional, and I was also worried that if I kept my replies short and direct, everyone would assume I was angry."

Machiavelli's Lesson: The Strategic Softener

Softeners: damned if you use them, damned if you don't. But never fear: There are solutions! One powerful option is something I'll call the Strategic Softener. Remember, softeners work. The trick is to find softeners that achieve the goal of relaxing people's defenses but not at the cost of your credibility.

Dr. Cecilia L. Ridgeway recommends pairing softeners with confidence. For example, at a meeting, instead of saying "Sorry" or "Could I just say something?," Cecilia recommends something like, "This might sound crazy, but what if we tried X?" or "I totally get why everyone is wanting to change directions, but I really do think we should stick with what we're doing." Those are still softeners, but they have some swagger to them.

In writing, try playing around with different softeners. It doesn't have to be a bunch of exclamation points or a smiley face; it could be a warm tone or taking a couple of sentences to ask about your boss's trip to Florida. Part of being a new prince in the workplace is finding ways to assert yourself and advocate for your ideas without being too obvious or direct about it. As Machiavelli so beautifully puts it, a prince should have "all the fierceness of the lion and all the craft of the fox" (Chapter XIX, DTE). With Strategic Softeners, you can dress up your roar a little and make sure it's heard and taken seriously, but doesn't scare the fellas too much.

Respect in Action

Of course, a lack of respect in the workplace doesn't just show up in words, it also shows up in actions—everything from being shut out of key meetings and social events to sexual harassment.

Machiavelli's Lesson: Bring Your Own Chair

Women are often left out at work—left out of conversations, meetings, and after-work socializing. This can have a very detrimental effect on one's career over time.

Lisa Davis has worked in the military and tech industries for decades and says getting excluded is something she has come to expect. Lisa learned to take a head-on approach to workplace exclusion. She started just showing up to meetings even if she hadn't been invited: "Like, 'I'm here,'" she asserts. "'Your dislike of me being female or whatever is not going to stop my drive and my motivation and my initiative.'" Her advice to women: "You need to have a level of tenacity here that you probably didn't know you needed to have. If you're sitting around, waiting for someone to invite you to the table, don't. Bring your own chair and make your own space at the table. Nobody's going to invite you." Lisa says the discomfort of this is worth it, because being "in the room" has proven to be so valuable. A lot of things happen in meetings: You learn about upcoming projects, meet clients, hear crucial information. Lisa says forcing a place at the table has been an effective way to survive and thrive in the sometimes hostile environments in which she's worked: "It's helped me find my voice," she says. "I have basically learned to become fearless."

Machiavelli was a huge advocate of showing up and forcing a place for yourself at the table. His advice: If you're feeling excluded or ostracized or ignored, show up. And then keep on showing up. He recommended, for instance, that princes who needed to secure a new territory go and live in that new territory. The stranger and more hostile the land, the more crucial it was for the new prince to be there physically, to make his position "more secure and durable" (Chapter III, MPE). Machiavelli thought being physically present was the best way for a prince to avoid conspiracies and sabotage.

Machiavelli's Lesson: Fox Your Way to the Table

Samantha Hubner also experienced exclusion when she started her job in the technology and defense industry, but she opted for a more fox-like approach. Samantha was working with a small team of men and she really liked her colleagues, but often felt left out. "They would always be talking to each other about life and work and what they read in the newspaper," she says. "I never really felt like I had anything to add, but I started to get really tired of being quiet, because I'm not a quiet person." Worse, Samantha noticed that she wasn't being included in key meetings. She brought the issue up multiple times and though her colleagues responded with concern and apologies, the exclusion continued.

So Samantha took action: "I would stalk the calendars of the guys in my office," she says. When Samantha spotted a pitch meeting with an outside client, she would make sure she was at the front door to greet them when they arrived. "I would play into this stereotype of being the hospitable, welcoming woman in the office," she says. "I would take them to the conference room. I would offer them water or coffee and then I would wait until all the guys had taken their seats. Then I would bring over the coffee, shut the door, and sit down at the table before anyone had a chance to throw me out."

Samantha found that it worked: "The guys were like, 'Nice power play! We'll make sure we get you included in more of these meetings.'" She admits her tactic could have had a very different outcome, but she thinks the key is that she was honest and direct first, and when the results didn't happen, she took action.

Be the Social Activities You Want to See in the World

Of course advancing in a workplace isn't just about meetings. After-work happy hours, social outings, and get-togethers are a really important way to bond with colleagues, get information, and network. Women, especially women of color, are often left out of these informal networking events.

Christine Pride took a proactive approach at her workplace. She felt like a bit of an outsider in the very exclusive, insular, and white world of publishing. Publishing is a relationship-based business, and Christine knew that being a part of the social network was key to success. So she found a way to put herself in the center of things: "I started organizing social events, like an annual softball game and happy hours." Christine really enjoyed those activities and her involvement also made her feel more a part of the organization.

Sexual Harassment and Me Too

In the past few years, thousands of women have come forward and hundreds of men in prominent positions have lost their jobs because of revelations sparked by the Me Too, Black Lives Matter, and Time's Up movements. What has become clear is that harassment in the workplace is not the exception; it's the rule. Many women find the office to be a place where they endure humiliation, degradation, racism, and, in the very worst cases, assault. This sends women the message that they are not only not welcome in the workplace, but they are also not safe there.

Studies estimate more than 80 percent of women experience sexual harassment in the workplace. Dr. Stefanie K. Johnson, from the University of Colorado Boulder, thinks the actual number is higher. Stefanie studies workplace harassment. She says sexual harassment isn't about sex at all but about power. It's a form of bullying. "It's putting women in their place," she says. "You're stripping away their accomplishments and saying, 'At the end of the day, you're just a hot piece of ass.'"

Stefanie points out that women who are attractive but who have masculine characteristics (i.e., are assertive, ambitious, etc.) are far more likely to be sexually harassed than extremely feminine women. If a woman is hyperfeminine, "the men might ask you out," she says, "but they likely won't harass you, because they're like, 'Okay. She knows her place.' But if you're tough and you're cute, then you're really in for it."

Stefanie says women tend to experience more harassment the higher up they move in a company. She is quick to add that women with less power are often more victimized by the harassment they experience, because they have fewer ways to fight back or respond.

LGBTQ workers are frequent targets of sexual harassment in the workplace. Sharita Gruberg, of the Center for American Progress, points out that this harassment is often couched in a joke: "People think, 'Oh, I'm not gay' or 'I'm not queer, but this person is, so I'm going to make jokes.' Like fake sexual advances." Sharita says this harassment is so common and so scarring, LGBTQ workers will avoid companies, and even entire professions, where they feel they are likely to encounter it again. "It's really common for folks to just hide," she says.

But why sexual harassment instead of, say, calling someone names or ignoring them or stealing their parking spot? Stefanie K. Johnson says, for men, feeling powerful and feeling sexually aroused are linked. So sexual harassment is a way for a man to assert his dominance. "There's an unconscious association between power and sex for men," Stefanie explains. "Having power over someone is sexually arousing for men, and being sexually aroused makes men feel powerful." She notes that this is one reason why men will sometimes stand around in groups leering at women: "Like 'Oh, I'd tap that.' To diminish women makes you more of an alpha male."

Does This Count as Harassment?

In the midst of the Me Too fallout at NPR, I overheard a conversation happening between some male colleagues in the kitchen about hugging. Could you still hug women at work? Was that harassment? What if the woman initiated the hug? Was a short hug different from a long hug? "It's like a minefield," one of them said, sounding panicked. I walked into another room to start laughing, but I also had to admit I didn't know the answers myself. I realized in that moment how nebulous the definition of *harassment* felt and how fast the rules were changing.

I asked Stefanie Johnson about this and she said she hears this kind of thing a lot, mainly because there is a great deal of uncertainty about what counts as sexual harassment. She says there are a lot of very well-meaning people who are not sure where to draw the line.

But there is a line. Stefanie says sociologists and psychologists break sexual harassment down into three categories: sexual coercion, unwanted attention, and gender harassment.

Sexual coercion is the quid pro quo kind of harassment: "If you sleep with me, I'll give you this promotion." Stefanie says this is the most extreme and obvious form of harassment, but it also tends to happen less frequently than the other two kinds.

The second form of harassment is unwanted sexual attention. "That goes from leering, all the way to touching and making sexual comments," Stefanie says. This kind of harassment often has a very destructive, cumulative effect on victims.

One woman I spoke with—I'll call her Kelly—worked for a small sports marketing company. She was frequently asked to work with a senior member of the team who, she says, was notorious for harassing women: "I became a frequent target of the creepiness," she recalls. "Every morning he would come into my office and kind of gesture for me to stand up at my desk, and [he'd] look at my outfit and comment on it and then give me a hug and a kiss on the cheek." Kelly tried to speak to the higher-ups about what was happening, but she says nobody wanted to take any action, because they liked the man's work. She felt helpless. "I didn't feel like there was any recourse."

Finally, there is the most common form of sexual harassment, which isn't necessarily sexual at all: gender harassment. Gender harassment is essentially negative or disparaging comments about women, like "Women are too emotional to do this job," or "Women aren't as good at this kind of work."

This kind of harassment happens all the time, right out in the open. Nobel Prize–winning biochemist Tim Hunt famously said female scientists cause trouble in labs, because they tend to cry when criticized and because everybody starts falling in love with each other. There was the infamous "Google memo" in which an engineer at Google wrote a manifesto claiming the reason there were fewer women in tech was because women are naturally less apt at programming. And in 2005, famed economist and then president of Harvard Larry H. Summers was trying to explain the shortage of women in senior posts in science and engineering at the university and said men tend to outperform women in sciences and math because of biological differences.

These are highly publicized examples and in every case the men who said these things took enormous heat, but they were merely echoing what people say all the time, in much lower-profile settings.

This might not seem like it should be in the same category as creepy outfit scans or unwanted touching, but Stefanie points out the effects of gender harassment are extremely destructive. Remember, we are creatures who live and die by stories, and stories have a powerful effect on us. Studies have found that women actually perform more poorly when they are told that women aren't as good as men are at whatever task they are performing. In one case, a math test was given to a group of people, all of whom were told that women tend to perform badly on math tests. Guess what? The women performed worse than the men. When a different group was given the same math test without the gender commentary, the women's scores were equal to the men's scores. And the impact extends beyond job performance. Stefanie points out harassment can cause health problems and create trauma. It can push women to leave jobs and even entire fields.

Lesbian, Slut, Tits, Anal

Harassment isn't always just an individual issue. In some cases whole companies or professions have cultures of harassment. Back in 2016, Alice Wu, an undergraduate at UC Berkeley, was excited about majoring in economics. She heard about an online gathering place for young economists called Economics Job Market Rumors. It had started out as an informal chat room for economists to talk shop, but over the years it had developed into a go-to site for job openings, professional opportunities, and industry gossip. It was also notorious for being an incredibly toxic place for women.

Alice visited the site and was horrified at what she saw: "A lot of very sexual stuff." Alice was a budding economist, and economists love data, so she started thinking about how she could quantify what she was seeing. Alice decided to use language software to do an analysis of the words people used when they talked about men versus women on the site. The results were pretty alarming: The words most strongly associated with women included: *lesbian, slut, tits, anal, feminazi, hot, vagina, naked, boobs, pregnant, gorgeous, horny, crush, beautiful, secretary, shopping, date,* and *prostitute.*

The words most associated with men included some offensive terms, like *homo,* but were mostly neutral professional terms, like *advisor, Nobel, recession, Wharton, mathematician, pricing, textbook,* and *brilliant.*

Worst of all, Alice says, if you were serious about a career in economics, there was no avoiding this site.

Dealing with Harassment

Figuring out how to respond to sexual harassment isn't easy. Companies will tell you to go to the human resources department, but that might not be the best starting point. It is the job of someone in HR to protect the company, and that can often mean protecting the people in power. If the person harassing you is powerful or well-connected within the organization, HR might not be willing or even able to censure him or her. This happened at NPR: The head of the newsroom was accused of systematically harassing women at the company. The harassment was reported to HR many times over many years, but nothing ever came of it. Why? Probably because he was a very powerful figure at the company. It wasn't until an outside organization (the *Washington Post*) reported on the accusations that the man was put on leave and eventually resigned.

Machiavelli's Lesson: Fight Back

Sexual harassment might be tricky, but it's essentially a power game and there are ways to respond that can be effective. One thing everyone agrees on is that you should keep a record of the harassment: Save emails, voice messages, and texts. If it's an incident, write down a description of what happened with a date and a time. If you go to your manager, HR, or even a lawyer, a written record is crucial.

Whatever you do, don't put yourself through that situation any longer than you have to. I know (personally) that can be easier said than done. Some situations might seem nebulous or complicated. Also, responding can come with consequences. Even still, in the words of Machiavelli: Shut. It. Down. Right. Now. At least, that's how I interpret this: "Whoever shall fortify his town well . . . will never be attacked without great caution, for men are always adverse to enterprises where difficulties can be seen" (Chapter X, MPE). Translation: Make harassing you as hard and troublesome and unpleasant as possible and it will be less likely to happen.

Above all, be understanding and kind to yourself. Being harassed is terrible and it is not your fault. I have been there and I wish I had not spent so much time and energy beating myself up for not responding perfectly.

Machiavelli's Lesson: Ask an Honest Question

Dr. Stefanie K. Johnson says one effective response to harassment can be asking an earnest question—"Like, 'What do you mean?' or 'Why are you saying that?' or 'Why are you asking me that?'—with some ounce of empathy, like as 'I'm really curious: What's your goal here?'" Stefanie says this accomplishes a few things. First, it gives someone the benefit of the doubt. You are not attacking anyone or accusing anyone; you are asking them a question. Stefanie says this is also a good way to call out behavior, because if someone said something without thinking, it gives them a moment to reflect on what they've said. "If you have to think through, for a second, what you've just said out loud," she explains, "you might realize the folly of your ways, and that's probably better than me telling you, 'Asshole, knock it off,' because then people just get defensive. This way they can actually listen."

Also, this is an understated yet firm way to stand up for yourself.

It's mild but proactive and will make you a less attractive mark for a harasser without creating a big scene or lots of drama.

Lawyer Up

Talking to a lawyer can be incredibly helpful. It sounds extreme, but it really isn't. The initial consultation with a lawyer is free and can be very empowering. The lawyer will most definitely be on your side and sympathetic. She can talk you through your options and the information that you should be collecting. Even if you never officially report an incident, just knowing that you have the resources to take action can provide a strong mental shift: You're not helpless. You have power and options and people (and the law) on your side ready to fight for you. Actually taking legal action is a step that you can consider; obviously, that is more extreme. The initial consultation, though, has no real downside, costs no money, and can help you start to navigate a difficult situation.

Machiavelli's Lesson: Tell Someone

If you are experiencing harassment, tell someone: a lawyer, a friend, a family member, a supervisor. Speaking out about what you've witnessed or experienced can be helpful and healing. And it's gotten much easier to do. Dr. Stefanie K. Johnson says she used to see a lot of reluctance on the part of women to talk about the harassment they'd experienced. "People didn't want the stigma," she says. In the past, when people complained about harassment, it was not uncommon for them to be asked questions like, "What did you do to deserve that?" or "What were you wearing?" Stefanie says Me Too has done much to change that attitude, and talking to someone who is sympathetic and will listen can be empowering.

Finally, Stefanie says, it's crucial that women be a resource for other people experiencing harassment. If you see someone else getting harassed, stepping in is important. "If no one steps forward, it kind of validates the behavior to other people. It's so important that we speak up for others."

Economist Alice Wu discovered this when she did her language analysis of the online economics forum. Her UC Berkeley research got a lot of attention and was even written up in the *New York Times*. Alice was initially reluctant to have that attention: She was wary of being so publicly critical of a profession she was just entering and feared being attacked on the site itself. Instead, after the article was published, she received an enormous outpouring of gratitude.

"I got all of these emails from female economists thanking me for bringing this to light," she says. "Some women I talked to had dropped out of economics because they'd had such bad experiences. And the male economists were like, 'Thanks for doing this. We didn't realize how bad it is.'" The article's publication also sparked a huge conversation within the field of economics: The website started to be monitored and the American Economic Association, the main professional group for economists in the United States, highlighted gender issues the following year at its main conference.

SALLIE KRAWCHECK:
She-Wolf of Wall Street

It's hard to think of a bigger boys' club than Wall Street: big money, big egos, steak dinners, strip clubs, the dreaded "boom boom room." The stories of harassment and gender discrimination in the world of finance and banking are legendary. Succeeding as a woman on Wall Street is incredibly hard; achieving a leadership position is almost unheard-of. Sallie Krawcheck did both. Sallie has been a CEO and CFO at Smith Barney (part of Citigroup at the time) and an executive at Bank of America and Merrill Lynch, among other executive positions.

During her career, Sallie has run the true gauntlet when it comes to dealing with harassment and a lack of respect in the workplace. When she first started as an analyst on Wall Street, Sallie would arrive each morning to find Xeroxed copies of her colleagues' genitals on her desk. Once, when she was leaning over a desk to look at a spreadsheet, a man started pretending to have sex with her. "I only knew because there was laughter," she recalls.

And it wasn't just that colleagues were harassing her; Sallie's gender affected her ability to get promotions and jobs. She says once, after many rounds of interviews, she got a verbal job offer from a bank that she was incredibly excited about. Then one of the executives saw her on the sidewalk with her baby—she had been careful not to mention that she had a baby in the interviews—and the offer was rescinded. Sallie was devastated. "When I literally said, 'You wouldn't do this to a man,' they literally said, 'No, of course we wouldn't.'"

Sallie says in meetings she would often be talked over or her ideas would be attacked or ignored. In one place Sallie worked, one of the male managers would immediately start shaking his head every time she spoke. "I must have looked like the gal who didn't go to prom with him," she says, laughing. "Whether it was my Southern accent, whether it is that I was blond . . . there was something about me that he just viscerally, desperately disliked."

Sallie says she can laugh about it now, but at the time it caused her enormous stress. "Professionally, this was world-ending," she says. "I mean, it can have sort of a big effect on your day . . . and your career."

Sallie's Lesson: Fight White Man with White Man

Sallie employed a few tactics to deal with the harassment and lack of respect she experienced on Wall Street. For dealing with hostility in meetings, she found an ally: a higher-up at the bank who could help her find direction amid all the head shaking: "He'd be like, 'Don't let it get to you. You're on the right track.'" This helped her figure out which ideas to focus on and where to direct her efforts: "I was successful faster because he would review my research and critique it and advise me."

Sallie was an extraordinary worker with unique ideas, and in spite of the obstacles, her rise in the world of banking was pretty meteoric. Before long, ambitious, cocky Wall Street men had to answer to her. They were not necessarily excited about this. When Sallie was promoted to the position of director, a bunch of the analysts she was in charge of left because, she believed, they didn't want a female boss.

"It was terrible," she recalls. "But every time I started freaking out, I'd think, 'Okay, I'm hiring. I keep hiring.' And I focused on, 'How can I help the people who are here? What can I do that will make them more successful?'"

Sallie's work and management skills somehow broke through the sexist noise, and eventually the head of Citigroup, Sandy Weill, asked to meet with her and said, "You call a spade a spade. You see things differently from other people. You put the client at the center . . . You don't play the political game. How would you like to be the CEO of Citigroup's Global Wealth Management Division?" It was a true dream job and one of the best moments of her professional life. Still, says Sallie, the Hotbox and Cinderella Syndrome did not disappear. If anything, they got more intense, so Sallie developed a few strategies.

Sallie's Lesson: Leave 'Em Laughing

The first trick Sallie learned was to joke around and keep the tone light: "I learned that humor softens things," she explains. "If someone is laughing with you, it's hard for them to hate you at the same time."

Sallie's Lesson: Whose Idea Was It, Anyway?

Another technique Sallie used when introducing a controversial opinion or disagreeing with someone would be to put a little distance between herself and her idea. This technique helped other people be open-minded and loosen their grip on their own ideas. Sallie says: "So instead of saying, 'Your team is heading in exactly the wrong direction. We should go here,' I would say something like, 'How about, just for fun, we explore a completely different alternative?' and then help navigate the team toward the alternative when it became clear that I was right. I also learned how to say things like, 'Hey, you know, I don't even know that I believe this, but just for argument's sake, how about A, B, C?'"

Sallie's Lesson: It's Not Me, It's You . . .

The biggest lesson Sallie learned from her years on Wall Street was that no matter how smart you are and how hard you try, being a woman in the workplace will sometimes just bite you: "Sometimes it doesn't matter how much you contort yourself and sugarcoat it. It's not going to make a difference." In those moments, Sallie's best advice is to understand that the situation is not your fault. And if you are interrupted or have your ideas stolen, or are called "sweetheart," or some creep in upper management gives you a shoulder massage, you should not feel like you've failed because you wore the wrong clothes or didn't think of the perfect witty comeback. "Some advice that I don't think is given often enough is 'This is not your fault,'" Sallie says. "It's the culture."

Sallie's Lesson: Silver Lining Discrimination

Sallie says an essential survival skill on Wall Street was noticing some of the tactical advantages that came with being a woman: "You couldn't forget me; you could forget the man with the brown hair and the glasses who wears the tie; but if you are the lone female, then it's impossible for people to forget you." This helped Sallie's ideas stand out and helped her make connections with people in the industry. Everyone, even the people at the very top, noticed her and wanted to meet "the woman."

Also, Sallie began to realize that some of the more "womanly" ways she spent her time proved to be major advantages: "I always said that having a baby and having to get my hair done actually helped me. The men would work and work and work and work, and I would be jealous because they would get to keep working and I would go home and play with the baby for a couple of hours and bathe him, feed him, and put him to bed." But that time with her baby and getting her hair done gave Sallie her best ideas: "My differentiating insight as a Wall Street analyst . . . came to me while I was getting my hair colored. And many of my ideas came after I played with my son, and the research tells you that the right way to be creative is to take a break and then let your subconscious go to work. And so the guys never stop working, and I beat them because I had a baby."

A Little Respect

In the workplace—and every place—people will try to tell you who you are and how you should be treated. Getting the respect you deserve requires drawing boundaries and standing up to the powers that try to push them. This can feel like it has to be aggressive or confrontational, but it doesn't. What it does require is knowing in your bones that you have a right to be in the workplace—without being looked over, interrupted, excluded, or massaged. You have as much a right to be in the workplace as the white man you're sitting next to (and probably more if statistics are to be believed). Drawing boundaries and standing up for yourself aren't easy things to do, but they're worth the trouble, and every time you do, you will be contributing to a more respectful, inclusive workplace where everyone can thrive.

5

Support

Janet Yellen: The Power of Preparation and Pulling Up Your Socks

"The first method of estimating the intelligence of a ruler is to look at the men he has around him."

—Machiavelli, *The Prince* (Chapter XXII, MPE)

S upport. This is not an obvious manifestation of power and may even sound like the antithesis of the independent career woman machete-ing her way to the C-suite. But the truth is, without support, you won't get very far in this world. You simply can't rise to the top of an organization or a profession alone. And in the workplace, women are not getting the support they need.

The Mentor Problem

The support problem begins at the very start of women's careers, in the crucial taking-under-the-wing phase—in other words, finding a mentor.

It can be a tricky thing to get a mentor if you are a woman. For one thing, as a woman, people are less likely to want to mentor you. In a study out of Yale University, discussed earlier, researchers cooked up fake résumés for students in STEM fields who were applying for a lab manager position (a job for people starting their careers—very important for future success). Identical résumés were topped with the name "John" or "Jennifer." The result? Faculty members thought

"John" was more qualified and expressed a greater willingness to mentor him. This wasn't just male faculty members, either. Even the *women* were more excited about mentoring John. (*Et tu,* ladies?) This probably helps explain why fewer than half of women report having a mentor at work. This lack of mentorship has real consequences: People who are mentored get promoted more often, make more money, and report being happier in their careers.

Part of the problem with finding a mentor is that people tend to mentor people who remind them of themselves. If the higher-ups at your workplace are a bunch of older white men who are all die-hard Pats fans and you are a Latina from Oregon who's really into performance poetry, chances are you will not remind any higher-ups of themselves. And even if there are women in leadership roles at your company, they may hesitate to support you because they might see you as a threat. This is known as the "queen bee syndrome," and it often crops up in places where there's a feeling of tokenism among women. After all, if there are only a few slots for women and you have one of those slots, why would you champion some pretty young thing who is cheaper and hungrier and knows how to use Slack?

Women of color have an especially difficult time finding mentors. Christine Pride encountered this problem in the publishing industry. It wasn't that there was a lack of women in senior roles; the problem was, none of them looked like her. Christine is African American and most of the women in publishing are white. "I can count the number of editors of color on two hands," she says.

This posed a particular challenge for Christine, because publishing is an apprenticeship industry, and to rise through the ranks in a publishing house, it's crucial to have higher-ups advocating for you and mentoring you. "A lot of publishing folks went to the same three schools," she says. "They've summered in the same place in the Hamptons or Maine; they love the same writers and they go to the same sample sales. And so when those women look at the next generation of editors, they're like, 'I see myself in you. I'm going to help you succeed.' But I don't look like them."

Christine has always gotten along well with people and was able to create a broad network of colleagues she truly liked, but she suspects the lack of diversity and mentoring in her industry held her back. "I've had a long and successful career in publishing, but you always wonder," she says. "I don't know what kind of career I would have had if I were white. I mean, it's unknowable and unprovable, but, all things being equal, I probably would have had a more successful career. I don't know, but it's a sense."

Me Too and Mentoring

Ever since the Me Too movement started, I cannot tell you the number of times I've heard men talk about how they avoid certain situations with women entirely now, including mentoring roles. A man championing a woman can be viewed with a certain degree of skepticism. One woman I spoke with said her husband works at a teaching hospital and has decided not to mentor any female surgeons going forward because he has seen colleagues' mentoring be misconstrued. This is actually the rule rather than the exception. Research has shown that the majority of male managers do not feel comfortable mentoring a woman at work or even socializing with one. And that number has been on the rise. This is a major disadvantage if you are a woman trying to find a mentor or even just trying to do a little networking. The person who might best be able to help you might not feel comfortable helping you. And even if he does, his help might be viewed with suspicion.

Mentor Hunting

To get the support you need in your workplace and your industry, you should prepare to go mentor hunting. Think about who might be able to help you—people whose work you admire or who have a job you want or who are top decision-makers at your company. Send them an email telling them you admire their work and are inspired by them, and that you would love to take them out to coffee or for a drink to talk about their career. Definitely say you want to talk about *their* career and not *your* career; it will make them way more likely to say yes. (If there's one thing I've learned in fifteen years of reporting, it's that people like talking about themselves, and the promise of getting to wax philosophical about one's successful career to an adoring young person is pretty powerful bait.) If the person in question doesn't respond, try one more time and then email someone else. You are mentor fishing. You want to find someone you click with and who will be available to you.

Mentor hunting might take a little time: There's a certain je ne sais quoi involved in a mentor/mentee relationship. "It's kind of like finding a friend," says Wall Street CEO Sallie Krawcheck. She recommends looking for a mix of qualifications and chemistry.

Ideally, you should have more than one person mentoring you. Try for a range of mentors: people who are very high up in the company (maybe you meet with them less frequently and it's more formal, but these people can give you a lot of help when opportunities open up at the company) and people who are midway up in the company (maybe you have a closer, more social relationship with them and they can help you deal with day-to-day things). Also, consider mentors who work at different companies; they can help you tap into opportunities and networks outside your bubble. Mentors are your wilderness guides for the workplace. Having a diversity of experiences and advice to help you navigate the professional wilds will always serve you well.

With male mentors, or mentors where there might be a concern about the relationship being misconstrued, consider asking to meet for coffee during the day rather than a drink after work. You can even suggest meeting in the office, if there's a lounge area or a kitchen. When you meet, you can be a bit more formal and earnest than usual—make it clear that you are seeking advice and meeting in a strictly professional light. Things can become more relaxed later on, but being overly formal at first might help to put the mentor at ease.

Calling All Mentors

So now that you have your mentor, use them. Ask them for help. Women tend to be shy about asking for things directly or voicing their ambitions, but just do it. Be direct and honest about where you want to go in your career; don't hedge. Make sure your mentors know what your goals are. Also, be sure to ask them what they would be doing if they were you. They might suggest something you've never thought of. So much of the destructive effect of discrimination happens in one's own head when we start to scale back our ambitions or limit our own sense of possibility. A mentor's vision can snap you out of that.

Defining the Relationship

One thing to keep in mind is that your mentor is not your friend— not that you can't be friendly with your mentor, but this is not a typical friendship. The boundaries in these relationships can be tricky, and getting them wrong can have major consequences. In the early part of my career, I tended to drink too much when out with mentors. I was excited to be out with people I admired and was nervous, so I drank until I wasn't nervous. In one case, I was out with a very senior woman at my company and I drank five glasses of wine, talked about a recent breakup for more than an hour, cried in front of her, and still can't remember how I got home. She was very gracious and kind, but, OMG, DON'T DO THAT.

Make no mistake, I would absolutely recommend bringing important issues to your mentor—even emotional or sensitive issues. I also think you should feel free to express emotions, and yes, even have a glass of wine (maybe not five). But don't be too raw in front of a mentor. If you find out your male colleague is making twice your salary, go out with friends, blow off steam, cry, and curse the skies, but when you call your mentor, those emotions should be in the background. You are going to them for help and for actionable advice. This is a powerful person who could recommend you for opportunities or go to bat for you. You want them to see your best, most professional self.

Machiavelli's Lesson: Be the Mentor You Want to See in the World

No matter where you are in your career, you will always be senior to someone. So find a mentee! Find a person who is just starting out, someone you really believe in, and tell them that you think they have talent and offer to be of help. This does a few things: First, it's good karma. Second, if there's a promising young person, they are likely to go places and be a great connection for the future. Third, people in junior positions can be helpful allies and sources of information for you.

Finally, mentoring people can help your profession evolve: You can single-handedly make someone feel more welcome or secure in a job or career.

After her experience of feeling like a bit of an outsider in the publishing world, Christine Pride made it a point to promote and champion people of color in her field. She says whenever a person of color reaches out to her for advice, she makes time to talk with them and help in any way she can. "It's my way of paying it forward," she says.

Machiavelli's Lesson: Beware the Mentor Trap

While finding a mentor is beneficial, you also want to be mindful of your mentor's limitations. So many times I've spoken with people who have gotten bad or limiting advice from mentors. Remember, a mentor's advice is coming from his or her own personal experience, and even if it's coming from a good place, it can be destructive or mislead you. If it's advice about how something isn't possible or advice that seems questionable or isn't sitting well, don't take it as gospel. As Machiavelli says, if "the armour of others is too wide, or too strait for us; it falls off us, or it weighs us down" (Chapter XIII, DTE). In other words, what worked for your mentor might not work for you and might even hold you back.

Machiavelli's Lesson: The Almighty Network

Ultimately, your goal in the workplace is to build a network: peers, mentors, mentees. These people make up your professional network—a source of information, advocacy, support, advice, and sanity. Machiavelli preached the importance of a network hard. The smart prince, he writes, "is defended by being well armed and having good allies" (Chapter XIX, MPE). Having a strong network is essential to rising in any profession. Wall Street CEO Sallie Krawcheck says she always remembers advice she got from her friend Carla Harris (a senior banker at Morgan Stanley): "All the important decisions about your career are made when you're not in the room. People decide to hire you, fire you, promote you, fund you, send you on the overseas assignment, all when you're not there. So how do you ensure that you have someone in the room fighting for you? I would strongly argue that you need to have in place your Personal Board of Directors. Those are your mentors, your sponsors, your confidants . . ."

Support and Resources

In mid-career, support in the workplace will often manifest itself as resources: equipment, space, time, staff, and money. Here, too, women struggle.

In 1999, MIT did a review of its female staff. At the time, MIT's faculty was 92 percent male. They were trying to hire more women and make sure the women who did work at the university felt supported. It turned out, they most definitely did not. In spite of the nearly endless resources at MIT, women faculty members were struggling to get workspace, equipment, staff, assistants, and grant funding—far more so than their male colleagues. MIT publicly released the report and started trying to make changes. One female faculty member was quoted as saying: "I was unhappy at M.I.T. for more than a decade. I thought it was the price you paid if you wanted to be a scientist at an elite academic institution. After the committee formed and the dean responded, my life began to change. My research blossomed, my funding tripled. Now I love every aspect of my job. It is hard to understand how I survived those years—or why."

Negotiating for Support

If you want to claim your share of limited resources, you will probably need to push to get them. Here is another area where having a multifaceted approach to negotiation can get you some real benefits. When you're starting a new job or gunning for a raise, don't just think about money; think about resources that would help your work be the best it could be: an assistant, more space, better equipment, a bigger team, etc. What would make your project a success? What would make you enjoy work more? What do your male colleagues have that you would like to have?

Money, Money, Money

Support doesn't *only* manifest itself in money, but, truly, money is a big one. And women simply don't get the financial backing that men do. Women head about 17 percent of the start-ups in Silicon Valley. That is an alarmingly low number, but even more alarming is the fact that female-led start-ups get only about 2 percent of venture capital.

Tech superstar Lisa Gelobter got some of that 2 percent and lived to tell the tale. Lisa is now the CEO of her own start-up, tEQuitable, a software company that helps businesses address workplace biases and discrimination. But before she started her company, Lisa had a hugely successful career in Silicon Valley: She was part of the team that created the technology behind Hulu and web animation; she worked for the Obama administration, and she was profiled by the History Channel for Black History Month, celebrating her contributions to technology. To put it mildly, investing in one of Lisa's projects should feel like a very safe bet. But despite all of this and the fact that Lisa had a solid business plan that involved a short path to profitability—not to mention that money was flying around Silicon Valley like crazy at the time—Lisa had a lot of trouble raising the cash for tEQuitable: "I had one prominent investor say, 'You are too technical.' And I'm thinking . . . 'Too technical? Is this because I'm Black? Because I'm female? Because the idea is terrible? Because I didn't pitch it well?'" What made matters worse, a short while later, Lisa was at a social gathering and started talking to a young, white Stanford grad. He began describing a project he and his friend were working on, involving an industry they wanted to "disrupt." They weren't sure what kind of company to start, but they decided to see if they could raise some money to research that question. "He told me, 'Yeah, we raised $2 million in a week just to explore and figure out what we wanted to build.'"

Eventually, Lisa and her business partner were accepted into the prestigious Y Combinator start-up incubator and got their funding, but even so, it wasn't as much as she had hoped: "Literally every single person I talked to raised more money in less time than me." Her company, incidentally, *was* a good bet. It's been a major success, and the product they make has been in high demand. But Lisa's difficulties are the norm. Women simply don't get as much support as men do for their projects, ideas, and companies. The small-business loans women receive in the United States are, on average, about a third smaller than the loans approved for men, and women-owned businesses are far more likely to experience cash shortages and to have their growth hindered by a lack of funds.

Girl Angel

A lot of the reason women and minorities aren't getting the money they need is that they are held to higher standards. Freada Kapor Klein has made a lot of money off that fact.

Freada is one of the most powerful venture capitalists in Silicon Valley. Her firm, Kapor Capital, makes a point of funding companies that are founded by people who are underrepresented in tech: women as well as Black and Latinx entrepreneurs. Her group has some of the highest returns of any venture capital firm in the country. Freada credits that to the fact that female and minority entrepreneurs are almost always much better prepared and organized than their white, male counterparts. They represent extraordinary investment opportunities that many people don't see because of unconscious biases.

"A business plan with a different name on it, whether it's a gender-specific name or an African American–sounding name— that identical business plan or pitch for a start-up gets evaluated entirely differently," Freada says. "I personally know of situations where white folks with mediocre track records raised twice as much money in one-tenth the time as African Americans with stellar track records. There is no explanation other than the racism that is embedded in the networks."

Freada says the situation isn't just unfair; it's also hurting our economy and our society. "We are shutting ourselves off from a whole bunch of ideas," she says. "We are not resourcing people who have different perspectives on problems, so those problems are less likely to get solved: people who have been homeless, people who have been incarcerated, people who live in neighborhoods with high rates of crime, people who are food insecure. We're not hearing ideas that can address those problems." The problems that *are* getting solved: chocolate chip cookies delivered to your door 24/7, finding a discounted hotel room at the last minute, finding someone to walk your dog, finding the fastest route to the airport. All of these are very successful businesses that have created jobs and provide important services to people, but they also all reflect the needs of only one part of society.

Freada's Lesson: The Warm Intro

One of the keys to success in getting support for a business is something known in Silicon Valley as the "warm intro." The warm intro is a personal referral, often from someone you know to someone of power and influence (and hopefully with tons of money). "Somebody will write and say, 'Hey, my friend/my colleague/my former team-mate is starting a company and raising money and I'd like you to take a meeting with him,'" Freada explains. She says the warm intro is how the lion's share of companies get funded in Silicon Valley. It's also where a lot of racism, sexism, and socioeconomic exclusion come into play, because a warm intro depends on insider networks. Getting a warm intro is a powerful way to start solving the support problem. But if you're not in one of those self-selecting groups, how do you get one?

Start with your mentor. Can she help? Try a college or high school alumni network. Maybe this person grew up in your hometown or is an avid stamp collector or a Lakers fan like you, or maybe you follow each other on Instagram. Maybe they're a friend of a friend of a friend. Find any commonality or excuse you can and reach out to people who might be able to get you a warm intro or who might, themselves, have the resources you need.

If you're feeling timid about asking someone you've never met to do you a solid, consider that Machiavelli thought asking for a favor was actually a power move. He observed that when someone helps you, not only do they feel a connection to you, but they will also often feel like *they* owe *you*. "It is the nature of men to incur obligation as much by the benefits they render as by those they receive" (Chapter X, DTE). It's a strange phenomenon, but it makes sense: If someone asks us for a favor, it makes us feel powerful, connected, and successful. It's natural that we would feel grateful to a person for making us feel that way.

Vivienne's Lesson: Hang in There

Vivienne Ming, neuroscientist and artificial intelligence expert, experienced the fundraising gender divide in a unique way. Vivienne is transgender, and when she was a man in her twenties, she went to work raising money for a film industry start-up. "The only useful part of that experience was seeing how easy it was to raise money as a man, just so I had a point of comparison," she recalls. "I had flunked out of college, flunked out of life. Why anyone ever offered us money is a complete mystery to me." Vivienne had a remarkable and life-changing turnaround, went back to school, graduated at the top of her class, and ended up, a decade later, with a PhD and an expertise in artificial intelligence and machine learning. She and her wife put together a business plan and a formal presentation, and went around to venture capitalists and angel investors to try to raise money for their company. "Before my transition, with my being homeless and being a dropout . . . no one ever questioned me," says Vivienne. "As soon as I had long blond hair and a dress, no one would give us money. They absolutely did not want to fund a company started by two women. And they loved our technology—didn't question that at all."

Vivienne says, for her, the key to unlocking venture capital as a woman was getting her first company to turn a profit. "Once you prove yourself that first time out, it does change, but that first time becomes a fundamental barrier." Vivienne's message: Keep pushing. Don't get discouraged. The initial success is, by far, the hardest, so expect to struggle at the start and know that it will get a lot easier after that.

Boss Bitch

When women reach leadership positions, they can also experience a lack of support—from the people they are managing as well as from the higher-ups who put them there. The reason points us right back to our favorite place: the Hotbox. Here's how it manifests itself in leadership roles: The further a woman advances in her career, the harder it gets to walk the line between "good woman" and "strong leader." After all, when you take on a leadership role, there are moments when you can't be nice or soften what you say or be self-deprecating: You have to make a hard call, pull rank, tell somebody their work isn't good enough, fire someone, or deny someone a promotion.

"That's where the trouble starts," says gender researcher Dr. Cecilia L. Ridgeway. "There's a sense of it being improper or illegitimate. And that immediately, implicitly arouses questions of motivation: 'Why are you doing this?' And then people think: 'Self-interest. You just want to grab for yourself.' That's where you get the B-word." If a man gives orders, he's being tough and strong and doing what needs to be done. If a woman gives orders, she's a self-interested bitch who's stepping on people to grab more power.

Machiavelli's Solution: The Meta-Softener

So what's a lady to do? One solution comes back to our old friend the softener. But instead of a warm tone or a smiley face, this situation calls for something bigger: a Meta-Softener.

Remember the Erin Brockovich Exception? People can get behind a woman fighting for something or speaking out, as long as she is doing it on behalf of someone else. Or, in this case, something else. If you're a leader and a woman, "the team" is your Hotbox escape hatch. "When women make it, they almost always make it by doing it this way," Cecilia notes. This magical formula is something management consultant types call "transformational leadership."

Here's how the "Go, Team!," Meta-Softener, transformational leadership trick works: Whatever you're doing or pushing for, frame it as something that is for the good of the group. You're asking people to stay late *for the team*. You're demoting Joe *for the team*. You're promoting Barbara and hiring Mickey *for the team*. This tactic will enable you to get support for your vision and your leadership a lot more easily.

For example: "Listen. I know how important our work is. That is why I care so deeply about this team and this project. Evan and Marie, I like where you're going, but it's not enough. I am going to need you to work this weekend and start from scratch: Put together something that is more in line with what we discussed. I will be here to support you however I can. If we pull together and do our very best work, I know we can make this happen. I really believe this team is exceptional."

There is a bonus: Transformational leadership turns out to be more effective at motivating people than an authoritarian approach.

Managers, male and female, who use the transformational leadership tactic are perceived as more effective and are better able to accomplish their goals.

There is a Machiavellian bonus here, too: If you can pull this off and lead effectively, minds will change and the Hotbox will start to cool. Machiavelli observed that when people see a leader who benefits them—a person who is creating a situation in which they can thrive, feel appreciated, and do their best work—they will drop their prejudices and get on board. "Men are attracted more by the present than by the past," he writes, "and when they find the present good, they enjoy it and seek no further . . ." (Chapter XXIV, MPE).

JANET YELLEN:
The Power of Preparation and Pulling Up Your Socks

One of my very favorite photographs in the world is, weirdly, of a bunch of bankers. It was taken in Jackson Hole, Wyoming, at the annual meeting of the heads of central banks from all over the world. The photo features a sea of men in dark suits, and, right in the middle, is a petite woman with a white pageboy wearing a mint-green suit jacket, standing perfectly erect and looking relaxed and totally in command. It is Janet Yellen, the first woman to head the U.S. central bank and the first female Secretary of the Treasury.

There aren't many economists who rise to the level of superstar, but Janet Yellen most definitely does. Janet headed the Council of Economic Advisers under President Bill Clinton, ran the San Francisco Federal Reserve Bank, headed the U.S. Federal Reserve from 2014 to 2018, and then took the post of Treasury secretary under President Joe Biden.

As Federal Reserve chair, Janet Yellen oversaw the biggest drop in unemployment of any Federal Reserve chair in modern history. Under her watch, inflation remained low and the stock market thrived. Pretty much everybody agreed she was aces. Democratic Senator Elizabeth Warren called her "one of the most successful Fed chairs in history." Republican President Donald Trump described her as an "absolutely spectacular person" who had "done a terrific job." Janet Yellen achieved what can seem impossible as a woman: She got to a top leadership position; she was an extremely effective leader; *and* she was well-liked by her bosses and the people who worked for her. For a woman in a top leadership role, that is basically a miracle on the order of loaves and fishes. Janet Yellen pulled it off.

Love and Economics

As soon as Janet started college, there was no doubt in her mind what she wanted to do with her life. "It really was kind of love at first sight," she says of economics. Janet says she loved the analytical approach to problems and the ability to use economic principles to find real solutions to things. Throughout her schooling, Janet felt very supported by her professors, but there were not many women in the field. "I recall three women in my class," she says. "It was a very isolating experience."

When she took her first teaching job at Harvard, Janet encountered the lack-of-ladies issue again. The male economics students would hang out in a big group, socialize, and collaborate on research. Janet was mostly excluded from all of that. "It was socially isolating," she recalls. "It wasn't natural for them to include me. I was handicapped . . . though I thought at the time I was just screwing up."

That all changed when Janet happened to sit next to a handsome young man in the Federal Reserve cafeteria one day. They started talking about labor policy (as you do). "We realized from the first minute that we were very compatible in terms of our views," she says. They dated, fell in love, and married. They also started collaborating on economics research. With her husband's partnership, Janet says she felt like she was finally "in the club." "That gave me a sense of professional involvement and belonging that I didn't have [before]," she says.

Janet very quickly began to stand out in the field of economics in her own right. Her work started to get a lot of attention, and she was asked by President Bill Clinton to head the Council of Economic Advisers at the White House in 1997. It would mean working fourteen-hour days, running a team of dozens of economists, and helping set policy for the country. It would also mean a major disruption for Janet's whole family. At that point Janet, her husband, and their teenage son lived in the Bay Area, and taking the White House job would mean a cross-country move. Janet says her husband didn't hesitate for a moment: He told her to take the job. "I have a terrific spouse," she says. "We have an extremely equal relationship, or if it's unequal, it's that he does more than his share." Janet's husband took on the lion's share of the household responsibilities, took every bit of leave he had from his job as a professor of economics at UC Berkeley, and even did a cross-country commute for a while. (GO, MR. YELLEN! Incidentally, "Mr. Yellen" is Dr. George Akerlof, one of the most respected and renowned economists in the world, who won the Nobel Prize in economics in 2001. His support of his wife's career certainly does not seem to have held him back.) Janet says her husband's support was absolutely crucial to her professional success and enabled her to pursue her stellar career. "Without that support system, none of this would have ever been possible," Janet says. "Without him, it would have been challenging beyond words."

At the White House

Once Janet Yellen took her post at the White House, she discovered it was not always an easy or supportive place: "It was tough sledding for women," she recalls. "Clinton was very keen on having women at the table, but the atmosphere was a tough environment and there was a gender issue." At the White House, everybody was desperately trying to grab the president's attention and have their ideas heard and turned into policies. Janet says she spent a lot of time talking with the economists she oversaw—men and women—about the difficulty of speaking up in a roomful of "smart people . . . all yelling at once."

Janet's Lesson: Be Prepared

Janet says it was at the White House that she learned her most important workplace lesson for handling tough, competitive environments and getting support while swimming with alpha-male sharks: preparation. "For me, being prepared is the most important thing," she says. This was what Janet recommended to the women she managed who, like her, were feeling frustrated in trying to be heard and building momentum for their ideas. "Fortify yourself by being as prepared and as knowledgeable as you possibly can. That works to bolster self-confidence. It certainly does for me. And that's what I do to this day. I do not wing it. I never wing it."

Janet's Lesson: Have the Courage of Your Convictions

Preparation, though, was only the first step for Janet Yellen. At the White House it was also necessary to find the courage to speak up in an extremely intimidating environment. Janet says one of the keys to this was making sure people had the courage of their convictions—that they understood and felt the value and urgency of what they had to say. "Most of the people at the table aren't economists," she says of White House meetings. "We would take pride in bringing in the best possible economics to the table and in helping policy makers decide on sensible policies." Janet developed a code of ethics for the team, which inspired people to believe in what they were doing and which could also inspire them to speak up when they were feeling intimidated. "Our values are: We're super ethical; we operate with integrity; we're not political; we value expertise; we try to look at facts and make reasoned judgments." Janet says believing in the importance of what you are trying to achieve will help give you the courage to speak up, even in the toughest environments.

Janet's Lesson: Pull Up Your Socks

When Janet Yellen took the job of Federal Reserve chair—head of the U.S. central bank—the U.S. economy was still recovering after the Great Recession, and all eyes were on her and how she planned to move the economy forward after such a terrible blow.

The job involved a lot of public speaking, not to mention hourslong interrogations from Congress regarding the debt the country had racked up during the housing crisis and the bank bailouts. All of this was being closely watched by the world and, if not handled just right, could easily send global markets skyrocketing or spiraling. It was an almost unimaginable amount of pressure. To complicate matters, Janet does not particularly like public attention or giving speeches.

Her advice: "You often have to do things that are scary at some level. You just have to force yourself to face up to it and do it . . . You have to pull up your socks and do what you were hired to do."

One way Janet found the courage to do everything she had to do was from the support she got from other women. Janet says when she was appointed to head the Federal Reserve and, subsequently, to serve as the Secretary of the Treasury, she got messages of support, encouragement, and gratitude from women all over the world: "I found it enormously motivating," she says. "People felt, 'This is really shattering the glass ceiling.' A lot of people were looking up to me and they wanted me to do a good job. You do take pride in that and feel it shows that women can accomplish a lot and deserve to be in positions like this. So I certainly did not want to louse up."

Janet's Lesson: Machiavelli's Golden Rule

A big part of each of the jobs Janet Yellen held was managing teams of people. At one point she had thousands of people answering to her and the whole U.S. economy was in her hands. She was extremely successful in managing this and was also admired and liked by the people who worked for her. "Janet Yellen was known to be the hardest-working person around," says Julia Coronado, an economist who worked with Janet. "She led unapologetically with a 'feminine touch.' She was respectful and personal with colleagues, asking about family, always communicating calmly and methodically, even as she was absolutely unafraid to express her views and challenge those of others. She set the bar so high, and as a result of her hard work, she was ahead of the curve on so many things . . . I'm the biggest Janet fangirl."

But according to Janet, managing people was the easy part of her job: "It really was not hard to do," she says. "Managing people meant things like motivating them and encouraging them to be assertive in expressing their views." I think there's a hidden lesson from Janet Yellen here: One key way to get the support you want as a leader is to *give* support. Support people when they do good work and support them in their ambitions and goals. If you are managing people or working alongside them or even under them, encourage them and notice the good work they do; that will go a long way in helping you get the support you need to lead.

Machiavelli greatly admired good leaders, and the way he measured good leadership was by how well the people did under that leader. Were people happy? Did they prosper? Ultimately, Machiavelli thought an ideal prince created a place where people could do their best work, live their best lives, and feel the support of their prince contributing to their prosperity and dignity. "Collectively they will be better," he writes, "seeing themselves commanded by their own Prince, and honoured and esteemed by him" (Chapter XXVI, DTE).

We Are the Network

Gaining the support you need to succeed in your profession is all about creating a network of mentors, colleagues, mentees, and confidants. These are people who can back you up when times are difficult and propel you forward when times are good. This network will be a crucial source of information, ideas, opportunities, critique, advocacy, and support. They are your professional family. Wherever you go in your career, you will always be connected to them, and they are a key to your success now and in the future.

6

Title

Neha Narkhede: True Grit

"It is not the title that honors the man, but the man that honors the title."

—Machiavelli, *Discourses on Livy*

What's in a name? Kind of a lot, actually. Probably the biggest and most important way power manifests itself in the workplace is title. Title, of course, is not separate from money. Often the best way to get a raise is to get a promotion. More important, your job title dictates what you do every day: how you spend your forty-plus hours a week, who you're in charge of, and who's in charge of you.

Title-wise, women struggle. In fact, the situation with gender and job title is, in many ways, worse than the pay gap, which gets all the attention. About 80 percent of company CEOs are men. Women make up fully half of first- and second-year law associates but only about a quarter of law firm partners and federal judges. Similar statistics apply to congressional seats, corporate boards, and start-ups. This is in spite of the fact that companies with a larger percentage of women in high positions tend to be more profitable and do better during downturns.

The fact is, men get more promotions than women and they get them faster. If women do get a shot at a top spot, they are more than twice as likely as a man to be hired from outside the company—in other words, not to be promoted from within.

Here's the conundrum: Women are getting the degrees and getting hired at the companies and working their butts off and climbing the ladder like the fearless warriors they are, and then . . . something happens and they seem to end up, as Lester Bangs so memorably put it in the movie *Almost Famous*, on a "long journey to the middle." So what is happening? What is keeping women out of the upper echelons of power?

Mind the Gap

Katie Green experienced the promotion gap in a particularly visceral way. She was working at a marketing agency in New York City as a coordinator, an entry-level position. She befriended an intern at the time, a white man I'll call Ray. Three months into Ray's internship, he was promoted to Katie's level. "He totally deserved it," recalls Katie. "He was working really hard." But roughly a year later, Ray was promoted to management and Katie was still in the same position. "I have more relevant experience in the field," she says. "I'd been a coordinator longer and all my reviews had been great. So, you know, that kind of hurt."

But Katie was not one to wallow in despair! She was going to work so hard, her promotion and raise could not be denied! Katie put her head down and spent the next six months working as hard as she could. But it didn't work. Her requests to her manager didn't seem to be going anywhere. She remained friends with Ray, who noticed all of Katie's efforts and took her aside one day. He told her he thought their workplace was unfair and wanted her to know the details of his experience so she'd have facts that could help her. Katie describes the conversation as "eye-opening." "I realized I was making significantly less than he was from the beginning, even from when he was hired as an intern." Katie says it was particularly frustrating because the company prided itself on being progressive. When Katie asked Ray how he had gotten the promotion, "he told me that he was just given the promotion. He didn't even ask for it."

Katie took this new information to her manager and demanded a raise and a promotion. Her manager agreed the situation wasn't right and went to the head of the office on Katie's behalf. Months later Katie finally got promoted and got her raise. Sort of. "The monetary offer made my jaw drop," Katie recalls. The salary they were offering was lower than what Ray had been making when he was first offered the promotion months before.

Katie wrote a letter to the head of the office detailing her work and making the case for why she deserved equal pay. Six months later Katie got the raise she was asking for. At that point she was a year behind Ray. And just as her raise came through, Ray informed her that he had just been offered a raise himself. "The gap was just getting bigger and bigger," she says.

But, Katie points out, the most troubling thing about the whole experience was the attitude of upper management when they finally gave her the promotion and the raise—a promotion and raise that were, by all accounts, long overdue. Instead of apologizing to Katie for the delay or even expressing gratitude for her years of work, upper management expressed doubt about moving her up: "The head of the office said, 'I hope you know, we're really going out on a limb here.'" In that moment, Katie realized her raise and promotion had come at a price—management now felt resentful and skeptical of her and her work. Ray had not had to deal with any of that.

Katie's experience is the rule, not the exception. All over corporate America, women find themselves staring into that same gap. In one massive study involving millions of women (done as part of a lawsuit against Walmart), researchers found female employees earned less and were promoted less often than their male colleagues in spite of having more qualifications and better performance reviews.

Why is it so much quicker and easier for men to get promoted than women? Dr. Cecilia L. Ridgeway, gender researcher at Stanford University, has spent her career looking at this question. The answer? Our old friend "power": to be able. Men are not necessarily seen as smarter or even better at their jobs than women. But they are seen as more capable—*more able*—in the workplace, so they are more likely to get promoted. After all, it's a gamble to promote someone. Employers are taking a risk when they put someone in a new job. And men will typically seem like a safer bet than women. "Employers think men are going to perform," explains Cecilia. "It is that sense of 'Who's the long-haul producer? Who's more competent?'"

The result: When a position opens up at a company and a male and a female candidate emerge, things are more likely to break the man's way. It's the Cinderella Syndrome coming back to haunt us. You can mop the floor, polish the silver, and snake the drains like a champ, but your male colleague is probably going to seem just a little bit more promising and capable. More "royal ball" material.

Part of the reason for this is that women are viewed more critically in the workplace than men are. Women's evaluations tend to be more negative and more personal than those of their male colleagues. In a 2014 study of job performance reviews, researchers found that women's personalities came up in about 75 percent of them. In men's reviews, personality came up only about 2 percent of the time. This is super annoying, of course, but it also does material damage to women's careers.

Natalie Johnson is the cofounder of Paradigm, a consulting firm that focuses on diversity and inclusion. She says the feedback issue is one of the biggest obstacles standing between women and positions of power. "Not only are women getting criticized based on their personality traits, which could impact their opportunities; they are missing out on feedback that is more actionable, that could actually make them better at their job." The result? If there's something a woman needs to do more of, or if the quality of her work could improve in some way, she might never hear it. She might hear instead that she's too negative or dresses too casually or is too terse in her emails.

So how do you deal with this? If people are going to see you more critically and judge you based on things that have nothing to do with your work, what can you do? We're back to Machiavelli 101: You face the monster. In this case, the feedback monster.

The F-Word

Feedback.

I feel like your manager saying she has feedback for you is the professional equivalent of "We need to talk." Nothing good can come of it and it might very well end with you packing your witty mug, family photo, and half-dead succulent into a box and leaving the building forever. Actually *asking* for feedback seems almost masochistic: You are opening yourself to criticism, and it might be unfair criticism from someone you don't respect. But *do* it. Ask for feedback. A big part of getting a promotion is knowing how you are being perceived by the people giving the promotions. And even if those perceptions are not fair or totally wrong, they are impacting your career. You need to know about them.

Be proactive: Ask your manager, your boss, your mentors, and your colleagues for their feedback about your work and about you as a worker. And when they give their feedback to you, just listen. Do not respond or challenge what they say. Only respond to ask more questions: "What about my work? How are you finding the quality?" or "What part of my work feels sloppy?" Write everything down. Nod and don't react. Hear what the other person is saying and take it in. Make the whole conversation about that. When people see you are listening without getting defensive or argumentative, they will open up more. They will tell you the really useful stuff: the stuff people say about you (good and bad) behind your back. That information might hurt and it might not be fair, but you need it if you're going to rise within the organization.

Machiavelli's Lesson: The Feedback Defense

Machiavelli, incidentally, was big on feedback. "A Prince," he writes, "ought always to take counsel" (Chapter XXIII, DTE). Machiavelli saw honest feedback as the primary way a prince could protect himself against flatterers and yes-men. (Machiavelli was death on flatterers and yes-men.) "There is no other way of guarding oneself from flatterers except letting men understand that to tell you the truth does not offend you . . ." (Chapter XXIII, MPE). Feedback feels like risky exposure, but Machiavelli saw it as powerful protection for a prince and a way to get necessary information. The ability to hear the truth—or the "truth" of people's impressions and opinions—will make you stronger and smarter and help you succeed. Machiavelli was careful to say that you should not open yourself up in this way to just anybody. Ask the people who are key to enabling you to move up within a company; ask people you respect; ask the people you trust.

Caveat: This experience might suck. You might get feedback that is personal or unfair or is just straight up incorrect. Listen to it, get through it, and take note of it. Remember, all of this information— even the personal stuff—is useful. You are learning how you are perceived by your peers and by the people in power. It might be unfair and sexist and total BS, but it's good information. The more you know, the better.

If there is a factual misperception—say your boss tells you he's disappointed your productivity is down and you *know* your productivity is up—you will need to address it, but don't be emotional about it. Use data. Say something like "Thank you for telling me. I'm surprised to hear that you're disappointed in my productivity . . . I was thinking I had produced a lot more in the past few months. I'm going to check that and I'll get back to you. But in the meantime, I'd love to hear more of your thoughts. Are you satisfied with the quality of my work?"

Machiavelli's Lesson: Life Is a Cabaret

Of course, *getting* the feedback is just the first step. To make the feedback work for you, you have to find a way to act on it. Personal feedback is probably the hardest, so we'll start there. This feedback is very likely going to point to a Hotbox situation: how you dress, your attitude, the way you communicate. Are you too nice or not nice enough?

The origin of the Hotbox problem is rooted in gender expectations. It's frustrating and destructive, but it can also offer solutions.

For example, if you are getting feedback that you're too aggressive and pushy and people don't like you, it probably means you are expressing a lot of masculine energy at work. (Silver lining: People probably respect you and think you can handle a lot of responsibility.) If you get feedback that you don't seem "ready" for big projects or that there are questions about your abilities, it probably means you are bringing a lot of feminine energy to your job. (The upside: People probably like you and want you to do well.) We all have masculine and feminine energies and we all express both differently in different situations, so one thing to consider doing is to start playing around with your masculine and feminine sides. Think about how you speak, your tone in emails, how you dress, and what you say (or don't) in meetings. Where are you leading with masculine qualities and where are your feminine qualities coming out? Then think about shaking things up. Try getting a little playful about it. Experiment.

Legal scholar and gender researcher Joan C. Williams first started experimenting with this in the extremely competitive and extremely male field of academic law. Joan tends to lead with masculine qualities at work: She is assertive, outspoken, and confident. But, she says, that wasn't serving her well. She wasn't well-liked or thriving in her job. The women who were popular in her workplace tended to display more "feminine" traits and were very deferential to their male colleagues. "One woman I actually liked a lot was at this public event and said, 'Oh, Mr. X knows *everything*. I'm just following in his footsteps.' . . . That was kind of the coin of the realm."

That particular coin was not going to work for Joan. She knew she couldn't extol the amazingness of her male colleagues and keep her lunch digested. Still, she noticed the powerful effect this tactic had on the male faculty and began to think about how she could achieve the same thing. Joan started to think of femininity as a toolkit. "I very consciously femmed it up," she says. "And, believe me, my life's been a hell of a lot more pleasant since I did."

Joan's two-year-old daughter was her inspiration. "She was obsessed with dresses and refused to wear pants," recalls Joan. As a scholar and a feminist, this was mildly distressing to Joan, but she decided to take an academic perspective on things. "My daughter was like, 'Okay, I'm two years old. Time to give a hegemonic gender performance.' So she would wear dresses and I would wear dresses, too, to kind of keep her company, and I thought, 'Why not dress with a little more attention to the aesthetic dimension of dressing? That's not inherently stupid; it's just devalued.'" (The fact that this is what Joan's inner monologue sounds like makes me love her and her dress-obsessed daughter *so much*.) For Joan, dressing "like a girl" actually changed things. She started to notice her male colleagues being more pleasant to her, and her work life started to become a bit easier. There were limits to the power of the dress, of course. That particular workplace was still very toxic and, in the end, Joan decided she should leave that institution for another job that would be a more supportive environment.

Joan continued to use what she had learned about masculine and feminine traits at work and experimented with all kinds of things. One of her favorite discoveries was using a "feminine" skill she truly enjoyed: "I have the ability to connect with people at a very genuine and deep level in a very short period of time . . . And so I used that."

If you tend to be a more feminine type at work, try using some masculine approaches: Try wearing a suit jacket, or take the exclamation points out of your emails. Smile less. Make direct eye contact. Force yourself to speak up in meetings. Try (respectfully) disagreeing with a higher-up. Try asking for something you think is totally outrageous. Express one of your opinions as a fact. Try one thing one week and another the next.

If you have a more masculine energy at work, you can consider wearing dresses, as Joan did, or be warmer or more expressive in your emails. Smile in meetings. Try agreeing with a colleague: Say you really like her idea (if you actually do). Try to connect with one of your colleagues in conversation. Ask him to coffee.

To be honest, it's a little difficult for me to give this advice. I think it's really smart and I think Niccolò would give two enthusiastic thumbs-up, but it's also a little hard to swallow. I want to be my authentic self in the office, and that authentic self has lots of potted plants and a wool wrap at my desk (because I'm always cold) and a photo of Emily Dickinson on my cubicle wall with a heart around it. DO I HAVE TO GET RID OF MY EMILY DICKINSON HEART PHOTO IF I WANT TO GET PROMOTED? Still, playing around in this way can help you navigate the Hotbox with greater ease.

Can You Be Less . . . You?

Of course, some of this feedback could be truly hurtful and offensive. For women of color, gay women, and nonbinary workers, getting feedback can mean, basically, getting asked to look "less gay" or "less Black" or a whole host of other horrifying, racist, and bigoted messages. Not that these messages will usually be quite that direct. Often the language used to express things like this is coded. For example: "Some organizations will say you need to be *professional* and *neat* and *tidy*," says Dr. Tina Opie of Babson College. Tina says that can be code for Black people that they can't have a natural hairstyle. Tina says when she worked in banking and consulting, she was given offensive feedback all the time. "I had a beautifully tailored red suit . . . I felt so powerful in that suit. It was like my armor. I loved that suit. And I was told, 'You need to work harder to look like the people we work for.' And what they were basically saying is, 'White people don't wear red suits.'"

Tina also found that her hair was a frequent topic of comments and criticism. She recalls one instance when she had styled her hair in a twist out, which required hours of effort and styling. Tina loved the result: "I was taking pictures of it and posting it online and I'm getting compliments from my friends." But at work, when Tina was chatting with a white female colleague about her years working in consulting, her colleague said, "You wouldn't wear your hair like that if you were still consulting or banking, would you?" Tina says she was gut-punched. What was worse, the woman in question had not put any effort into her own hairstyle. "Her hair was wet," Tina recalls. "She hadn't even blown it dry from her shower." Tina says this moment perfectly illustrates the destructive messaging that women of color receive at work all the time: They're often expected to look and act in ways that deny their identity. Figuring out how to navigate that situation can be complicated and painful. "Everyone is expected to wear a suit," says Tina, "but not everyone is expected to straighten their hair . . . or to cover particular aspects of their identity so that they're less salient."

Tina often discusses this with her students as they are preparing for job interviews: "Black women, Latina women, and even some white women will come to me and say, 'Professor Opie, I have this job interview. What should I do with my hair?' And I tell them, 'Look, I'm not going to tell you what to do, but what are you trying to convey in the workplace and in the interview? Do you think that your hair conveys it? You know, I love natural hair, but I'm known in my field and I'm almost fifty and I have a job. You have to count the cost, because if you go with your Afro . . . it is beautiful and glorious, but I've done research, which shows that natural hair is perceived as more militant, more rebellious, and less likely to conform. So they may not want to hire you. And so you lose a job.'" Tina says this is hard advice to give, because it's essentially telling her students to consider downplaying their race or ethnicity or sexuality in order to get a job.

"What I say to my students is, 'On one hand, being inauthentic has psychological costs. Your well-being will take a hit. If you're authentic, that feels great, but you also need to pay your bills and eat. So you have to make a trade-off.'" I asked Tina if maybe a job that wouldn't hire someone because they had a natural hairstyle would not be a place her students would want to work. That kind of bias seems like a red flag: "Oh, it's everywhere," Tina replied. "It's a red flag about this country."

Tina's Lesson: The Red Underwear Rebellion

Tina says one solution she's found to help counteract the discomfort and trauma of having to dress or act in a way that doesn't feel authentic is to find ways to express yourself that will not cost you professionally. She first gave this advice to a woman who was a lawyer in the United Kingdom and was required by her profession to wear a white wig and a long black robe in court. "She said, 'I hate it. And I know I don't have the authority to just not wear what they tell me to.'" Tina's solution? "What about your underwear? What if you wear bright red lace underwear underneath your clothes? Or socks with purple hearts or whatever? A way to signal to yourself that 'I'm still my authentic self. I'm still a rebel, even though I'm being forced on the outside to conform.'"

Question: Do they make Emily Dickinson underwear?

The Discrimination Is Coming from INSIDE THE HOUSE!

Another thing holding women back from promotions is . . . us: our own ambitions—what we allow ourselves to want and strive for. Rather than risk rejection, discrimination, and other painful experiences, it can feel safer to stop reaching for certain things.

Katie Green, who works in marketing, noticed this after she had to fight so hard to be promoted to the level of her male colleague. Katie eventually left that job, but the experience has stuck with her in all kinds of ways. For instance, she has shied away from applying for jobs that seemed like a stretch. "Looking back, maybe I should have been applying for director-level roles," she says. "And I wasn't, because my confidence has been totally stripped from me. I find myself obsessively documenting everything I do to prove that the money they pay for my salary and my health insurance is worth it." Katie says her new bosses clearly appreciate her, but she still doesn't feel as if she can relax. "I have my own secret personal documentation, because I'm worried I'm going to be in a position one day where again I have to prove that I am good at my job and that I am worthy of my salary. I think that directly comes from being told that I was not worth the same as a male counterpart . . . I take that trauma with me to every meeting, to every call. And it's so hard and it's so draining."

It's so hard and it's so draining, and millions of women do exactly this every day. Studies have found that people who experience discrimination tend to stay in jobs longer, rather than risk a bad experience at another job, and may even avoid entire fields they assume would subject them to harassment or bad treatment. The destructive relationship between experiencing discrimination and discriminating against oneself shows up in all kinds of situations at work. But there are methods to make sure you're not getting in your own way.

Machiavelli's Lesson: Raise Your Hand if You're Unsure!

Never say no to an opportunity because you feel like you're not qualified or don't have the skills. This is simply impostor syndrome BS and it is to be ignored.

When Ginni Rometty, who was the CEO of IBM, first got the offer to become chief executive, she said, "Tsk, it's too early. I'm not ready." Ginni recounted this at a commencement address at Northwestern University. "Just give me a few more years and I'd be ready for this." She went home and told her husband what had happened. "He said, 'Do you think a man would have answered the question that way?' . . . And you know what? He was right. And I went in the next day and I took that job."

I have personally noticed this phenomenon during my fifteen years of economics and business reporting. Most of the people in the world of economics, business, and finance are men. When I reach out to a male expert with a question, he will almost always respond right away and enthusiastically agree to speak about whatever topic I'm reporting on, even if it's not his specialty. But many times, when I reach out to a woman, she will hesitate. She will want to see a list of questions and will express worry that it isn't her exact area of expertise. Very often, women will suggest a colleague I should call—someone who *really* knows the topic. Almost invariably this colleague will be male.

In one case, I was doing a report on a paper that had recently come out. The paper had two authors, a male and a female. I opted to call the female economist, who was the lead researcher on the study. The woman agreed to talk with me the next day. But shortly after that, she sent me an email saying her male coauthor would do the interview. "He's a huge fan of your show and wants to take over this interview," she wrote, adding a smiley face. I noticed that the man had been quoted in all the articles about their work. The man was doing all the press. He was quick to give his female colleague credit, and I enjoyed talking with him, but I was also angry. Why was he getting all the attention? Why was she letting him do all the press for their work?

He was pushing for his interests and she wasn't pushing for hers. As a result, he was publicly getting credit for work they had done together.

"I Know What Boys Like"

There is also a Machiavellian reason women undershoot in their careers—a *socially* Machiavellian reason: Many women worry that career success will mean a trade-off with social or family life. As women, we receive extremely mixed messages about succeeding at work. On the one hand, there's Rosie the Riveter flexing and calling on women everywhere to take the workforce by storm! On the other hand, there's Glenn Close's character in *Fatal Attraction*—the successful career woman who ends up boiling her married lover's bunny in a psychotic rage. Her lover's wife, incidentally, is a sweet, virtuous (and sane) homemaker.

As women, we get this message pretty consistently: *Be careful! Focusing on your career could mean other parts of your life will die on the vine. Better grab a man now!* Men don't get this messaging. Their worth is not tied to their youth or to the person they choose as a partner. Their worth is tied to the work they do (which, of course, comes with its own set of difficulties, but that is a subject for another book). One time a friend of mine got a huge career-changing opportunity. She was ecstatic and called her dad to tell him the big news—but instead of him saying "Congratulations, honey, that's wonderful!," he said if she was going to take such an intense job, she should freeze her eggs.

Research does back up some of these toxic messages. Studies show that when people hear about a woman who is succeeding in a traditionally male field, they assume she is less likable, less attractive, less happy, and less socially desirable than a woman who succeeds in a career that people associate with women. Also, when women hold higher-status jobs than their male partners, the risk of divorce increases.

In the workplace, men can aim for the top, with all of society and the workplace itself yelling, "GO, GO, GO!" If a woman aims for the top, not only does she not get that encouragement, she gets voices of *dis*couragement: "Should you be working so hard?" "What about your social life?" There's also a worry (often unspoken) that being too ambitious and successful will mean, at best, you will not be attractive to men and, at worst, you will end up crazy and alone, boiling your married lover's bunny.

Big-Dick Energy

One of my guilty pleasures is a show called *Younger*. It's about the publishing industry and it's filmed right around my office in New York. In the show, young, ambitious Kelsey (played by the delightful Hilary Duff) has been rising through the ranks of a publishing house and actually takes the helm of the company in her late twenties. She's out for drinks with her girlfriend and remarks that her online dating profile isn't getting any hits. Her friend offers to look at her profile to ferret out the problem. Kelsey (Hilary Duff) hands over her phone.

"Oh, Kelsey, no, no, no. This says that you're Publisher of Millennial Print."

"Yeah. That is my job."

"Yes. And it is a great job, and I am in constant awe of your accomplishments, but this kind of overachieving only works if you're trying to pick up women. All right? Men don't want to deal with your big-dick energy."

"Oh, my God! Okay. I don't have that energy, and you're shouting."

"You have BDE, Kelsey. You do. I mean, you are basically wielding a giant psychic schlong."

Her friend changes Kelsey's job title on the dating app from *publisher* to *creative director*. She explains to Kelsey that nobody actually knows what a creative director does, so it's less intimidating. Immediately, Kelsey starts getting messages from guys who are interested in her now that she has a job title that isn't so impressive.

Also, I am a woman in the world and I have seen men visibly flinch or even get defensive when I have talked about my work. I've gone on dates with men who talked about their own jobs for hours without ever asking me about mine, presumably because my professional life was of no consequence. I know culture is tricky and not always fair, and I have felt, at moments, that if I were less ambitious or less excited about my work, dating might be easier. Truthfully, though, it's just who I am. I am ambitious and hardworking, and it's very important to me that I am able to support myself. I could pretend otherwise but not for long. My dating life, in fact, got much more fun and *easier* when I stopped underplaying the importance of my career to me. We all have to make the choices that feel right for us, but I, for one, think there's a way that women don't have to choose between achieving everything they want at work and being considered attractive and desirable.

In fact, these entrenched cultural norms are changing quickly: Studies have shown that fewer than 30 percent of men say they want a relationship with strict gender boundaries. And families in which the breadwinning is shared have fewer problems over the long run and are generally more stable than families in which the household has one person earning all the money.

Slaying Cinderella and Escaping the Hotbox

Why do I think you should push for a better title? Because, statistically speaking, it's long overdue. Also, getting a promotion is one of the best and easiest ways to get more money. To get around the obstacles in your way, the best thing you can do is make a plan.

First things first: Where do you want to go?

If you don't know exactly what you want right now, that isn't a bad thing. You don't want to be one of those people whose entire life is laid out in a joyless, albeit very thorough, five-year plan. But there is a great deal of power in clarity.

So often in a workplace, there's a kind of fog around where you are and where you want to go—meaning there's not a clear and concrete path to getting what you want, or, very often, there's a concrete path up to a point and then there's a kind of mysterious anointment that has to happen, a fog that envelops the path.

I have definitely spent non-negligible swaths of my career lost in the fog with no real plan for how to get out of it or even of where I wanted to go. The reason was not that I was lazy or didn't care. It was actually the opposite: I was scared to name exactly what I wanted because I was afraid I wouldn't get it. After all, you can't really fail if you don't know what you want. But the fog is not our friend. Cinderella loves the fog. She will spend a hundred years polishing bannisters in the fog. If you want to slay Cinderella, you need to get as clear as you can.

It's Homework Time

I know. It's so unsexy and it's so unavoidable. To get your promotion, you need to get some information: Seek out people who have made the transition you want to make and find out how they did it and how long it took them. Of course, just because it took Bill, Jerry, and Carol two years does not mean it needs to take *you* two years. But if it took Bill, Jerry, and Carol two years and you've been grinding away for *three* years, you know the time is probably ripe to ask.

Now look at the official description and requirements for the job you want. How many of the tasks for your dream position are you already doing? What skills do you need that you don't have? How can you get those?

If the position you want requires ten years of experience and you have seven, don't write yourself off. Remember, a man will shoot for a position when he meets 60 percent of the requirements for the job. Do you meet 60 percent of the requirements for that job?

Mapping the Fog

Now it's time to start mapping your path through the fog: What are the steps between where you are now and where you want to go? Are there things you could be doing now that you're not doing? Can you find a way to start doing them? There might be mysterious, fog-enveloped parts of that path, but as my high school math teacher Jean Parker used to say, "Tiny little steps for muddy little feet." Jean worked in the Air Force and then as a science and math teacher for years, always encouraging women to enter STEM fields. She helped a lot of young women through this fog, and her advice is just as true for navigating the modern workplace as it was for tackling algebra problems: "Don't panic. Focus. Start with what you know."

Professional Herding

One big obstacle on the path to promotion is something known as professional herding. A man and a woman starting out in the same profession will often be nudged in very different directions. This is part of why charting your own path through the fog is such an important step: It prevents you from getting herded someplace you don't want to go. Women will often be herded into support or service roles and saddled with a lot of busywork that men don't have to deal with.

Dr. Alice Eagly, coauthor of *Through the Labyrinth: The Truth About How Women Become Leaders*, stresses that it can be hard to know the difference between what you want and what other people encourage you to do. We all want the approval, the admiration, and the respect of others. These things can be powerful shapers of our professional destinies, especially since they often come into play very early in our lives. Alice says women will often be encouraged and praised for considering jobs that are traditionally female: "Oh, you're going to be a teacher of young children? That's really nice.

You'd be good at that." Maybe not so much if they express the desire to be a bull rider or a fighter pilot. The effects of this herding are not subtle—a lot of professions are starkly segregated by gender: Around 90 percent of elementary school teachers and nurses are women; 80 percent of social workers are women; meanwhile, more than 80 percent of engineers and architects are male.

Within companies, women often get herded into support roles, which typically involve a lot of work and little glory. Machiavelli, incidentally, saw support roles as a trap for an up-and-coming prince. "He who is the cause of another becoming powerful is ruined . . . ," he writes (Chapter III, MPE). If you succeed at your job, the person you are assisting will never want to see you promoted: You're too useful to them right where you are! And if you're bad at your job, you won't get anywhere, because a top person at the company doesn't like you. Of course, these kinds of jobs are often the places we start out in our careers, but get out of there as fast as you can.

Office Housework

Office Housework is a term coined by legal scholar and gender researcher Joan C. Williams, and she defines it as a necessary task that will drain your time and life force and will not help get you where you want to go. Joan considers office housework to be the opposite of so-called glamour work: the work that will get you promoted.

Of course, every job involves a little dues paying and drudge work, especially in the early part of a career. But Joan says men will often naturally stop getting asked to do office housework when they reach a certain level. Women will typically continue to get assigned these tasks and end up in the tricky situation of figuring out how to deal with it.

Office housework usually falls into one of four categories:

1. **Social coordination/hostessy-type stuff.** Party planning, ordering lunch, fetching coffee, and organizing happy hours, birthdays, and other events.

2. **Administrative-type work.** Finding times and places to meet, booking reservations, coordinating schedules.
3. **Emotional labor.** People will often expect to confide in women about personal problems. Also, women are frequently asked to tend to upset colleagues or difficult clients.
4. **Drudge work.** This is undervalued work and will vary from job to job. "In architecture, this could be designing the elevators or the bathrooms," says Joan. "In law, it's managing the paralegals, rather than arguing in court."

In academia, office housework consists of serving on committees. Dr. Isabel Escobar has served on "about a million" committees. This started when she began teaching chemical engineering at the university level. She says the fact that she is female and a minority made her very popular on committees of all types. "You've checked two boxes with one person," she says, laughing. This gave the committee a sheen of diversity and credibility, and because Isabel only had one vote, the status quo was not threatened by all of that shiny diversity. At the end of the year, when all the university professors were submitting their annual reports, this disparity became especially apparent to Isabel: "I would always run out of space under the 'service' category and my male colleagues would be like, 'What else can I put here?' or 'How can I stretch this?'" Isabel realized she was spending hours of her time on committees that her male colleagues could spend on research, publishing articles, and other work that would get them ahead and advance their careers.

Again, Machiavelli warns against this kind of work. He says being known as the person who will do thankless work *for the team* will actually make people resent you and, ironically enough, end up thinking you're selfish. The reason? If you are doing lots of grunt work, everyone will identify you as the person they can give their grunt work to. You will either exhaust yourself doing this work or, if you ever try to draw a boundary and say no, the person asking will get angry. Like, "Hey! Why won't you do this for me? You did it for

Ralph last week!" And, just like Niccolò says, you end up "either poor" (drained of all your time and energy) or "despised" (Chapter XVI, MPE).

Avoiding Housework

If you realize you have been saddled with hours of thankless housework, don't panic! You are a woman in the workplace. Housework happens. Here are eight ways to get out of it (or even spin it to your advantage).

1. **Don't volunteer for office housework**—"ever, ever, ever, ever, ever," stresses Joan C. Williams—even if you feel "only you" will do it correctly; even if it seems easier and faster to just do it instead of trying to get out of it; even if your inner Lisa Simpson is exploding like a lotus flower inside of your chest, saying, "BUT I LOVE SANDRA AND I *WANT* TO PLAN HER GOING-AWAY PARTY AND BAKE MY FAMOUS CHOCOLATE CHOCOLATE CHIP CUPCAKES!"; and even if the boss tells you, "Man, we really appreciate you coordinating all of these meetings. I can't tell you how valuable it is." According to Joan, this work may be appreciated but it is not valued. And those sweet words are part of the office housework honey trap—a reward for you "knowing your place." "Don't get confused that any of this will get you promoted," warns Joan. "Playing the nice card, which is kind of the default mode of many women, is not a good strategy." Quash your inner Lisa Simpson and get in touch with your inner Mr. Burns. Mr. Burns would NEVER bake chocolate chocolate chip cupcakes for Sandra (unless, of course, he had poisoned them).

   So, okay, you aren't volunteering for office housework, but a lot of times these tasks get assigned. So what do you do if your boss asks you (or tells you) to do office housework?

2. **Just do it . . . once.** "Do it once. Do it graciously," Joan advises. "And then find a way out of it." She recommends setting up a rotation or recommending someone else who could do the task the next time. Whatever happens, she says, do *not* become known as the office party planner or event booker or lunch orderer.

3. **OMG, sorry! I'm just so bad at this!** My mom is an extremely fast and accurate typist, but when she was working in Los Angeles in the sixties and seventies, she made a point to type slowly and badly when she was starting a new job. That's because, at that time, the second a woman showed any aptitude for typing, she would get funneled into secretarial work and taking dictation faster than you could type "WAIT! THIS IS NOT THE JOB I WAS HIRED TO DO! WHY CAN'T YOU TYPE YOUR OWN DAMN 'NOTES TO SELF?!'" Typing was the office housework of my mother's time and she made sure she was terrible at it (or at least that everybody *thought* she was terrible at it). So if you keep getting asked to order lunch, maybe get some of the order wrong? Maybe order from the *bad* Thai place by accident. You're far less likely to get asked again.

4. **I'd *love to* but . . .** One effective way to avoid office housework is to have other work that makes doing the housework impossible. But not just any work—work the company highly values. This makes you look like a team player *and* gets you out of office housework. "Oh, I'd love to help, but I'm finishing up the X project. I know how important that project is to the company. I just won't have time to arrange those meetings for you."

5. **Just say no.** Or . . . you might just have to say no. You will probably take a hit for that, but it's better, in the end, to be a little less liked but associated with valuable work than to err on the side of being adored and associated with grunt work. This is not an easy call, but it's what Machiavelli recommends in these situations. As a leader, you need to be okay with people not liking you. "A reputation for being mean," he writes, "is

one of those vices which will enable him [a prince] to govern"
(Chapter XVI, MPE).

6. **Get someone else to say no for you.** This was the rather masterful solution Dr. Isabel Escobar found for the constant barrage of university committee requests. At the time she found this solution, Isabel was feeling truly powerless in her situation. She was dutifully saying no to the endless committee requests, but they didn't stop coming. "When you're saying no once a day to an invitation, people start saying that you're not a good colleague," she says. So she went to talk with the head of her department and the two of them came up with a system. Every time someone asked Isabel to serve on a committee, she would say, "Oh, absolutely! But I need permission from my department chair." And then the department chair would say no. Isabel got to look like a positive, supportive, collaborative woman and didn't have to spend all her time in committee meetings.

7. **Get help!** If saying no isn't working or you're getting lots of blowback, ask a mentor or higher-up for help. Tap into the network you have at the company, or get advice on how to get out of the housework. Remember, all of this is a journey. If you get stuck with office housework for a month or two, it's not the end of the world. The important thing is that you've noticed it and you're working on getting out of it.

8. **Own the housework.** If you have to set up a meeting, sit next to someone you want to talk to or use organizing the event as an excuse to make a new contact (possibly a mentor). If you're stuck on a hiring committee, get a look at salary ranges and job descriptions; that's information you can use in future negotiations. Isabel says after she and her department chair developed their system, she would still sometimes serve on committees: "At one point I got a phone call from the university president, who asked me, as a favor, to be on a committee . . . When the university president is calling you to ask you to do a 'small favor,' that's a committee that's of high value."

NEHA NARKHEDE:
True Grit

Neha Narkhede is one of the most successful humans in the world. Even more impressive, her success has been achieved in an arena that is notoriously difficult for women: tech. She is the founder of one of the legendary Silicon Valley "unicorns"—that is, a privately held company that is valued at more than a billion dollars. There are only a few hundred of them in the world, and 90 percent of them were founded by men. Neha is in the mythical 10 percent of unicorn founders who are female . . . a unicorn among unicorns! She is the founder of Confluent, a data-streaming technology firm that is currently valued at around $4.5 billion. Before that, Neha worked her way up the corporate chain at LinkedIn.

Neha grew up in India, where her parents encouraged her to dream big. When she was very young, tooling around on her first computer, playing games, and using Microsoft Paint, Neha's parents began telling her stories about successful women from all walks of life, "from Indira Gandhi, who was prime minister of India, to Indra Nooyi, the executive of PepsiCo, to Kiran Bedi, the first female to join the Indian police," Neha recalls. "Ceiling crashers. Women who were truly paving the way." Neha says hearing those stories as a girl was a crucial factor in her drive and success as an adult.

Neha came to the United States for college and started working in tech after graduation. She saw the gender problems in the industry almost immediately: "You look around and you suddenly realize you're amongst very, very few women." Neha noticed that as she moved up in the industry, the number of women got even smaller, and she could easily see why: "You get the opportunities you deserve much later than a man. Men are evaluated much more on potential. Women are evaluated on experience, and it takes a while to gather that experience." Neha ran into this the first time she asked for a promotion—to lead a team of engineers. "There were some initial questions and pushback: 'Well, you know, it's very hard' or 'You've never done it before.'" Neha saw that the men she worked with did not get this kind of pushback. In fact, they were actively supported and encouraged, and they thrived and took more risks as a result.

Neha saw that this culture in tech was not only slowing women down; it was also making them question themselves. "A lot of us have the impostor syndrome," she says. "But it's a lot more magnified for women because of the external skepticism that feeds into it."

Neha's Lesson: Say Yes to "No"

Neha was not one to be intimidated or discouraged by an unfair environment. She figured out how to work the system. The first thing Neha trained herself to do was not to be afraid of being told no. She forced herself to ask for the promotions, assignments, and positions she wanted, even when the ask seemed ridiculous or far-fetched.

"It's hard for sure," she says. "But I want to stay open to hearing a no. I think most people don't ask for the things they need because they're very concerned that the no is actually the final no." Neha says one of the ways she overcame the fear of no was by thinking of nos as temporary. Like a "No for now." "I just sort of mentally prepare myself. Like, 'This is a first no, it's not a permanent one.' And it's completely okay to hear no . . . until it becomes a yes."

Neha's Lesson: Slay Cinderella with Feedback

Getting to yes was the next step for Neha. After being told no, Neha would always make sure to ask why: Why can't I get this promotion or this raise? This meant getting feedback. Neha says asking for feedback is one of the secrets to her success. Many times over the course of her career, Neha would ask for a promotion or a new position and would be told no. Her response: "Tell me what I should be doing. Tell me, what are the outcomes I should be driving at to address those concerns?" I asked Neha if this was difficult for her and she said it always is. "The reality is, if we are going to change the status quo, we're going to have to swim against the currents a little bit. And you do need a lot of stamina and grit to swim through those currents. So my approach is usually, 'I want to listen.' Sometimes people have actual, real concerns. You never want to ignore those, right? That hurts you in your learning curve."

Neha says the key to getting feedback is to get specifics. What *exactly* do you need to be doing to get where you want to go? Anything quantifiable is key. If your manager is concerned you don't work well on a team, ask what she would like to see from you, specifically. What could you or the team do or produce that would mitigate this concern? If she's concerned with the quality of your work, ask what you could do to bring that quality up. If she's concerned you don't have enough experience in a certain area, ask what you could do now to start getting that experience.

Neha says once she got the feedback and the specifics, she worked like crazy to do everything on the list and then went back to her manager and said, "Okay! I did all the things and got the skills. Time for a promotion." And she assumed that she would get it. After all, she had done everything they asked. She had earned it on their terms.

Neha's Lesson: True Grit

There is a word that Neha uses a lot. It came up dozens of times when I spoke to her: *grit*. "Grit and persistence have taken me very far," she says. Neha explains that when she would bump up against obstacles or be told no, as she was many, many times, she would rely on her grit to move forward. "I respond back by saying, 'I'm actually going to prove you wrong. I'm going to continue learning what you asked me to learn and grow into the role I feel is made for me.'"

Where did her grit come from? Neha says a lot of it came from those stories her parents would tell her as a girl—of the women who had broken barriers before her: "That was possibly the biggest supporting factor to me. Making it to a different country and starting a company, you have to believe that someone like you has done it before."

Eyes on the Prize

Getting the title you want is about having a plan. Where do you want to go? What are the ways you can get there? Obstacles will always come up. Herding and housework will happen. Make sure you're focused on where *you* want to go and direct your energies there. That has been the secret for Neha Narkhede. "When I come across anything that looks like a ceiling," she says, "I assume, first, that it's a glass ceiling. And that I can crush it."

The Parent Trap

Alysia Montaño: Supermom

"It may be possible to make them believe by force."
—Machiavelli, *The Prince* (Chapter VI, MPE)

Most women will become a parent at some point in their lives, and when they do, the workplace difficulties they face are compounded. Women with children are paid less, their work is viewed more critically, they are kept off important projects, and they are held back from promotions. This is, of course, in addition to the actual parenting of a child—the picky-eating phase, the preschool lice outbreak, the not-sleeping phase(s), playdates, potty training, and the dreaded princess obsession. The mommy discrimination women face is so harrowing that a huge number of mothers drop out of the workforce entirely. And the worst part is, everybody thinks they're doing you a favor.

Welcome, ladies, to the Parent Trap.

Dr. Cecilia L. Ridgeway has studied gender discrimination for decades and considers the discrimination against mothers to be "the most formidable." Cecilia points out that for many other kinds of discrimination there are laws, workplace rules, and policies protecting you. These don't necessarily prevent the discrimination, but, Cecilia says, they do "provide a basis for a complaint—something you can refer to when you're arguing for better treatment." Discrimination against mothers is talked about much less, and the awareness around it and rules preventing it are not as common or well-established. In many workplaces, mothers can feel like they're totally on their own.

The Motherhood Penalty

Mothers are consistently sidelined, overlooked, kept off important projects, and paid less (in fact, the pay gap between mothers and women without children is roughly the same size as the pay gap between men and women). In one particularly interesting study out of Cornell, participants were given a stack of résumés and asked to evaluate several fictional job candidates for the position of marketing director at a small communications company. The résumés were written to be equal in nearly every aspect: education, years of experience, recommendations, etc. There was one difference: Some of the résumés were modified to indicate the job candidate had children. The subjects of the study were then asked a bunch of questions about the various candidates, the most basic being: Would you recommend this person for this job? The results were stunning. People were almost twice as likely to recommend women without children than mothers. Adding insult to injury, study participants recommended offering women who didn't have children a starting salary that was, on average, $11,000 higher than the salaries they recommended for mothers.

To be clear, this wasn't a parent penalty: Some of the fictional job candidates were male and they did not experience daddy discrimination. In fact, people favored dads slightly over men without children and recommended paying them more.

Why are we hating on the moms? Dr. Cecilia L. Ridgeway says there is an unconscious belief that mothers don't *need* the money, because there is a man taking care of them. (Never mind that nearly one-quarter of the children in this country are being raised by single parents and most of those single parents are women.) "What becoming a mother does is trigger that most traditional aspect of the original gender stereotype: the passive, feminine mother," says Cecilia. You say you're about to have a baby and suddenly everyone imagines you spend all your time knitting and breastfeeding and pulling the latest batch of cookies out of the oven, all while being cared for by your devoted, high-earning husband.

If women become mothers, they and their work are viewed more critically. In the Cornell study, participants answered questions about how strict they would be with each job candidate—for example, how often they thought this person could come in late to work without it affecting their chances at a promotion. Women with children were held to much harsher standards than women without children. With men, the opposite proved true: Dads could get away with more late mornings and still be seen as "management material."

Cecilia says the reason for this extra strictness is that once women have children, they are automatically considered to be less committed to their work—their *real* job is raising babies now and work is more like a hobby. And it's not just in studies: Cecilia has seen this in her own profession. She recalls one particularly striking case of a young assistant professor who was getting a lot of buzz in academic circles until she mentioned that she'd just had a baby: "The tone changed," Cecilia recalls. "Suddenly the work was looked at in a different way. Instead of 'Okay, there are some flaws here, but it's very promising,' it went to 'It's promising, but it's got bugs.' No one fired her. No one said she was dumb all of a sudden because they knew she had kids. But people wanted to do the equivalent of giving her prize assignments, and then they thought, 'Well, maybe not.' No longer was she the rising star."

Benevolent Paternalism

One of the things that makes discrimination against mothers so insidious is that a lot of it happens under the guise of looking out for the mother's best interests. The perpetrators of this discrimination often feel they are acting out of consideration for the woman in question. Mothers can suddenly find themselves on the receiving end of something known as "benevolent paternalism": "We can't put Lila on that account—she just had a baby! We need someone who can basically live and breathe this account all year. We'll put Jim on it. Let's cut Lila a break and let her spend some time with her kid!"

And if a woman pushes back against this and lobbies to get onto big projects or jump back into the work she was doing before she went on maternity leave, she will often be scolded or criticized by colleagues and friends. Dr. Isabel Escobar, a chemical engineer at the University of Kentucky, experienced this at a previous workplace after she adopted her daughter. Isabel was always a person who worked nights and weekends—the department workhorse. Nobody ever had a problem with that. But once Isabel had a daughter, some male faculty members started telling her she should take it easy and step back from certain projects. "It was never meant in a negative way," she says. "It would always be a comment like 'If you take this position, you'll likely be neglecting your child, won't you? You should remember that you're a mom and your child is the most important thing in the world.'"

In the diplomatic profession, women with children will typically get passed over for the more dangerous posts in places like Afghanistan and Iraq. That's according to a career diplomat, whom I will call Elizabeth. Elizabeth says those more dangerous posts are key to advancing in the profession. If a man has a family and young children, she says, this won't factor in "because his wife is usually safely in the United States" with the kids. Elizabeth pushed for dangerous assignments and eventually got them, but, she says, it was always an uphill battle and she dealt with a lot of questions and criticism about her professional choices.

This is the mommy version of the Hotbox: If you *do* manage to get the dangerous assignment or the big account, you may face a lot of judgments about the kind of mother you are: "Wow. Lila's working late. Didn't she just have a baby? She's kind of a workaholic, no?" If it were Lyle, the new dad, working late, people would likely see him as working hard on behalf of his new family.

On the other hand, if women do cut back their hours or shy away from big assignments after having a baby, they'll be punished for that, too. Christina Hildebidle encountered this in her work at a major nonprofit. "One day I had to leave in the middle of the day because my kid had actually fainted at school," she says. "And my manager said something like, 'Remind me never to hire any other working mothers, because they never stick around.'" Even more shocking was the fact that her manager had children of his own.

If a woman with children leaves early for some reason or makes a mistake in her work, it will often be attributed to her being distracted by motherhood and seen as proof that she is no longer serious about her job. Anya Kamenetz is an education reporter at NPR and the author of several books on parenting and education, including *The Art of Screen Time: How Your Family Can Balance Digital Media and Real Life*. She says this discrimination is so pervasive, it has become common practice for parents to lie about childcare duties. "Jobs have rewarded parents who were able to hide the fact they were parents," Anya explains. "It's so much easier to say, 'I've got to leave work for a dentist appointment,' versus, like, 'My kid has a dentist appointment.' Or 'I have to leave early to train for a marathon' instead of 'I have to leave work because my kid is sick.'"

The Flextime Ghetto

Many workplaces have tried to deal with the Parent Trap through flexibility programs that allow people to work from home or work part-time, or otherwise tailor their schedules to better fit childcare duties. The problem is that flexibility programs tend to backfire. They often ghettoize mothers into obsolescence. Even in established programs at large companies, like Deloitte, McKinsey & Company, and Boston Consulting Group, the number of women who participate in those programs is tiny, and the number of women who participate in those programs and become managers and leaders is minuscule. In fact, workplaces with no flexibility programs tend to pay mothers more and promote them faster than companies that have a flextime program in place.

Bad Timing

Motherhood can be especially hard on working women, because it often happens at a crucial moment in a woman's career. Şebnem Kalemli-Özcan, a University of Maryland economist, says the time when many women are having children—in their thirties—is also the time when they are expected to be paying their dues and establishing themselves in their careers, "meaning they should be in the office from six a.m. to midnight." Şebnem noticed this when she was trying to get her first professor job while raising two young sons. "It's six p.m. and my male colleagues were still in the office. I had to go home, breastfeed, make dinner, and pick up the kids. It was very, very hard for, like, the first ten years."

According to Dr. Cecilia L. Ridgeway: the whole way the American workplace is structured encourages men to stay at work and women to leave if they have kids. "The rigid structure of work implicitly assumes that ideal workers will not have direct, personal responsibility for the daily care of dependent children."

The Result

The result of this discrimination is striking: Nearly a third of working mothers end up leaving their jobs. In her 2007 book, *Opting Out? Why Women Really Quit Careers and Head Home*, Pamela Stone, a professor at Hunter College, explored why women were leaving the workforce in such high numbers after they had children. Conventional wisdom was that these women had simply found childcare to be more rewarding work, but Pamela discovered the truth was a lot more complicated.

It turned out the combination of being underpaid, held back from promotions, and benevolently paternalized was pushing women out of the workforce after they had children. The phenomenon was concentrated among women with advanced degrees (for example, of the women who graduated from Harvard's prestigious

MBA program, only about a third ended up working full-time). The reason for this seemed to be that these women were more likely to be in a financial situation that allowed them to leave their jobs once they had a compelling alternative—in this case, raising their children full-time.

Many of these women wanted to continue in their careers and most would eventually try to go back to work, but getting back into the workforce wasn't easy, and most of these women never went back to a full-time job.

Dream Job Nightmare

One woman who left the traditional workforce after she became a mother is Anne-Marie Slaughter. Anne-Marie was rocketed to workplace-gender-issue fame after writing an article in *The Atlantic* titled "Why Women Still Can't Have It All." The article was about the real struggles Anne-Marie was experiencing trying to be a present parent for her two sons while working a top-level job in the State Department. To sum it up: Anne-Marie had achieved everything she had ever wanted in life and it was making her miserable.

Anne-Marie was working at Princeton University as dean of the school of public policy, she was married to a Princeton professor, and had two boys in middle school. Then the Obama administration asked her to serve at the U.S. State Department as the first female director of policy planning, working directly under Secretary of State Hillary Clinton. "It was a dream job," says Anne-Marie. "I loved Secretary Clinton. I loved what we were trying to do."

Anne-Marie's husband had tenure at Princeton and her boys were nearing high school, so instead of uprooting the family and moving to Washington, DC, she decided to commute. Anne-Marie would spend the week in DC making international policy decisions, hobnobbing with world leaders, and helping the United States chart its course through global politics. Then she would jump on a train on Friday evening and spend the weekend in Princeton, New Jersey, with her family. At 4:00 a.m. on Monday morning she would wake up and hop on the train back to DC. Anne-Marie had it all: a perfect family, a dream job, a boss she loved. "What I realized was 'Wow. This is incredibly hard. It's not fun,'" says Anne-Marie. She was exhausted all the time and felt like she was doing everything badly: Being away on weekends meant big compromises for her work. "You can't tell Egypt to put their revolution on hold until Monday," she says. Also, part-time parenting wasn't panning out so well. Anne-Marie's son started getting into trouble: He was failing some of his classes and had several run-ins with police. "He was acting out and he was making really bad choices," she recalls.

Anne-Marie wasn't sure what to do. She had worked her whole life to get to this place in her career and she'd *gotten* there! She didn't want to give any of it up. But her home situation was getting serious and she realized she needed to make some choices. She decided to leave her State Department job to be home with her son. "It was wrenching," she recalls, "but I don't think I could have lived with myself if my son had really spun off the rails. Not that going home was any guarantee. It wasn't. But at least I knew I was going to give it everything."

Anne-Marie went back to New Jersey, her son soon got back on track, and she thought about returning to her career in government. But she found that she kept putting the decision off. Finally she had to admit to herself that she didn't want to go back. It was too hard to be a present parent *and* have her dream job. She had to choose. Anne-Marie chose her family.

That decision sent her spiraling into a kind of identity crisis: "I thought, 'Who am I? This isn't Anne-Marie Slaughter, who has known what she has wanted to do for all these years and always pushes her way through problems. This is not me!' It's not the choice I thought I would have ever made."

At that moment, Anne-Marie says, she realized much more fully how being a woman in the workplace involves choices that men don't necessarily have to deal with. She realized the feminist line she'd been believing and preaching for years—*You can have it all if you just work hard enough!*—didn't feel true. Anne-Marie thought if *she* couldn't make it work, almost nobody could. After all, she had every advantage: plenty of money, a supportive spouse who was an active parent, and the ability to commute and hire help. And in spite of this, she couldn't do it all without making enormous compromises. In her article for *The Atlantic*, she discussses her decision to leave Washington and how she felt like the "lean in" mentality was not the whole truth and resulted in women working themselves to death and feeling like failures. Anne-Marie's article went viral: Tens of thousands of people read it and commented. "My life was turned upside down. It was like a tsunami," she says. And not always in a good way. Many women were angry at her over the article. They felt like Anne-Marie was taking feminism back decades. "I lost friends over it," she says.

Anne-Marie's conclusion: "The woman who does it all" is a lie. Women who have childcare responsibilities are in a real bind in the workplace, and solving it on an individual level is almost impossible. Anne-Marie thinks the solution needs to come from the workplace itself. Companies need to make real accommodations for families; the way we value childcare needs to change; the roles we see as *male* and *female* need to change. And until that happens, she says, "having it all" means you're either "superhuman or self-employed."

Incidentally, Anne-Marie did go back to work. She is currently the CEO of New America, a public policy think tank, and she also does a lot of independent work, writing and speaking all over the world.

Working from Home

The COVID-19 pandemic put the difficulties of working mothers on steroids. Starting in March 2020, millions of people saw their workplaces close and started doing their jobs from home. At the same time, schools across the country shut down and children began schooling from home. Parents and children were suddenly all home together, trying to work and go to class online and adapt to a whole new routine. "A lot of us just were not okay," says Anya Kamenetz. I was pretty shocked to hear this from Anya. I know her from NPR, where she has always been my work-life-balance hero. She produces amazing radio, writes books and articles, travels the country giving speeches, has a vibrant social life, is raising two girls, and always manages to look totally put together. I figured, if anybody in the world was winning quarantine, it would be Anya. But when I spoke with her, she said it had been incredibly difficult and overwhelming, even with a really involved husband at home. Anya says before COVID-19 she'd had a lot of help: school, day care, grandparents, a nanny, her synagogue. "It was *It Takes a Village*–type parenting," she says. "And then it was like the village had been set on fire . . . We were all in our houses with our kids *all the freaking time.*" Instead of commuting to work in Manhattan, grabbing a fancy coffee, and spending her day reporting and chatting with her colleagues, Anya suddenly found herself in a blur of fixing meals; setting kids up with their devices for e-learning; fielding texts, emails, and work calls; and trying to get stories reported on deadline. Anya says the barriers between working and parenting totally broke down (along with everyone's sanity). The "pretending not to have kids" act that most workplaces had rewarded didn't fly any longer. "There's just no hiding anymore." Her kids were making themselves known. And heard. On one particularly memorable occasion, Anya was doing a video interview from her home office and her daughter stormed in "and threw an absolute fit about My Little Ponies. I was picking her up and putting her outside the room and she was screaming and banging on the door." The woman Anya was speaking with was very understanding. Still, it was rough: "It was a total meltdown," Anya says, laughing. "It was really embarrassing."

And Anya points out she had it easy compared to most people. She had a partner, resources, space for a home office, and access to some childcare. But even still, being a working mom in quarantine felt untenable. And for millions of women who didn't have Anya's advantages, the situation became a crisis. "People were losing pay and losing hours because they were having to parent while they were working," says Anya. "And for single parents, the challenge has been unreal."

This became very evident as the pandemic dragged on. Even as men started reentering the workforce at the end of the summer of 2020, hundreds of thousands of women started dropping out of the workforce every month to take care of children and family members.

Why was it mostly women who were dropping out of the workforce? Because as progressive as we might think we are, women still do most of the childcare and housework in the United States. This holds true in most heterosexual households where both partners work full-time. In fact, during the pandemic, mothers were more than three times as likely as fathers to be doing the housework and childcare. Also, because of the gender pay gap, if a couple was making a choice about who should work and who should stay home with children, it often made more financial sense for the woman to stop working, because her male partner was probably earning more and had better prospects for promotion.

The consequences of women leaving the workforce are serious. First of all, these women are losing years of earning, which sets them up for financial hardship later in life. Also, even the women who go back to work will have lost years of professional ground. This affects women's representation in government, on corporate boards, in environmental matters, in tech, in academia, in medicine, in law, and in the arts. Women's voices are not being heard at the level they should, and their intelligence, ideas, points of view, and voices are critically underrepresented.

Machiavelli's Lesson: Show Up

At the heart of the mommy discrimination problem is the fact that once you become a mother, people will often stop seeing you as an individual: You are no longer Sandra the shark, who never loses a case! You are Sandra, a mother and a caretaker . . . who also wants to continue working as a lawyer. So one of the keys to combating the Parent Trap is to constantly remind the people you work with of your individuality, agency, and power. Be present at work. Show up. Machiavelli, remember, was big on new princes living in the places where their power was most shaky. "Because, if one is on the spot," he writes, "disorders are seen as they spring up, and one can quickly remedy them . . ." (Chapter III, MPE).

What does this mean in terms of having a kid? It means that the time around having a baby is critical. The first thing you should do before you go on maternity leave is set up a meeting with your boss to discuss your return. Make it very clear that you are coming back and plan to hit the ground running. "Just act like you're taking a business trip," advises Dr. Cecilia L. Ridgeway. The more specifics you give, the better. "When I do come back, here's what I'm doing . . . I'm going to start here on that project." Even if you're not sure how you are going to juggle everything or what your childcare situation will be or even if you want to go back to work full-time, pretend that there's no question in your mind, and everything's all squared away. Set a firm date for your return to work and be very clear about it with everyone. Also, up until your maternity leave, do your best to stay focused. Don't give anybody an excuse to say you've checked out.

When you're back, it's very important to be fully present at work, at least for the first few months. You need to make good on your pre–maternity leave plans. Set up a meeting with your boss and get right back into things.

To be honest, I feel weird giving this advice. It seems kind of monstrous. I don't have kids, but I can't imagine how overwhelming a moment like that must be, especially if your baby isn't sleeping through the night and you are figuring out childcare and barely getting yourself to work as it is. But all the research shows that this is a pivotal moment in your career. All eyes are on you; people are dying to shoo you into the Mommy Hotbox. It's important to send the message that you are the same person you were before you left and that you're serious about your career.

Also, when you're first back at work, be vigilant about people keeping you off assignments or commenting on your workload.

Dr. Isabel Escobar did this after her male colleagues began cautioning her against taking on demanding roles. She learned to speak up and smack them down—gently. "Well, you know, this is *my* child. This is *my* family," she told one colleague. "Let me be the one to determine with *my* family what is best for *my* family. But thank you for your input." Isabel says a female colleague recommended that approach—emphasizing the word *my*. "It worked. The man backed off."

Machiavelli's Lesson: Mum's the Word

Before you leave and after you go back to work, Dr. Cecilia L. Ridgeway recommends keeping the baby talk to a minimum. To be clear, this sucks! A baby is a major life event! It's exciting and scary and it *should* be discussed at watercoolers across the land and shouted from rooftops! But the more you mention the baby, the more you risk fading into the stereotype of baking cookies and knitting onesies and definitely *not* being the point person on the flashy Jones account.

This does not, of course, mean that you are downplaying your kids in your actual life. You're just downplaying them at work. Machiavelli understood the power of a well-placed illusion in winning over the minds and hearts of people: "It is not essential, then, that a Prince should have all the good qualities . . . but it is most essential that he should seem to have them . . ." (Chapter XVIII, DTE). The good qualities, in this case, are the not having of children. I know. It's a messed-up world—which, of course, is why we need Machiavelli in the first place.

Machiavelli's Lesson: Work Like a Mother

"You don't talk about the baby," asserts Adele Lim when describing having children while working as a TV writer in Hollywood. "Writing on any show is just hard. And if you are a go-to member of the core team, that is a 24/7 job." Adele watched many women—and there were not all that many in writers' rooms to begin with—talk about their babies or leave early for childcare and get marginalized as a result. "People get annoyed. They're like, 'We were busting our ass on that outline and she's at the park playing peekaboo with her kid.'" Adele knew that this attitude was unfair and sexist, but she was also making her way in a very tough and very male-dominated industry and she was providing for her family. So Adele refrained from talking about her babies at work or showing off the millions of adorable photos she'd taken and worked as tirelessly as she had before she'd become a mother. "You run yourself ragged and become a crazy person," she says. "I have two kids, three years apart. And the first five or six years of being a mother are a complete haze to me." Adele would go to work from 10:00 a.m. to 7:00 p.m. (or later). Then she would get home and spend a half hour with her baby and then work until 2:00 or 3:00 a.m. She says because she was working so hard, the fact that she had a baby became an asset instead of a liability: "Like, 'Oh, she's a mother, but she also killed 24/7.'"

Dr. Cecilia L. Ridgeway says this is one way out of the Mommy Hotbox. You work so hard, nobody can believe you even have children. "Like, 'Who would've thought? She's really superwoman.'"

I know. I KNOW! That is yet more inhumane, monstrous advice. Cecilia says it's especially troubling because the systemic solution and the individual solution are at odds here. The systemic solution is that there needs to be pressure put on institutions to make real change to accommodate child-rearing and that pressure has to come from lots of women and men getting together and saying, "I HAVE KIDS AND SO DO MOST PEOPLE HERE AND WE NEED CHANGE!" And change *is* needed! But this isn't a book for companies or policy makers; it's a book for women. And if you are a woman in the workplace, working until you drop is one way out of the Mommy Hotbox.

The Daddy Hotbox

The bias against motherhood is really a bias against active parenthood. As we've seen, men who have children earn more and are promoted more quickly than men who don't have children. But if men ask for time off for childcare duties or if their childcare interferes with output in some way (for example, they leave early to pick up a sick kid a bunch of times or take extra paternity leave), they can be penalized and their earning and promotion potential can drop. The thought is that men who are active caregivers are seen as more feminine. They, too, get stuck in the Parent Trap.

Elizabeth, the career diplomat, says her husband took over childcare duties when their family moved overseas for her job, and he experienced a lot of discrimination and ridicule for his active parenting. "He tried to join the 'Diplomatic Wives' Club'—that's what it was called—and he got heckled. No one would invite our daughter to playdates because it was *dad* who was bringing her and not *mom*."

Machiavelli's Lesson: "Hey, Partner!"

One suggestion I heard from several mothers I spoke with was the importance of dividing up the childcare equally with your partner if you have one. "Couples need to be fully engaged in the beginning," asserts lawyer and entrepreneur Anne-Marie Slaughter. She says women need to insist their partners do an equal amount of the childcare from the very beginning and should have those discussions before the baby is born. "My husband and I always say, 'The person who does the taxes the first time will do them forevermore.' You need to be really careful to ensure that there is genuine, mutual responsibility from the beginning, because you are setting patterns."

ALYSIA MONTAÑO:
Supermom

Alysia Montaño is a professional runner and an Olympian. She's won national championships, broken two world records, and competed in the 2012 Olympic Games. Her career began in 2008, right after she graduated from college and signed a contract with Nike. Alysia says signing that contract was one of the best moments of her professional life, but the contract itself was extremely demanding. "You are expected to live, eat, and breathe track and field," she says.

Alysia says the contracts are very unforgiving for athletes who get injured or who want to take time off to have children. "They put pregnancy under the same clause as injury," she says. "So there's that." Alysia mentioned wanting to become a mother, and, she says, Nike's response made it clear they were not open to that discussion. "You have a target on your head even mentioning pregnancy."

Alysia's Lesson: Find an Ally

But Alysia and her husband wanted to start a family, and so she left Nike and signed a contract with Asics. There was a woman high up in the ranks at Asics, and Alysia thought that would mean more support for her decision to have children. And, indeed, when Alysia got pregnant, it was the female executive who extended support: "She's like, 'Oh my gosh, we want you to enjoy your pregnancy! Do not worry about your contract at all. It is safe.'" Alysia says this was an enormous relief. "I felt empowered and I felt very happy and open to do all the appearances they asked me to do." In fact, about eight months later, Alysia was invited to race at the USA Track & Field championships. She decided to run the race while eight months pregnant. She felt great, and she wanted to make a point that pregnancy and being a professional athlete could coexist. "People kind of freaked out," she says, laughing. "They're like, 'What are you doing? You're going to kill your baby!'"

Alysia ran the race with her baby bump and says it was a truly joyful experience. "I felt fantastic. I felt super empowered and grateful for getting the conversation started." Her race got a mountain of press. "It was incredible," she says. "I got way more attention for that than for my seven national titles."

Shortly after Alysia's daughter was born, though, the female executive left Asics and everything changed. Asics called Alysia and said they wanted to reduce her contract. She contacted a lawyer and got Asics to back off, but she was so anxious about her new job situation, she started training sooner than she wanted to. "I ended up winning nationals at six months postpartum," she says. "I was taping my stomach together . . . but we won the gold medal at the world championships at ten months postpartum." In spite of the wins, Alysia continued to get signals that Asics wanted her gone. She says it felt clear to her that Asics saw her as a "mom" now and not a committed athlete: "I knew I had the biggest target on my head. I knew if I didn't qualify for the Olympic team, I'm done." Alysia fell during the qualifying race for the Olympics and her fears were realized. Her contract was terminated.

Alysia's Lesson: Find Your People

Alysia tried to get another contract, but she and her husband wanted another child, and she was determined to be honest with potential sponsors. She says a couple of companies considered taking her on, but none did. Meanwhile, money was getting tight for her family. "I'm marching around the baby and a three-year-old and trying to go to the track to work out with the last bit of savings I have. It was just too hard financially. I needed to be able to contribute." Alysia took a job in marketing and tried to get her training in where she could, in the hopes of getting back to the work she loved.

Alysia says it was an awful feeling that the family she and her husband so wanted had to come at the expense of her career and her livelihood. "I felt alone and I felt just really worried about what my future held," she recalls. Alysia eventually told her story to the *New York Times*, explaining how difficult it is to be a female athlete and also to have a family. After the article came out, Alysia heard from hundreds of female athletes who were struggling with the same thing: "That's the thing that's really surprising to me and exciting . . . how many women athletes have been able to confide in me that they want children. I must have been the Lone Ranger, since nobody was doing it."

Alysia did eventually find a sponsor: a New Zealand–based company called Cadenshae, which makes active maternity wear. The company has been extremely supportive of Alysia having a family. She says signing with them felt like a true victory, not just for her, but for all female athletes. "I want to show people what it looks like to be a woman in my profession," she says. "I wanted to make a statement, like, 'Quit governing our bodies and support us through this amazing, monumental moment in our lives. Support us as we try to figure this out.'"

I, Mother

The key to navigating the Parent Trap is to assert yourself as an individual. People are trying to put you in a box—a June Cleaver box—where you have Ward paying all the bills and no time for the flashy Jones account because you have to get dinner on the table for Wally and the Beav. You need to fight that image. Be direct. Be proactive. Tell your boss that you are supporting your family financially. Tell your boss that you want the challenging assignments. Keep your conversations at work about work. When you first get back from maternity leave, work as hard as you can. Show up. Be present. This is a crucial and pivotal moment in your life and career, and too many women are getting pushed out of the workforce or onto some dead-end track simply because they choose to have children.

8

Women and the Dark Arts

"The ruler is not truly wise who cannot discern evils before
they develop themselves, and this is a faculty given to few."
—Machiavelli, *The Prince* (Chapter XIII, DTE)

F rustratingly (and horribly), some of the women who have made
it to the top or who are on their way there will target, sabotage,
or stab their fellow ladies in the back. *Why* would they do this?
Why would you turn on your own, especially when your own are
having a hard enough time as it is? OH, THE HUMANITY! As
the great Madeleine Albright said, "There's a special place in hell
for women who don't help each other." That place may be special,
but it's most definitely not uncrowded.

Still, many of the reasons for this phenomenon have everything
to do with the unfairness of the workplace itself. (Hate the game,
baby!) It is women trying to navigate an unfair system and seeing
gender targeting as their best option. They're not necessarily wrong
about that. Tokenism exists, and many women figure they're not
really competing with everyone else at the company, but rather
they are competing with the other women at the company. It's the
"queen bee syndrome" again and it tends to show up in workplaces
where there aren't many ladies in high places.

These women practice the dark arts, like in *Harry Potter*—except
with Outlook invitations and casual Fridays instead of capes and
owls. And they're not always so easy to spot; often they are very

charismatic and clever and their tactics work—at least for a while. Dealing with them is essential to surviving and thriving in the workplace. Machiavelli thought a good prince had to be able to spot the "hidden venom" of a dark arts practitioner in order to survive (Chapter XIII, DTE). The stakes in these situations can be incredibly high: Dealing with a bully or being manipulated or harassed at work can reduce productivity, cause depression and anxiety, and even push people out of a workplace altogether. "It's a serious emotional, physical, and financial issue," says Dr. Mariana Bockarova, a behavioral scientist at the University of Toronto.

So how do you spot these ladies? And how should you deal with them once you *do* spot them? I've broken dark arts practitioners down into four basic types and, in sticking with the Harry Potter theme, have identified a Patronus to disarm each one. One universal rule: Keep. Your. Cool. These ladies use fear and intimidation to knock people off-balance and get their way. Don't let them throw you. Remember, practicing the dark arts isn't something people do because they feel powerful. It's something people do when they feel threatened, vulnerable, and weak.

Write It Down

A key thing to remember when dealing with a dark arts practitioner of any kind: Write it down. Keep a log of the devious things they do. This advice comes from Dr. Susan Krauss Whitbourne, a professor of psychology at the University of Massachusetts, Amherst, and coauthor (with Richard P. Halgin) of *Abnormal Psychology: Clinical Perspectives on Psychological Disorders*. Susan has spent years studying dysfunctional personality types and says if things ever escalate to the point where you need to take official or even legal action, having texts, emails, and written accounts of incidents is crucial. "You need documentation," she says. Still, Susan asserts, there are ways to deal with, and hopefully neutralize, these ladies before things get to that point.

The Highlander

Some women rise to power on the unspoken agreement that they will not threaten the patriarchy. In exchange, they, by their very ladyhood, give the workplace a sheen of inclusivity and diversity and help the patriarchy protect its privileged position. I call them Highlanders, after the 1986 movie *Highlander*, starring Christopher Lambert (launching my forever-crush on Christopher Lambert), in which a bunch of immortal warriors battle it out for "the Prize," which is very vague and mysterious and appears to involve knowing all the secrets of the universe. There's an iconic battle cry in *Highlander* of "There can be only one!" (That is, only one of the immortals can claim this prize; all others must be killed.) That way of thinking is the hallmark of this particular workplace personality.

When a Highlander gets into a position of power, she will often do so by targeting someone who has the position she wants or is somehow in her way. (Usually it is not a man: That's part of her deal with the patriarchy.) The good news is, Highlanders are not subtle creatures and they are generally pretty easy to spot.

Spotting a Highlander

1. **The mean girl next door.** Highlanders will often come off as funny and sassy and outspoken. Really, though, these ladies are just mean. They enjoy picking on people; it makes them feel powerful. The easiest way to spot a Highlander is through her words. She will attack people openly and make jokes at the expense of others, very often in meetings or group settings.
2. **Suck-ups.** Highlanders are not subtle, long-game ladies. They don't spend time with people who are not immediately useful to them. If you notice this woman spending a lot of time in the office of a supervisor or manager and not really bothering with anybody else, you may have a Highlander on your hands. Of course, *you* may be the person this woman is schmoozing.

If so, beware. These ladies look out for number one. Full stop. The second you are no longer useful to the Highlander or are in her way, the knives will come out. Be wary if the office mean girl wants to be your bestie. Keep your distance and don't be lured in.

3. **Birds of a feather.** Highlanders don't tend to have many female friends; they gravitate toward men or, if they do have female friends, they tend to be in a mean-girls cabal.

Machiavelli's Patronus: We Need to Talk

If a Highlander slams your ideas in a few meetings or makes a snide remark about you or your work, she may be targeting you. Here are a few ways to deal with, and hopefully disarm, your Highlander.

1. **Calling all allies.** This is a moment to call on your allies, mentors, and friends for help. "Establish and maintain a strong network of individuals," recommends Dr. Mariana Bockarova. Talk to your allies before a meeting; make sure you have people speaking up for you, coming to your defense, and supporting your ideas. Highlanders are very sensitive to the dynamics of a group, and if she feels like her bullying doesn't have support or that the tide is turning in your favor, she will back down immediately.

2. **I think we're alone now.** Highlanders thrive on group inter-actions. They feed off the validation and energy of a crowd. To deal with a Highlander, get her out of that arena and into a one-on-one interaction. She is much more vulnerable there. Remember, a Highlander is just a bully, and bullies are, fun-damentally, scared. That said, dealing with a Highlander early is a good idea, because she will not back down if she senses weakness and she can be vicious and relentless. Ask the High-lander to coffee (or just ask for a few minutes of her time). The old "We need to talk" trick strikes terror into even the darkest heart.

3. **Calm confrontation.** A Highlander is not a subtle creature. You can't appeal to her sympathies or charm her into backing off. You need to make it clear that you're not afraid of her. Fear and a lack of fear are the only languages your Highlander speaks. Still, Dr. Susan Krauss Whitbourne recommends avoiding aggression or accusation. Keep everything pointed to you. Susan suggests saying something like, "I've felt over the past couple of weeks like there's been something wrong. I'm not really sure what it is but I feel like I'm disappointing you." This puts the bully on a back foot but also not in a position to be aggressive or lash out, which is a Highlander's go-to in a confrontational situation. If your Highlander says (and she very likely will) that she's not sure what you mean, recount the incident in very neutral tones: "I noticed you made a comment about how much I talk in meetings and I wanted to ask you about that. Does it bother you when I talk in meetings?" Don't be aggressive or emotional, but do be direct and unapologetic. Chances are the Highlander will wave it away or deny it. If she does acknowledge it or tries to make you feel like you're overreacting, or laughs it off by saying something like, 'Oh my God, you wouldn't shut up! Somebody had to say something!,' listen closely and respectfully and say you understand. Look right at her and don't betray any emotional response. When you respond, you want to give the bully a way to save face, but you also want to make it clear that you are not to be messed with. Something like, "It's true. I do love contributing in our meetings, and I know I can get carried away. If you feel like I'm hijacking the conversation, please just come and talk to me. I'm always open to feedback and I always want to hear what you think."

4. **Highlander manager.** If a Highlander is your superior, tell her you've noticed that she seems to have taken a critical tone toward your work. Say you look up to her as a woman in the workplace and you'd love her feedback. (Is this subtle shaming? You bet your Machiavellian ass it is!) You can also try appealing to her ego. You can be flattering, but don't say anything nice

out of fear, or the Highlander will see it as weakness. All compliments should come from a place of calm and confidence. For example, "I notice you didn't seem to think my pitches were working. Would you mind giving me a critique? I'm always impressed by your pitches and I'd love to know more about your process." Whatever she says, nod, take notes, listen, and thank her. Keep your good humor up. Don't come off as crushed or angry. Highlanders can smell victimhood like sharks smell blood. If your Highlander says something mean, don't flinch or register the insult. Say you'd love to schedule a follow-up to talk more. You're not running scared or letting her get away with taking swipes at you, but you're also not creating drama for her. This will make you a very uncompelling target.

The Highlander likes feeling powerful. If you don't seem afraid of her, it will throw her off. Also, if she knows that making a snide remark to you in a meeting will always result in an earnest thirty-minute conversation, it's highly unlikely she will keep doing it. Remember Machiavelli's lesson about dealing with sexual harassment. It applies here, too: "Whoever shall fortify his town well . . . will never be attacked without great caution, for men are always adverse to enterprises where difficulties can be seen . . ." (Chapter X, MPE). Make bullying you as unappealing, difficult, and troublesome as possible.

Most important, be gentle with yourself: You're in a tough position, and if you don't behave exactly the way you wish you had or if you lose your cool, don't worry. Highlanders are pretty obvious. Everyone sees them for what they are, and the workplaces where they thrive are undoubtedly toxic and probably not a place you want to be for long anyway.

The Queen of Hearts

The Queen of Hearts is a smart, quick-witted woman who is arrogant, erratic, and a little bit unhinged, which is where a lot of her power comes from. QOHs are often quite successful in workplaces early on in their careers. "They can be very charismatic," says Dr. Susan Krauss Whitbourne. "They have this magnetism that fools people into thinking, 'Oh, this is somebody who can really get things done.' People promote them because they just seem to have it all: the power, the confidence. They have a very charming exterior." The interior, though, is something of a hellscape. QOHs are deeply insecure, unbalanced, and toxic. They also have no scruples when it comes to attacking people or respecting boundaries. They are entirely self-centered and, in true queen fashion, see other people as subjects and useful tools rather than equals or colleagues or even sentient beings. QOHs aren't too hard to spot: They typically show their colors pretty quickly. "Over a short period of time, they reveal unhealthy attitudes and behaviors," says Dr. Mariana Bockarova. "They actively undermine those around them and create tension and anxiety, fueling a toxic work environment." If you are working for a QOH or if she is your manager, Mariana says, this puts you in a particularly hard situation. A QOH is extremely status conscious and will often abuse those below her and do whatever she can to "erode the victim's self-confidence or leave them feeling humiliated," Mariana also says.

Rest assured, these ladies will flame out: They don't typically have much self-control, and their actions become pretty outrageous pretty quickly, but the flaming out might take a while and they will probably create some serious carnage before they go. Like the Queen of Hearts in *Alice in Wonderland*, these ladies are unpredictable and vicious and will turn from mirthful to murderous at the flip of a card.

My Queen?

So how do you know if you're working with a Queen of Hearts? In the early days of working with one, it isn't always so easy to tell. They can be a charming and magnetic lot. But there are definite ways to spot them:

1. **They have jumped jobs a lot.** QOHs will often move jobs every couple of years, running away from the consequences of their toxic behavior.

2. **There are no *teams* in *I*.** All the work a QOH does will be 100 percent in service of making herself look good. A QOH will not do anything for a "team" or any supportive, behind-the-scenes-type work or any favors for anybody else (unless it's a higher-up—these ladies heart hierarchy). For a QOH, "everything is always done for *me* and *my glorification*," explains Dr. Susan Krauss Whitbourne. These ladies are domineering, grandiose, and obsessed with status. If you are in competition with a QOH, beware. This can bring out the claws. "The idea of losing a competition can really bring out the worst in them," warns Mariana Bockarova. "Lying, claiming credit for other people's work." Nothing is off-limits for a true QOH.

3. **"But enough about me . . . *What do you* think about me?"** If the lady in question keeps bringing every topic of conversation back to herself, there is very likely a QOH in your midst. "It all has to be from their own perspective," says Susan Krauss Whitbourne. "Even just chitchat. It always becomes a story about them."

4. **"Does this make me look fabulous?"** QOHs are often very vain. They spend a lot of time and money on clothes, hair, and makeup—like little peacocks. QOHs are also incredibly susceptible to flattery. They are deeply insecure and will often repeat compliments other people have given them and brag about their accomplishments. If actual compliments and accomplishments aren't sufficient, a Queen of Hearts will simply make things up. These ladies bow to nothing, not even reality. And it's not just praise for outward appearance these ladies are seeking. They are often very active on social media, where they can get the validation and attention they crave 24/7.

5. **"I don't feel so good . . ."** A key way to spot a QOH is by monitoring how you feel after you've interacted with this woman. "Inevitably, they're going to make you feel like you're lesser," says Susan Krauss Whitbourne. QOHs "build themselves up by putting people down." If you leave conversations

with this woman feeling bad, slighted, or marginalized in some way, you're possibly dealing with a Queen of Hearts.

6. **Destructive criticism.** QOHs cannot take criticism. They have extremely fragile egos and will lash out in an outsize way at anyone who makes even a small criticism of them or their work. "Their antennae are always out there for defection and disloyalty," Susan says.

When a Queen Attacks

QOHs make trouble. It's what they do. They're not particularly strategic about who they attack or how (except they will almost never attack superiors), and the attacks can be vicious. If we're going to get clinical, these women would be considered narcissists—or at least they have narcissistic tendencies. They are emotionally unstable, extremely self-centered, and have no boundaries. This toxic brew can make them frightening and intimidating adversaries. It can be tempting to drop everything and do what you can to appease them, because you know the horror show that will ensue if you don't.

Patronus: The Zen Babysitter

QOHs tend to draw in codependent types and people pleasers, who will bend over backward to manage their emotions and appease them. If you have any of these qualities (I do! I do!), check yourself around a possible QOH. One good way to approach a QOH is to channel your inner Zen babysitter. Imagine you are babysitting someone's child. The kid is a nightmare: screaming, refusing to go to bed, throwing things, locking themselves in the bathroom. How would you handle this? You're not in a position to discipline or punish the child, but you still need to assert yourself and take control of the situation. This is a good proxy for dealing with a Queen of Hearts attack. A calm, firm approach with these ladies is ideal. (If you can avoid them entirely, even better!)

When facing down a QOH, you have to make it clear that you aren't a doormat, but you cannot introduce any drama or emotion into the situation, because a QOH will feed on that. Likewise, avoid criticizing her actions or accusing her of anything, because that could send her into a gloves-off spiral, and you do not want to go gloves-off with a QOH. Instead, Dr. Susan Krauss Whitbourne advises appealing to her rational side.

1. **"Help *me* help *you*."** Queen of Hearts are always interested in advancing and looking good. So spin your request—whatever it is—in terms of her own interests. "Figure out a way that it will end up kind of glorifying them," Susan advises. For instance, "I'd love your input on this, and if you would feel comfortable speaking up on my behalf at the meeting, I would so appreciate that. I know management really respects your opinion and they *do* love teamwork and collaboration. Come to think of it, that's how everybody ends up getting promotions at this company."

2. **"Have you been working out?"** Flattery is an effective way to appease a Queen of Hearts. In fact, flattery can give you a bit of power over a QOH, because she is so thirsty for it. Tell her she looks nice. Tell her you loved her presentation or her Instagram post. She'll eat it up.

3. **Soft boundaries.** You need to be calm, gentle, and firm when you set boundaries with a QOH. Stay away from feelings or emotions or anything personal. Instead, lay out the facts and explain how her behavior and actions affect your work. For instance, "I always enjoy hearing from you, but when you asked me about my dating life when I was pitching my idea at the meeting, it made it hard for me to focus on work. I want to make sure people see me professionally. I know you didn't mean anything by it, but I'm very sensitive about that stuff."

4. **Line in the sand.** If the behavior doesn't stop—say your QOH keeps bringing up your dating life in meetings—you need to take action. "Put up boundaries with clear conse-

quences," Dr. Mariana Bockarova advises. "Then actually follow through on them . . . [This] will display to the narcissist that they cannot take advantage of you."

Remember, it's best to avoid criticizing the actions of a Queen of Hearts, so don't imply that her actions were wrong or bad; you just want her to stop. For example: "Like I told you before, it makes it hard for me to do my job when you speak about my personal life in front of our manager. It's really important to me that it doesn't happen anymore. I thought about talking with HR, but I felt like it would be much more productive to speak about it with you for now. I know you're a respectful person and I value our relationship. But please don't bring it up again." The QOH may try to make you feel guilty for setting the boundary or come back with a dramatic story. Hear her out but stick to your boundary.

The "Machiavelliannes"

It kind of breaks my heart to use Machiavelli's name like this, but psychologists have actually identified Machiavellianism as a personality type, characterized by people who are master manipulators and who use others people's emotions to control them.

Machiavelliannes are just as vicious and conscienceless as Queens of Hearts, but they are far more dangerous. They are the calculating Michael Corleone to the QOH's hotheaded Sonny. They often have high levels of emotional intelligence and will use vulnerability, anger, and hurt as a way to create loyalty, extract information, and bend people to their will. They're typically charismatic, clever, and charming. Dr. Susan Krauss Whitbourne describes them as always having a little gang of ultra-loyal minions. But Machiavelliannes are not loyal to anyone. They are looking out for exactly one person. Everyone else is a chess piece and Machiavelliannes play to win. Period.

A Machiavellianne attack will often seem to come out of nowhere or from someone you considered a friend or confidant. "They can work well with colleagues, and be friendly and charming," warns Dr. Mariana Bockarova, "only to turn on them in an incredibly malevolent and unanticipated way with no remorse, stealing every idea their colleague has had, spreading harsh rumors, and cheating their way to the top." With ice water in her veins, no moral compass, and a vicious, power-hungry nature, the ends really do justify the means for a Machiavellianne.

Spotting a Machiavellianne

Spotting a Machiavellianne isn't easy. They are shadow people and great actors. But there are some dead giveaways. If a Highlander is identifiable by her talk, a Machiavellianne's actions are her tell.

1. **"Did you do something new with your hair?"** Machiavelliannes are flatterers. They are masters of the ego and use compliments to mollify people and curry favor. Machiavelli—the man—thought flattery was a signature of snakes in the grass and saw flatterers as very dangerous to a prince. He even has an entire chapter in *The Prince* titled "How Flatterers Should Be Avoided" (Chapter XXIII, MPE). This is not to say that if somebody compliments your work or says something nice to you, you should respond with grave suspicion. But pay attention to who flatters you and when.

2. **Two faces.** Does the woman in question slam the boss and then spend hours chatting him up? Is she critical of upper management in private but silent and avoidant or even supportive of them in public? If the woman says one thing in private and something else in public, she's likely a Machiavellianne.

3. **They think people are the worst.** Dr. Susan Krauss Whitbourne recommends listening to how a Machiavellianne talks about other people. "There's a high level of distrust," she says. "They believe that most people are essentially bad." After all, the way we see the world is very often a reflection of who we

are. If someone assumes other people are devious, malicious, or underhanded, that can be a powerful reveal of who *they* are.

4. **Twenty thousand questions.** A Machiavellianne doesn't just want to chat; she wants power over you. The way she gets that power is by extracting information. Does she keep asking you about negative experiences or emotions? Does she keep insulting your manager or a fellow employee, trying to egg you on? Is she always fishing for gossip or stories about bad work experiences? Does she ask inappropriately personal questions? Painful emotions, vulnerability, and insecurity are the arena of choice for the Machiavellianne. If a colleague only wants to talk about those things and does not seem interested in anything constructive or positive, beware.

5. *Why did I just tell her that?* If you leave an interaction with this woman feeling like you said more than you wish you had or you find yourself doing something you aren't sure was actually in your best interest at the suggestion of a colleague, you could very well be dealing with a Machiavellianne.

Patronus: Poker-Faced Pollyanna

Machiavelliannes love the shadows, so plant yourself firmly in the sunlight. Try to avoid one-on-one interactions with these women. They will use those moments to try to get information out of you or manipulate you in some way. But if you can't avoid a Machiavellianne, there are some tricks.

1. **Mum's the word.** Say as little as possible to your Machiavellianne. Don't give her information about your ambitions or your thoughts about colleagues or your worries or insecurities or anything else. Any information you give her will be weaponized. "As soon as you have opened your mind to a malcontent," Machiavelli warns, "you have given him the material with which . . . he can look for every advantage . . ." (Chapter XIX, MPE).

2. **"Hello, My Name Is: POLLYANNA!"** When you talk to a Machiavellianne, be super positive. You love everyone! And everything! You are so sorry to hear about what she's going through. And about her bad experience with Russell. He's always been great to you, but that sounds terrible. You're totally shocked! You really hope things get better! Kthanksbyeeeee!

3. **Help me help you!** Just like with a Queen of Hearts, if you can convince your Machiavellianne that *you* doing well is somehow in *her* interest, that is ideal. "Try as much as possible to set up a work situation that is advantageous to both you and her," advises Dr. Mariana Bockarova. Of course, the second your interests diverge, you are going to want to duck and cover.

4. **Poker face.** Machiavelliannes will attack at key moments in front of key people in ways you won't expect. The sneak attack is her signature. If a Machiavellianne sneak attacks, try not to show emotion. Channel your inner poker player. For example, let's say you and the Machiavellianne are talking with your boss about who should lead a project and your Machiavellianne says something like "Well, if Joe's on the project, we all know *you* will want to be a part of it . . . Seems like you are *always* finding a way to work with Joe . . ." Classic Machiavellianne attack. She probably wants to get you to back down so she can take the project herself. Avoid anger or defensiveness. Go for firmness and clarity. Above all, do *not* let her see that you're upset or thrown off at all. For example: "I do enjoy working with Joe. That's very true. I respect him as a colleague and we work very well together. And, yes, I would love to be on that project." If the intimations continue, address them directly: "You've made several comments now that seem to be implying something about my relationship with Joe. Is that right? What are you saying?" Remember, Machiavelliannes don't like sunlight; they don't really do confrontation.

5. **Shiny, happy people holding hands.** Call in your allies. Machiavelliannes operate by hiding and creating a strategic

network of allies to do their bidding. You need to fight fire with fire. Make sure you have friends and colleagues who are aware of the situation you're in and the kind of person you are dealing with. This will create some skepticism and pushback for any rumors or tactics a Machiavellianne uses. They can also give you information about whatever your Machiavellianne might be planning.

Machiavelliannes can be scary adversaries in a workplace: They tend to rise quickly and, unlike QOHs, they can hold their positions of power for a while. Often a Machiavellianne is quite popular and well-liked by people across the organization: Her emotional manipulations make people feel attached to her, devoted to her, and even protective of her. Still, as strategic as she is, when a Machiavellianne goes down, she goes down *hard*. Remember, Machiavelli's very favorite Machiavellian, Cesare Borgia, met a terrible end. Eventually, someone he had wronged rose to a position of power (became pope) and made it his personal mission to take Cesare down. Machiavelliannes are ultimately very vulnerable and alone: All of their scheming and manipulating means they have a long trail of enemies, and their calculating nature prevents any kind of real relationship or connection from forming. Your Machiavellianne may rise very high, but when she goes down, it will *not* be with a whimper.

Darth Mentor/Darth Manager

I talked a lot about the importance of women finding a mentor, but the story does not always end happily. Some mentors practice the dark arts and it can create huge problems if you are the mentee—especially if your mentor is your supervisor or boss. Women report having far more complicated relationships with their mentors and managers than men do. Here's the issue: When a Darth Mentor or Darth Manager champions you, she will often feel great ownership over you. Because women are perceived as having less power in the workplace and are supposed to be all about teamwork and supporting others, the expectations that come with the mentoring and managing of women can be extreme. Women are often vulnerable to an "I *MADE* YOU: YOU *OWE* ME!" attitude from mentors and managers.

The new prince feels your pain. Machiavelli notes that very often the people who help a new prince rise to power will end up resenting him or turning against him. He writes, "You are not able to keep those friends who put you there [on your new throne] because of your not being able to satisfy them in the way they expected . . ." (Chapter III, MPE).

I have seen this happen in journalism countless times. One woman I spoke with for this book, whom I'll call Georgia, had a mentor/manager who was a great champion of hers early on in her career. At the time, Georgia was freelancing and one of her industry mentors (an editor at a well-known shop) started giving her a lot of work. Typically, these would be lighter, pop-culture stories: celebrity breakups, fashion, and social media trends. Those are common assignments for someone who is starting out. When a full-time reporter job opened up, Georgia's mentor helped her get hired. This was a dream: Georgia had the job she wanted and also loved her boss! They would often go out for drinks and socialize. But after about a year, Georgia started to feel boxed in by the light human-interest stories she was always being assigned. Georgia wanted to grow professionally and felt ready to tackle more serious topics.

This happens to women in journalism quite a bit—I've noticed it many times. When men do a good job with lighter stories early in their careers, they are often seen as versatile and creative and are subsequently rewarded with all kinds of high-level assignments. But when women excel at lighter stories, they often end up *only* doing those stories. They became pigeonholed as fluff reporters. Georgia began to worry this was happening to her.

But Georgia was friends with her manager, so she went to talk with her about the situation and said she really wanted to start reporting on more serious topics. The conversation did not go well.

Georgia's manager told her that wanting to do more serious, newsier stories was a mistake, because lighter human-interest stories were the ones people remembered. She also reminded Georgia, not gently, that she was her boss and that it was Georgia's job to report the stories she was assigned. Georgia's manager concluded by saying her assignments would not be changing and that if she wanted to report on different topics, she could get herself another job.

Georgia was rattled by this conversation, but she was more rattled by the prospect of being a fluff reporter for life. She started gunning for more serious assignments from other editors (a major breach of protocol in her newsroom). Her manager stopped speaking to her and even tried to have her fired for insubordination. Things calmed down, but Georgia left that job as soon as she could. Apparently, the men this manager worked with did not experience this problem, and many of them thrived under her. Several of the women she managed, however, also struggled with this extreme feeling of ownership, and they reached out to Georgia to get her advice on how to handle the situation.

"Luke, I Am Your Manager"

How do you know if you're in a Darth Mentor/Darth Manager situation? Look out for a few key tells:

1. **Opportunity cost.** Your mentor or manager should be supporting you and, ideally, opening doors for you and expanding your horizons. If you find that your mentor or manager is discouraging you from a certain kind of work or telling you a particular career path is not possible, this may be a DM situation.

2. **That's nothing.** If you go to your mentor or manager with a problem or an upsetting situation and she criticizes you for being upset or angry, you could be dealing with a DM. Gender researcher Joan C. Williams says she sees this across professions: "Older women get really cross with younger women

[and] basically say to them, 'Grow a spine,' or even, 'Grow a pair.' And the young women are like, 'Are you kidding?'" Joan says in many of these cases the older women experienced a lot of discrimination or professional herding when they were coming up in their field and their attitudes have been shaped by that. They may actually think they're doing you a favor by toughening you up. To be clear, they are not.

3. **"You will do what you're told."** If you express a desire to grow, advance, or make a change in your career and your mentor or manager reacts defensively, expresses inappropriate ownership over you, or moves to block your progress, you're probably in a DM situation. You are likely very useful to your mentor or manager right where you are and it's not in her interest for you to grow or evolve. You need to get out of that situation ASAP.

Patronus: The Fearless Octopus

If you find yourself under the thumb of a DM, never fear! It's a perfectly normal and escapable situation. You simply need to keep calm and reach out.

1. **Channel your inner octopus.** By that I mean reach out in every possible direction. You will need to get support and mentorship from others, especially if your current mentor or manager is, at best, not going to support you and, at worst, is going to try to undermine you. In your conversations with potential supporters and mentors, do not badmouth your DM. It's enough to say her support has been invaluable, but you really want to go in this other direction and you'd love advice about how to do that.

2. **Have a conversation.** Talk to your mentor or manager about what you want. Leave emotion out of it. A DM wants control, but you have every right to take your career in whatever direction you choose. It's *your* career! Your DM does not have

to agree or like it, but it is also not her decision. If your DM pushes back when you express your wishes, listen respectfully and say you understand and then calmly restate what you want to do. Tell her how valuable her guidance has been and say you would love her support in this next step of your career. She may become emotional or say things to try to scare you or discourage you. Say you appreciate what she's saying, but you need to do what is right for you.

3. **Draw boundaries early.** Georgia says that when she thinks back on her experience with her DM, she realizes she did not have proper professional boundaries in that relationship. Georgia thought not having traditionally professional boundaries with her boss would give her more power and influence in the relationship (she also just really liked her), but when it came right down to it, Georgia's boss pulled rank. And she had every right to do that. What should have been a professional outgrowing-a-job moment turned into a very dramatic personal-betrayal scenario. And Georgia nearly lost her job.

Much of the Darth Mentor/Darth Manager situation is a natural evolution. It's normal to have workplace guides who teach you something valuable and whom you eventually outgrow. It's also a human thing to want to push someone in the direction you think is best; if that were a crime, there would be no parents who were not in jail. A mentor or manager often assumes a parental-type role, and it's understandable and even natural that those feelings go a little haywire when you are ready to leave the nest. With a DM, it's important to stand your ground but also be grateful for what she has given you. Georgia tells me that without her own DM, she's not sure she would have been hired as a reporter or encouraged to be creative in her job. She says she deeply regrets the way things ended, because she feels she owes her DM a huge debt of gratitude. Remember, in *Star Wars*, when Luke removed Darth Vader's helmet, there was a sweet, human face underneath all the scary plastic. Your wonderful workplace champion and teacher is still in there somewhere! Sometimes the dark arts just get the best of us. Honor your mentor. Thank her. And then get the *hell* out of Dodge.

Machiavelli and the Dark Arts

Here's the thing about the dark arts: They work. And, honestly, one of my biggest fears in writing this book was this very thing: Does Machiavelli condone evil behavior? And, if so, what should I do about it? My tote-bag-collecting, Brooklyn-dwelling, Emily Dickinson–loving public radio soul could not abide telling people that they should be underhanded or backstabby, but I was also determined to tell the truth of what Machiavelli said.

I was greatly relieved when I reread *The Prince*. Granted, Machiavelli does not condemn evil behavior—far from it. He acknowledges many times that extremely cruel leaders can be very effective. Cesare Borgia—violent and treacherous though he was—brought order to a lawless and violent region of Italy. Machiavelli also waxes poetic about the legendary Hannibal, who is considered to be one of the greatest generals in history. Machiavelli attributes much of his success to his "inhuman cruelty," saying it enabled him to lead "an enormous army, composed of many various races of men, to fight in foreign lands, [and] no dissensions arose either among them or against the prince . . ." (Chapter XVII, MPE).

Machiavelli had seen firsthand what chaos and lawlessness looked like and what it did to people. It is probably for that reason that he valued order and stability so highly. He observes, and rightly so, that a cruel leader can bring order and stability to a chaotic situation by scaring the bejesus out of everyone and not being afraid to do what needs to be done. Still, Machiavelli was clear that his ideal prince was not evil. "To slaughter fellow-citizens, to betray friends, to be devoid of honour, pity, and religion, cannot be counted as merits," he writes, "for these are means which may lead to power, but which confer no glory" (Chapter VIII, DTE).

Also, strategically, Machiavelli did not think evildoing was a great idea. Scheming, crushing people, and toxic behavior ultimately leave people vulnerable. Villains might rise to the top, but they're always on borrowed time. Eventually somebody they've wronged will be in a position to exact revenge—as happened with Cesare. For this reason, Machiavelli recommends that a prince "crush" (slaughter) the people he's injured to mitigate the threat (Chapter III, DTE). But slaughtering people doesn't really fly in the modern workplace (say what you will about corporate America, it has its merits), so the modern villainous prince is always at risk of someone she's screwed over or abused getting into a position to strike back.

Finally, Machiavelli observes that the reason people practice the dark arts is usually because they feel powerless—it is the last resort of a wounded prince. "Many times, indeed, having been good, he becomes wicked as a result of the fear he has experienced," Machiavelli writes. "This leads to a vicious cycle, because fear leads the prince to seek ways of 'making himself safe' and 'making himself safe' . . . 'gives him reasons for doing harm,' leading to the ruin of the prince himself."

As a woman in the workplace, it's easy to feel overwhelmed, and the dark arts can seem like a reasonable solution to some of the difficult and unjust situations that arise. The system we live and work inside of is unfair, and that can twist people and make them crazy. We all have a little bit of the dark arts in us. But being full of fear and hatred is, ultimately, a weakness. Machiavelli understood this. Near the end of *The Prince*, Machiavelli writes that a leader's greatest resource—the only one he can ever really count on—is himself. "Those modes of defense are alone good, certain and lasting, which depend upon yourself and your own worth," he writes (Chapter XXIV, DTE). Having integrity and thinking well of yourself: That is the greatest tactical advantage in any fight.

9

You Can Go Your Own Way

Niki Nakayama: Loving the Ugly Parts and Finding Your Bliss

"I want you to get this pleasure from my distresses, namely, that I have borne them so bravely that I love myself for it and feel that I am stronger than you believed."

—Machiavelli, in a letter, writing about his imprisonment and torture

This book is meant to be a playbook for women in the workplace—a guide to help you find ways to succeed inside of a structure that has been built to thwart you. I want the workplace to be a space where women can thrive and find meaning, joy, and inspiration. (Shatter that glass ceiling, baby!) That said, some ceilings are unshatterable—or might not be worth the trouble of shattering. I heard this from many successful women I spoke with for the book: You go! You fight! You play your heart out! You fight again! And if that doesn't work, you walk away. You don't want to spend the precious time you have on this earth hitting your head against a concrete ceiling that some pencil-pushing middle manager put there. Part of being successful is knowing where to direct your energies.

I, myself, went my own way at a crucial point in my career and I am forever grateful that I did. Looking back, that decision was one of the most pivotal of my professional life. At the time, though, it was frustrating and scary, and I worried every day that I was making a mistake.

I started out in radio as a producer, as most people in my profession do. But I always knew I wanted to be a reporter. This was a tough leap to make. One colleague described the process to me as being "anointed." But I was determined. I would stay late almost every day, reporting stories after my official job duties were done. It meant that I was essentially working all the time, but it felt worth it: I was on the air regularly and was gaining experience. I told myself I was paying my dues.

After a few years of this, though, I started to feel stuck. Every time I applied for a reporter position at the company, I was passed over. In one case, I was passed over for a man who was several years younger than I was and didn't seem to have done as much reporting as I had managed to squeeze in after hours. To complicate matters, I was promoted to the position of editor, which came with a nice salary bump. I was on an exciting professional track at the company, but not the track I wanted to be on. The editor track would not lead to me being a reporter.

I finally mustered up the courage to confront my boss. At that point I had been at the organization for four years, reporting regularly for most of that time. I told my boss I wanted to be a reporter and asked if I would be a serious contender for a reporting position when one opened up. My boss smiled and told me reporting positions were extremely competitive, and though my reporting was good, it lacked "specialness." He said I was welcome to keep producing pieces for air, but that I probably wasn't going to be a serious contender for any actual reporting jobs.

I was both devastated and very unsure of what to do. Should I quit and freelance? The prospect was terrifying. I knew how little freelancing paid and I was worried my boss was right, that my reporting wasn't good enough for me to be able to support myself doing it. Also, I had just turned thirty and felt like this was the time by when I was supposed to have achieved success. And in many ways, I had: I had a cool new position and was finally making decent money. Also, I was on the air all the time, so I *was* getting a lot of reporting experience. Finally, there was the pride issue: Telling people I had a job as an editor at a major news organization (even if it wasn't *exactly* the job I wanted) sounded impressive, and the idea of saying I was "freelance" didn't sit well with my vanity. I went back and forth for weeks, and finally I did what any responsible adult woman contemplating a career roadblock would do: I called my mother.

"It sounds like you need to quit, sweetie," my mom said.

"Quit?!" I had not expected to hear this from my mother. I imagined she would want me to stick with the solid job that had an impressive title and benefits and not venture into the "here there be dragons" world of freelance reporting. "I can't quit!" I began to cry. "I can't be thirty and unemployed. What would I tell people?"

My mom was quiet for a moment. "Do you think it will be easier when you're thirty-one?"

My mom is good on the wisdom front. Her words rang in my head for weeks. I knew she was right. I saved up my money for six months and then walked into the boss's office and said I was quitting to be a freelance reporter. Shockingly, my boss offered me a full-time reporting contract on the spot.

I was stunned. What about my lack of "specialness"? What about all the legions of people who *had* this specialness and who were dying to report for the show? What I realize now is that not hiring me as a reporter had nothing to do with my work. It had to do with the fact that hiring me as a reporter would create a problem (they'd need to hire a new editor), and I was *already* reporting for them, so they wouldn't really be gaining anything. I realized I had spent years trying to make my work better and smarter and more creative, thinking that was the key to finally getting my dream job. But I had been fighting the wrong fight.

Of course, I could never have gone my own way at that moment if I hadn't been very privileged on many fronts: I had a very wise mother; I also had the resources to be able to quit. If I hadn't had enough money to support myself, or if I had children or family to support or had been in a ton of debt, I could never have taken the risk of quitting and would likely have remained in that editor job.

Going your own way is about looking at the options presented to you at an organization and saying "None of the above." It's a risky move—I myself have done it approximately once and I'm still talking about it. But remember what Machiavelli said about neutrality being "an exceedingly dangerous path." Avoiding risk won't keep you safe. Sometimes the safest thing to do is take a risk and bet on yourself.

Machiavelli's Lesson: Know When to Fold 'Em

Neha Narkhede, founder of the Silicon Valley unicorn company Confluent, says one of the keys to her success was knowing when to fold 'em: "You don't have to die fighting that one fight," she asserts.

Machiavelli offers similar advice in *The Prince*, saying good princes try their very hardest to get what they want, but they also know when to stop trying. "When men attempt things within their power, they will always be praised rather than blamed," he writes. "But when they persist in attempts that are beyond their power, mishaps and blame ensue" (Chapter III, DTE). If you give something your all and try your very best, people will respect and admire you. Who doesn't love a fighter? Rocky Balboa lost the boxing match to Apollo Creed in the 1976 classic *Rocky*, but everybody loved Rocky for the courage and pluck he had. That said, it's hard to keep rooting for someone who stays in a losing battle. Imagine how you'd feel about Rocky the fourth time he went up against Apollo Creed and lost? The fortieth time? You'd probably think he needed to get over it and move on. Similarly, you need to respect your own time and efforts, and other people will do the same. There is great wisdom and courage in knowing when to stop trying.

When to Walk Away

But how do you know when it's time to move on? Neha Narkhede offers a couple of key ways to know when to fold 'em. Remember, when Neha was told no or discouraged from a promotion, she would go to her manager and ask what exactly she needed to do to go from no to yes—to get the promotion or the raise or new opportunity: She would get specifics—quantifiable goals to meet—in order to get her raise/promotion/new opportunity. If her manager couldn't give her specifics, Neha says that was a red flag that this company might not be a place where she could thrive.

If she did get that list of specifics, Neha would work her hardest to do everything on the list—increase her productivity, build up her skills, make twelve widgets a day instead of ten—and then she would go back to her manager and say, "Okay! I did everything you asked. How about that promotion/raise/new opportunity?" Most of the time, Neha says, this worked, but not every time. Sometimes Neha would get another long list of things she needed to do. When that happened, she would start looking for another job immediately: "That's when you know the ceiling isn't a glass ceiling but a stone or a concrete one. I move on." Moving on is not easy; it's a leap of faith and it can be tempting to stay in the situation you know, as stuck and frustrated as you might feel. But that is the trap of the Cinderella Syndrome: If that workplace is never going to send you to the ball, don't keep waxing their floors. "You've got to move on," Neha says. "There are other environments that are more suitable for you. I'm just really a big believer that there is always an opportunity outside waiting for you."

Of course, in Neha's case, after climbing the corporate ladder with great success, she left and built her own company—a company now worth billions of dollars. No matter how masterfully she'd maneuvered in Silicon Valley, she would never have achieved the success or financial gain she got by going her own way. Knowing when to fold 'em wasn't just about escaping a limiting situation; for Neha, it was about achieving her own dream and making something that was hers. "Then you can build the company you want," she says. "Then you can build a company with no ceiling."

White Manlandia

Another way to tell that a ceiling you're hitting up against is unshatterable is to look at the company itself. Specifically, look at the people who are currently running that company. This advice comes from bona fide ceiling shatterer Sallie Krawcheck. As she was navigating the sexist waters of Wall Street, one thing she asked herself when she was thinking of joining a new company was *Do you see people who look like you in the leadership suites? Or are the people who look like you all in support roles?* Sallie, of course, has moved into C-suites many times at companies where nobody in a leadership position looked like her. Still, she says, look and see who this company has promoted in the past. Who are they choosing to lead them? "If you look around a company and everyone in positions of power are heterosexual cis white males," Sallie says, "well, then . . . that tells you a lot."

Dr. Isabel Escobar used this tactic and it paid off. Just after Isabel earned her PhD in chemical engineering, she started applying for professor jobs at universities around the country. There typically aren't many women in chemical engineering departments, so when Isabel visited schools where she was considering taking a job, she would specifically ask to meet with the women in the department. In many cases, she says, there were none, and she considered this a major red flag: "It's a climate thing, right? Why did the women all leave? Why did they not come here?"

In one case, a university introduced her to a female assistant professor. Isabel was excited to ask this woman about her experience, but as soon as she did, the woman burst into tears. That was all the information Isabel needed. She eventually visited a university where a female engineering professor met her at the airport. "There was this amazing, powerful woman who told me exactly how she felt," Isabel recalls. "And we met up with another woman in the department who was the exact same way." Isabel knew she'd found a place where she could thrive. It was still a very male department, but Isabel had mentors and colleagues who could help her feel that she was part of a community, and support and guide her in her career.

"But I've Put in So Many Years! I Can't Leave Now!"

One of the hardest things about moving on is walking away from all the time and energy you've invested in a workplace. First of all, there's a feeling that *maybe* if you just put in six more months, things will turn a corner and you'll start getting some traction. And there's also the nagging feeling that you've invested so much time and energy into building your seniority and paying dues in your current job that you should find a way to make it work instead of starting from scratch somewhere else. This feeling keeps many women stuck in situations where they have no real future. If you feel like this might be you, one useful thing to consider is an economic concept known as the "sunk cost fallacy." The idea is that people tend to spend a lot of time and energy trying to fix the status quo instead of moving on. And it costs us. Betsey Stevenson and her partner, Justin Wolfers, are both economists at the University of Michigan. They talk about this phenomenon in *Principles of Economics*, a textbook they coauthored. They explain the sunk cost fallacy in terms of romance, but it applies equally well to careers. "We all have that friend who's been in a relationship with someone for two or three years and it's not working out," explains Justin. "And they say, 'But I can't break up with him or her because I've been with them for so long!' That's sunk cost thinking, as in 'I've sunk two years into this thing. I can't walk away now!'"

Betsey says she was 100 percent a sunk cost fallacy dater in her twenties. "If I think back to the relationships I had before Justin," she says, "I stayed in each and every one of them too long." Her advice: Instead of focusing on all the blood, sweat, and tears you've sunk into something that's not working, look at what the status quo is truly offering you. Maybe there is a real path forward if you keep pushing. Maybe there's not. If you suspect there's not, Betsey recommends focusing not on what you've already invested, but rather on another economic concept known as "opportunity cost." What is staying in your current situation costing you in terms of time and opportunity? What jobs are you *not* applying for? What skills are you not developing? What are you giving up by staying where you are? "If you exit bad relationships quickly, you're more likely to find that one great love," Betsey explains. "This is where the opportunity cost principle comes in. Because you're sitting there and you think,

'This relationship is not working out, but I've put two years into it. I want to be absolutely certain that it's not going to work out before I leave.' You're forgetting that every day you spend in that relationship, you're giving up the chance to be out there trying to meet somebody new: That's the opportunity cost. I think that's where people make mistakes a lot." Focusing on the opportunity cost in a situation is the escape hatch from the sunk cost fallacy.

Did two decades of dating just flash before my eyes?

Yes.

But this is also very valuable advice for the workplace.

Look Before You Leap

I do want to add a note of caution here, because I've seen a lot of people jump out of jobs in a moment of rage or frustration when I could see many opportunities open to them if they'd just stayed and worked through a tough or confusing situation. If you're unsure about staying or going, talk to mentors and colleagues; talk to people who've risen through the ranks and ask them what future they see for you at the company. Ask what they would do if they were you. Also, look around, talk to people at other companies, and look at job postings in your field. Get a sense of the options and opportunities that are open to you.

Don't Stop Believing

Sallie Krawcheck ran up against many a ceiling in her career on Wall Street. Most she shattered, but eventually she realized the whole financial industry was holding her back. Sallie decided to go her own way.

Sallie says the banking industry's approach to women bothered her for years—namely, it ignored them. Investment advice and financial planning, Sallie says, were always geared toward men. The worst part was that women needed the advice a lot more: Women tend to earn less and live longer than men. Women over sixty-five are far more likely to be on food stamps and live below the poverty line than men over sixty-five. Sallie wanted to create a service that would give financial advice to women tailored specifically to their needs. The market was huge and untapped, and Sallie was sure she could make the big banks see this amazing opportunity; after all, it was socially important *and* had the potential to make lots and lots of money.

Sallie took her idea to a bunch of bank CEOs. "They could not see it," she says. Apparently, the idea of women managing their own money was not computing. "I said, 'Ninety percent of women manage their money on their own at some point in their lives.' And this CEO came right back at me and said, 'But don't their husbands manage the money for them?'"

Sallie realized that if she wanted this service to happen, she would need to create it herself. She had never wanted to start her own company, but Sallie felt this was something women really needed and she knew there weren't many people who would be qualified, resourced, and motivated to start a business like that. She also knew the service could help women in fundamental and profound ways. "If you have another hundred thousand dollars, that is life-changing," Sallie says. "That is 'Leave the job with the boss who chases you around' money. That is 'Leave the relationship where the person is not nice anymore' money." In 2014, Sallie founded Ellevest, an investment service for women. "We are out there now," says Sallie, "fighting this fight for women."

Leap Before You Look

Having a plan and a path to success laid out is ideal, but sometimes you just have to leap. That's what Heather Longhurst did.

Heather was a power player in the ballroom dance world for years. She ran the largest ballroom dance studio in the country near Seattle, Washington. Ballroom dance is about performance, drama, precision, and rhinestones. "Rhinestones on everything. I'm serious," she says with a laugh—Heather had been a competitive ballroom dancer at Brigham Young University along with her husband. Shortly after college, and with a new baby in tow, Heather and her husband moved to Seattle and she began working at a small, local dance studio, teaching choreography. The studio had about sixty students and Heather was paid $25 a month for her troubles. Heather says she would have refused the token sum, but at the time, this income was actually significant for her young family. Fifteen years later, Heather was the executive director of Pacific Ballroom Dance. The studio was teaching thousands of students a year, bringing in around a million dollars, winning national titles, and was known around the country.

Heather says building up the business came naturally to her: "I realized I could see certain things that other people around me couldn't see," she says. "I could see like five steps ahead." It was a very demanding job, though, and Heather says in many ways she was always "at work": "I never really turned it off. I worked most Saturdays and a lot of Sundays. Whatever needed to happen, I would do it." Heather was traveling the country, attending competitions, coaching dancers, giving talks, and fundraising. She says she realized how much her life had changed when she found herself standing next to Bill Gates at a party.

But the real crowning moment for Heather was opening a new studio space for Pacific Ballroom Dance; it was huge—thousands of square feet—the largest ballroom dance studio in the country. Hundreds of people came to the ribbon cutting, including dancers from around the United States and the mayor. "I had to give a speech," Heather recalls. "I was reading my remarks and looking out at this sea of faces, and I had this moment. Like, 'Wow, we really did this.' I just remember thinking of the beginning days, and we just never, never, ever could have imagined that we would be at the place where we were. I was really, really proud." She also knew, at that moment, that she was leaving.

The reason had to do with a health scare Heather had had a couple of years earlier. A brain scan showed she had a tumor, and the doctor's prognosis was grim. Amazingly, it turned out the scan was wrong and Heather did not have a tumor at all. But that experience gave her an enormous amount of clarity: "I would call it a deep feeling," she says. The deep feeling told her that she should leave ballroom dance behind and start focusing on building a career as a writer. Heather had always written essays and first-person articles on the side, but because running the studio was so demanding, she never had time to focus on it. Now she was in her early forties and her deep feeling told her it was time to focus. Heather felt absolutely sure about this, but it was a difficult decision. "I felt like I was blowing up my life," she says. "In the ballroom dance world, people don't leave jobs like the job I had. You're in it until you're retired. So for me to push the eject button surprised everybody, especially since it was not to go to some other fancy job but just to write. People were like, 'What happened? Were you pushed out?'"

Not only that, Heather's identity was very wrapped up in the business she had built. "It was mine," she says of the dance company. "There's this idea, like, 'I'm successful in this arena and people know who I am,' and all of a sudden you detach yourself from that and it's, like, 'Am I a successful person? Who am I?' There was this feeling of being untethered." Still, Heather had some things working in her favor: Her family was in a solid place financially and the timing seemed right. But mostly, she says, it was a memory she had of talking with her father.

Heather's father had worked at a paper company in Idaho for years, but his passion was writing. He had worked as a journalist for some local publications and had written several books about his life and his family; although they hadn't been published, they had been circulated in the family, and Heather had always taken her writing to him. She remembered, back when she was in junior high, telling her father she couldn't be a "real writer" because she couldn't write using the big, fancy vocabulary words her classmates were using. "He encouraged me," Heather recalls. "He said that I can use simple, clear language that was my own and tell my stories in my own words." He told Heather to trust her own voice.

When Heather remembered that advice, she realized it applied not just to her writing, but to her life as well. She needed to find her voice professionally—a new voice.

"I realized I could be really proud of the things that I'd built," she says, "but that I could also go build again. That was really liberating—to realize that I didn't need to cling to the successes I'd had in the past. I was a builder who could build again."

Heather left her job and began to write every day. She's had several essays published and she's currently working on a book about the world of ballroom dance. "It feels like a much smaller life right now," says Heather. "But it feels like mine."

Build a Group of Allies

Going your own way doesn't necessarily mean starting your own company; it can also mean making a space in your profession where the structure and limitations of your company or your field are not present. After the big gender dust-up in economics—sparked, in part, by the work of UC Berkeley undergraduate Alice Wu—women in the field started putting together women-only conferences. Economist Şebnem Kalemli-Özcan says she was skeptical at first, but after attending a few of them, she has become a total convert. "They're really neat," she says. "In a lot of ways, they're like a normal two-day conference: You come, you present papers . . . But during lunches and dinners and all these other activities, the conversation is very different. It's all about sharing experiences: about working while having children, about sexism in the field—things you can never speak about at a regular conference." Also, Şebnem says, the conferences are a lot more fun. "They did yoga on the beach as an activity. It was great. You would *never* see that at a regular economics conference." Şebnem says the best part of these conferences is that women present their ideas, debate economic policy, and don't have to navigate any of the interruptions, idea stealing, and disrespect they encounter in most professional settings: "It becomes really just about the ideas, and it's so nice."

NIKI NAKAYAMA:
Loving the Ugly Parts and Finding Your Bliss

Every fine restaurant in the world, wherever it may be and whatever kind of food it serves, has a common dream: the Michelin star. It's a system that originated in France (with the tire people) and it ranks restaurants using a star system. That star, if you get it, will drive tastemakers, snobs, and foodies the world over to your restaurant. It will put you on an international culinary map. The Michelin star is a powerful force. It's also a super-male force: There are only a handful of female chefs in the United States whose restaurants have a Michelin star (as opposed to more than a hundred male chefs). One of those women is Niki Nakayama, owner and head chef of n/naka in Los Angeles. And the reason Niki achieved this has everything to do with her going her own way.

Niki grew up in Los Angeles; her parents are Japanese immigrants who own a wholesale fish business. Niki started learning about food from them and eventually decided she wanted to be a chef. The restaurant industry is notoriously macho, and Niki says she learned valuable lessons for navigating that world early on in culinary school. "I remember, specifically, this one time I was trying to carry a bag of sugar and my friend was running over to help me. My instructor, she pointed out, 'When you're out in the real world, you have to do all those things by yourself.' That's so true. You have to do everything as if you were a male chef . . . Don't be a needy chick."

More than anything, Niki wanted to be a chef in the Japanese tradition. She went to Kyoto to work in one of the traditional hotels there, learning old-style Japanese cuisine. But the chefs there weren't necessarily excited about teaching newbies. "In Japan the mentality is very, very closed off," she says. "So you don't go there thinking, 'Please teach me this!' You had to be like a fly on the wall . . . you had to be the least noticeable person. There was a lot of cleaning and *a lot* of washing dishes."

But Niki discovered a secret superpower: Because she was a woman and was from the United States, none of the Japanese chefs took her all that seriously and they did not bother to guard any secrets from her. Niki soaked up everything she could. "It was a lot of watching how the chefs move, how they work, where they use an ingredient," she says. "It's not flashy; it's just a very deep understanding of the work that they're doing." Niki fell in love with a style of food in Kyoto known as kaiseki, in which many small dishes are presented. "So much thought went into the food and the whole feeling of it was so amazing," she says. "Everything felt like a gift. There was so much about it that was about experiencing joy and there were so many things that were tied to that."

When Niki got back to the United States, she wanted to work in a Japanese restaurant, but she didn't think anyone would hire her; Japanese restaurants, she explains, don't typically want female chefs. "I thought, 'If I apply, they're going to reject me.'" So she decided to open her own restaurant. Niki was still dreaming of kaiseki-style cuisine from Kyoto, but she felt that she should go a little safer. After all, starting a restaurant is risky: Most restaurants fail and even the successful ones often barely make a profit. Niki wanted a restaurant that would draw customers in, and Los Angeles loves its sushi. Niki found a location on the west side of LA and opened Azami Sushi Cafe in 2000. Almost the entire staff was female.

"I remember opening the door and thinking, 'Here we go!' And nobody came . . . Nobody. *Nobody*." Niki waited all day, but not one customer came through the door. That meant hundreds of dollars' worth of fish had to be thrown out. Her restaurant was only a day old and Niki was losing money. She was terrified, but she decided to double down. She went back to her menu and started trying different methods with different ingredients, perfecting and re-perfecting recipes. "I was like, okay, we're going to dive in here," she recalls. "I'm going to collect fishy vinegar recipes from like ten different sources and experiment with every single one of them. I'm just crazy like that." Niki says she was used to working extra hard in the culinary world:

"You don't start out having the kind of respect that a man would," she says. "You have to work twice as hard to earn that respect."

Niki's Lesson: Embrace the Ugly Parts

Niki's work paid off. Azami Sushi Cafe gained a devoted following and a stellar reputation: It was a hit! But running a restaurant was a lot different from what Niki thought it would be. She says everybody always thinks being a chef sounds sexy and glamorous, but, she insists, it's not: "It's just fixing problems," she says, laughing, "like the ice machine. You get the scrubber and clean it out. It's really hard to feel glamorous when you're scrubbing out the ice machine. Being a chef is only glamorous in short spurts, and I love that. I think that it keeps us grounded." In fact, Niki thinks the ability to embrace scrubbing out the ice machine is key to a chef being great. "When people start out in the field, they see all the beautiful parts," she says. "But I always think if you can survive the ugly parts, then you can be successful."

Azami Sushi Cafe thrived for nearly a decade. Still, Niki kept dreaming of the food she'd made in Kyoto and decided she wanted to start a restaurant featuring the kaiseki-style cuisine she'd learned there. It was a risky move. First off, she had created a hit restaurant—a very difficult thing to do—and closing a hit restaurant is not a thing most chefs ever do. Also, Niki had built her reputation as a sushi chef, and now she would be switching to a style of cuisine most people hadn't heard of. Not only that, Niki wanted the menu to be prix fixe, and for the restaurant to be high-end and reservation only—no walk-ins. This was basically restaurant suicide. But the more Niki thought about it, the more passionate she began to feel about the idea. "I had this *Field of Dreams* moment where I'm like, 'If I build it, they will come,'" she remembers. "I spend so many hours of my life doing this work, I wanted that work to have a lot more meaning for me and I wanted a place where I would get to play around a lot more."

Niki's Lesson: If You Build It . . .

Niki opened n/naka in 2011. It was exactly the restaurant she wanted. Just like at Azami, she staffed it with mostly women.

Niki was right: She built it and the people did come. N/naka opened to rave reviews, and people started coming from all over the city to try her food. Her sous-chef, Carole Iida, is Niki's life partner and partner in cuisine: "She brought something really incredible to what we were already doing. She was able to make it a more far-reaching experience and expression than I could have imagined."

The world noticed. In 2019, n/naka earned not one but two Michelin stars. Niki became one of a handful of female chefs on earth to receive that distinction. "Honestly, it was a relief," she says, "like, 'Oh my God, we did it! We did good!'" Niki was inundated with attention and praise. People began coming from all over the country and the world to taste her kaiseki cuisine. She was also profiled on the first season of the Netflix series *Chef's Table*, the lone woman among six of the greatest chefs on earth. Niki stood out for her humility and her sly humor. But her fierce dedication, passion, drive, and creative badassery matched with all the male chefs the series profiled.

More important to her, Niki and Carole have created a kitchen unlike any other. Restaurant kitchens, especially in top-tier restaurants, are notorious for being toxic, super-macho places run by explosive genius chefs who rule with an iron fist and hurl pots across the room if the sauce hasn't been properly strained. That was not the kind of atmosphere Niki wanted to create. "It's a lot more like a nurturing environment," she says. "We're really a family at n/naka. The people who work here feel like they can tell us anything."

Niki says going her own way allowed her to cook the food that really spoke to her and explore her creativity. It also allowed her to create a new kind of professional kitchen—a space where she could thrive and be creatively inspired, and where people feel supported and respected. Going her own way turned out to be a transformative career move for Niki—one that elevated her to the top of her profession. She says her experiences have inspired her to always follow her own path, trust her instincts, and find her voice in everything she cooks: "I follow my intuition a lot," she says. "At the end of the day, you can have great ideas, but if it doesn't feel right, it's not right. Never ever let the cerebral take over. I do what feels right. That's how I cook. That's how I live my life."

Dream Bigger

When a situation doesn't work out or is no longer serving you, the decision to move on can be very difficult. It can be tempting to hold on to what you have, rather than to risk letting it go and taking a leap into something new. But if the place where you're working or the profession you're in isn't suiting you, supporting you, or offering you a real future, it might be time to stop investing your time and energy in a losing fight. Sometimes, when your hopes are dashed or your dream dies, it is in service of something much greater. After all, even our dreams can be products of our own limitations. A new start might give you something greater than you can imagine right now. If you're feeling boxed in or held back by your current situation—if a workplace or a profession is making you feel limited or trapped—it might be time to go your own way.

10

A Lady's Guide to Negotiation

"What remains to be done must be done by you."
—Machiavelli, *The Prince* (DTE, Chapter XXVI)

Negotiating.

It can be painful, uncomfortable, and emotionally wrenching, and if you want more money or a different job or more resources, you are going to have to do it. Negotiation is where the rubber meets the road—all the thinking, soul-searching, fog mapping, and homework you've been doing comes down to this.

Going into a negotiation can feel scary. If you're anything like me, a little gremlin emerges from the depths of your brain, saying things like: "They're not going to give you that—are you crazy? Why are you so greedy? Your work hasn't been *that* great over the past few months. Can't you be happy with what you have? They don't have the money for this!"

The first step in negotiation is to kill the gremlin—show no mercy to the little guy. Trust that the company will do its job by trying to get the most work out of you for the best deal possible. That leaves you to do *your* job: valuing your time and work as highly as possible and letting the company know what you need to be happy. Remember, it is in everybody's interest that you do this. If you feel good about your job, you will do better work, be a better colleague, and are more likely to stay with the company. If you are underpaid and seething with resentment, you are helping no one. And know this: A company will *never* pay you more than they can afford.

So now that the gremlins are dead (at least for now; they're pretty resilient little guys in my experience), it's time to get ready to negotiate. And by *get ready* I mean: It's homework time! If you think of the negotiation itself like a boxing match, the day of the fight is, of course, very important, but it's the training you've done to prepare for the fight that's probably going to determine whether you win or lose. It's back to that old Machiavellian idea of good defenses being a prince's best friend. In fact, everyone I talked to said the homework phase is the most important part of any negotiation. In their excellent book, *Negotiation Genius: How to Overcome Obstacles and Achieve Brilliant Results at the Bargaining Table and Beyond*, authors Deepak Malhotra and Max H. Bazerman say the more homework you do, the easier the negotiation will be and the less people will try to mess with you. "If the other party perceives that you have done your homework," they write, "their willingness to deceive you decreases . . . [and] you are likely to be taken more seriously."

Step 1. Homework: Ladies, Get In-Formation

Whether you're asking for a raise or a promotion or negotiating the terms of a new job, you want to know a few key things: How much do other people get paid in that job? What kind of resources do they have? How much experience/what skills do people generally have when they get that position? This is your "market research," and as you will see, it's one of your most valuable cards to play in a negotiation.

There are a few key places to go for that information:

1. **Power from the people.** By far, your best resource is people. Call in your network—ask your friends, colleagues, and mentors to help put you in touch with the people who will have the information you need. Ex-employees and those who used to have the job you are gunning for are often very open with

salary and job information. People currently in the position can be quite helpful as well. Try to ask a few people, especially men, to get a range of salaries and other information. If you feel strange asking about salaries, you can employ a reporting trick I've learned in my fifteen years of asking people uncomfortable questions about money: Ask for a *salary range* for their position. The word *range* makes things less personal, and people will generally open up.

Also, be sure to ask workers who have similar positions at other companies what they make. This is equally crucial information for your negotiation.

2. **Online.** Was the job posted on the company website or on a job website? Sometimes these listings will include a salary range in addition to the experience and skill requirements for the job. Glassdoor and other websites can also give you salary information. Keep in mind that publicly posted information probably isn't entirely accurate, but it's a good place to start.

3. **HR.** You can contact the human resources department at the company and ask for the official salary range for a posted position along with all the officially listed duties and experience requirements.

4. **Union/workers collective.** If your job is associated with a union, contact the union and ask for a salary range and a list of duties for the position. Even if you're not in the union, tell them that you have a job offer and are likely to be in the union soon.

To be clear, this process can be horrifically awkward and embarrassing and you might be stonewalled, denied, or ignored a few times. But in the words of Janet Yellen, pull up your socks and do it. Put in this work. It is the foundation of your negotiation, and it will determine what you ask for, how you advocate for yourself, and your confidence level in the negotiation. As Machiavelli wrote in a letter to a friend, "It is not a wise plan to risk all one's Fortune and not all one's forces." When it comes to the painful homework phase, go all in.

Step 2: What a Girl Wants

Now that you have the information, it's time to start thinking about the big questions: What do you want out of this negotiation? How much do you want to get paid? What title do you want? What resources do you need?

I've talked about the importance of not fixating on any one thing in a negotiation. A major pitfall I've had in past negotiations is going into the room wanting one thing. *Make me a senior reporter OR ELSE!* If I get it, I've won! I'm over the moon! If I don't get it, I've lost. I'm crushed and I want to quit. Don't get stuck in a tunnel vision mindset. Let your mind be flexible.

Remember the advice of negotiation expert Dr. Linda Babcock and try to think of ten things you want: Do you want the opportunity to travel? A particular title? An assistant? Your own office? The ability to work from home? A later start date? Training that would help you move forward? A certain number of vacation days? Better equipment? A six-month salary review?

Write all of these things down and list them in order of importance. Think about different combinations that might work for you: Is a lower salary okay if you get a better title? Is a lesser title okay if you get to work from home every Friday or join a certain team for a couple of months?

An Offer You *Can* Refuse

I realize this kind of flexibility might seem weak. After all, doesn't the confident person just swagger into the boss's office, make her demands, and swagger out? I mean, the Godfather didn't go around giving people different options that would make him happy so everyone could come to a mutually beneficial agreement. Never! The Godfather took what he wanted with guns and ultimatums and the occasional horse's head!

But in a (non-Sicilian) negotiation, a flexible mind is a powerful mind. I used to take aikido, a martial art that is all about the power of yielding to the force of your opponent and using that force against them. One of my teachers made the excellent point that, in a stream, the rock looks strong and the water rushing around it looks weak and malleable, like it's yielding to the rock. But look a hundred years later and you'll see the water has worn down the rock. Ultimately the water is stronger. This negotiation isn't about this one issue; it's about your career. Flexibility and open-mindedness will keep you away from the limitations that come with rigidity and tunnel vision. You don't know what might be available or what projects might be opening up in the future. Keep your mind open to possibilities and ideas. *Be the water.* (Obviously, you don't want it to take a hundred years to get your raise, but we'll get to that.)

Step 3: What a Firm Wants

Think about what the company wants: What are they looking for out of this job? What do they want out of *you*? What broader goals do they have? Do they want more customers? More social media reach? Do they want to promote more women or people of color? Do they want to seem younger and hipper and tap into a different audience? Do they want to avoid rocking the boat (i.e., not to have to find someone to replace you in your current job)? Think about how what you're asking for could align with that.

"We always think about what *we* want in a negotiation," says Linda Babcock, coauthor (with Sara Laschever) of *Ask for It: How Women Can Use the Power of Negotiation to Get What They Really Want.* "But it's almost as important or more important to understand how *they* see it and what *they* want."

Step 4: "I'm Special"

The next part of homework is all about the self-love!

Look at your own skills and contributions and attributes: What are you bringing to the table? What kind of work have you done that might warrant getting this promotion/raise/job? Do you have a particular degree? Years of experience? A particular skill? Are other people trying to recruit you? Have you produced a certain number of things or earned a certain amount of money for the company? Is your work especially fast/excellent/innovative?

There's the concrete stuff and the fuzzy stuff in this mix, and both are important. Concrete stuff includes things like: How much did you produce? Did you win any awards? Did you snag an important client? Did your sales go up? Did you win cases? What measurable success did you achieve? It may take a little digging and some math, but if you produced 20 percent more than everybody else last year, that's really great to know going into a negotiation.

The fuzzy stuff is easier and faster to get and is equally important. It's feedback and comments you've gotten or other things that might not be measurable but point to your value and the quality of your work: If someone sent you a nice email about a project or about working with you, you can quote it. If your boss said you helped a team work better together, write it down. If you got good feedback from a client, make a note of it.

Also, think about your personal qualities. Claire Wasserman, author of *Ladies Get Paid*, calls these superpowers: Are you enthusiastic? Detail oriented? The workhorse? Are you the cheerleader of the team? The one who tackles the really hard stuff? The closer? The glue? The creative spark? "The story you want to tell with this information," says Claire, is that "the team does better because of the work that I'm doing."

Step 5: The Position in Question

Now take a look at the job you're applying for or the promotion you're gunning for and think about reasons the position itself might call for higher pay or for a certain title: Is it a new project? A key project for the company? Does it involve a lot of responsibility? Did the job start out as one thing and change into something that involves more work? Does it involve a professional risk on your part? Will it likely involve working overtime for a while, start-up–style? Will it involve bringing people or teams together? All of these are reasons to ask for more money and/or a beefier title.

Step 6: The Shane Situation

Now that you've got your facts, you need to put them to work. The first thing you should think about is your Shane Situation. This is named after the 1953 film *Shane*, in which a handsome, taciturn gunslinger starts working for a family on their little ranch in Wyoming and—after saving lives, making all the ladies fall in love with him, and rescuing the town from a terrible marauder—decides, abruptly, to leave, saying, "I gotta be going on . . . A man has to be what he is." The iconic ending of the film haunts me to this day: A little boy who has become attached to Shane hollers his name over the prairie as Shane gallops off into the night. Let me tell you, whenever I imagine leaving a job, I always imagine leaving like that . . . ideally, with a devastated manager hollering my name over the open prairie, or at least a conference room.

Your Shane Situation is the situation you're in if *you* gallop off into the night. What happens to you if this negotiation goes up in gun smoke? Are you going back to a job you hate or have totally outgrown? Are you going back to a job you like just fine? Can you pay your rent? Are there a bunch of opportunities you could explore? Is it pretty bleak out there? Don't be afraid to be honest with yourself. If you need this job to pay your rent, that can feel scary because you might feel like you've just lost all your power, but the opposite is true. Now you know exactly where you stand and what you need out of this negotiation, and you can make decisions accordingly. That is powerful.

Also, even if you *feel* powerless, it's definitely not true. How do I know this? Because I'm an economics reporter. If this is a job you already have, the company almost certainly does not want to lose you. It's expensive and time-consuming to do a job search, hire a new person, and train them. According to Glassdoor, the average company spends two months and $4,000 hiring a new employee. That is expensive and a huge pain in the neck.

If this is a new job you're applying for, you also have a great deal of power. If a company has made you an offer, they *want* you. A lot.

They do not want to say, "Yeah, we loved Patrice, but she asked us for more money than we wanted to pay, so we went with the second most awesome person." Trust me, I have been on a bunch of hiring committees, and by the time the company is making you an offer, they *want* to put a ring on it. You have a lot of leverage.

Step 7: Finding the Floor

Now, with your Shane Situation in mind, think about the minimum salary/position/title/conditions you would need to take this job and feel okay about it—okay as in not jumping up and down but also not feeling like a sucker and waking up angry in the middle of the night. That is your floor. It might take some time to settle on this number, but take that time. Knowing your floor is crucial: It is the psychological underpinning for your negotiation.

Step 8: You Should See the Other Guy

Now it's role-playing time. Channel your inner middle manager and think about things from the company's perspective: What will happen to them if you walk away? What would it mean for their business? Would it be pretty easy for them to replace you? Would it be a total disaster for them? What skill sets, institutional knowledge, projects, and clients would they lose if you walked out the door? That is *their* Shane Situation. Looking at the two Shane Situations will give you an idea of your power in the negotiation.

It may be that you don't feel like you have much power in a particular situation; maybe the economy's terrible and there's a lot of competition for a particular job. Maybe you desperately want this job or you're broke and can't afford for this job to fall through. That's okay! We can't be the most powerful person in every situation. Machiavelli was almost never the most powerful person in his negotiations on behalf of little, broke, unarmed Florence, but he was able to achieve great success in his work and go toe-to-toe with popes, tyrants, and kings. If you don't have a lot of power in one particular negotiation, that's good information, but it doesn't mean you can't ask for things and it doesn't mean you won't get them. It just means that you may need this company a bit more than they need you right now. That could mean you decide to play things a little safer in the negotiation, because that might be better for you and your life—which is, after all, the whole point of this.

Step 9: ZOPA!

Now that you've thought about what the company wants and what you want, it's time to figure out how you might come to an agreement: How can you and the company both get what you most want? Business school types call this the ZOPA: the Zone of Possible Agreement. To me, *ZOPA* sounds like a kind of pasta, but it's a useful concept. You ideally want to reach a place where everyone is happy. Have a few ZOPAs in mind before a negotiation. This can help you lead the discussion to a place of mutual satisfaction.

For example, if you have been at a company for a few years and you really want to start doing a certain kind of work—let's say (since I know media) you have been a producer and getting reporting experience is your top priority. You also feel like you are underpaid by $10,000. Let's also say the company is in a budget crunch—those seem to be perpetual in media—but they also want to attract a younger audience and more advertisers. To complicate things, they *really* need you in the job you are currently doing and nobody is trained to fill in for you at the moment. Finally, you know that they are a little risk averse: They promoted a couple of people to reporters in the past and it didn't work out. They don't want to be burned again.

One possible ZOPA would be: You are given the time and space to report two stories a month, during which time you offer to cover X, Y, and Z topics, which you think would draw a younger, more diverse audience. Also, you've identified two colleagues whom you could quickly train to fill in for you and who would be really excited about that chance. Of course, *you* will need compensation for this new work and for the training, especially since you know you are currently earning near the bottom of the salary range for your position. Finally, you would need a new title to reflect these new responsibilities or a commitment to become a full reporter in six months if things go well.

If management counters that it's having money issues and they are not promoting or giving raises to anyone right now—not to mention they have a lot of doubts that you're ready to report—you can pivot to ZOPA 2: A one-month trial period, during which you get to try reporting (after training someone to fill in for you, of course). After the trial, you will reconvene to discuss how best to move forward. At that point two of their concerns will hopefully be alleviated: They know you can report really well and you've trained someone to replace you. But even if you don't get a promotion or a raise, you will come out of that month with reporting experience and a body of work that you can use to apply for other jobs. So your Shane Situation has actually improved. ZOPA!

Step 10: The Story of Us

You have your information, your Shane Situations, and your ZOPAs. Now it's time for the final phase of your homework: Write your story.

In this story, you are the amazing, loyal, hardworking, innovative badass who is excited to be at this company and wants to grow here and is simply making sure she is paid what she's worth so everyone can move forward together in a haze of symbiotic bliss.

Your story should be positive: If this is a company where you are currently working, tell the story of an evolution. Talk about how you have grown and what you have brought to the company. Talk about where you want to go and what you need to do that job with maximum enthusiasm—for example, "I'm so excited about the work I've been doing on this project and how much this team has evolved. I think we're at a pivotal moment and I'm so inspired about where we can go. To get there, I'm going to need to be putting in a lot of hours and taking on a lot more responsibility. I'm thrilled about that, but my current title/salary no longer reflects the work I'm doing. I've done a lot of market research and I think the work

I'm doing now is more of an X level job. I think it's time for a promotion. How does that sound to you?"

If you're applying for a job, the story should be about how much you will bring to the company and what beautiful music you will make together: "I really think I'm a great fit for this job. Your company is so innovative and dynamic and fearless, which is exactly what I'm looking for. You know, I'm a really dedicated worker and I love the chance to be creative, and together we could do some amazing work. I've thought a lot about what I'll need to do my best work and I've done quite a bit of market research. Here's what I need: . . . How does that work for you?"

We, We, We, All the Way Home

Whatever story you tell, the magic word is *we*. Remember, as a woman, one very effective way to get around the Hotbox and the Cinderella Syndrome is the Meta-Softener. This holds true in negotiation: "It's all about the team! It's all about *us* moving forward *together*!" This will be your touchstone in the negotiation itself. No matter where the negotiation goes or whatever crappy things your manager says or how many times she tries to reframe the discussion as your interests versus company interests, you hang on to *we* and you never let it go.

Smile like You Mean It

If it's a salary adjustment you're after—let's say you've found out incompetent Rick is making more than you—it can be tempting to go into the negotiation waving the flaming sword of righteous anger. But don't go into a negotiation with a victim story. A manager isn't going to want to spend money or promote you in order to correct a wrong. Framing a raise in that way means if they give you what you're asking for, they are acknowledging they have been unfair and are in the wrong: "Yeah, I underpaid Bianca because she is a woman of color and I'm unconsciously pretty racist and also sexist and even though I want to think of myself as an enlightened man, I am really a knuckle-dragging troglodyte who supports the

patriarchy. Bianca found out I was underpaying her and she'll probably sue us for discrimination if we don't give her a raise. My bad."

Nobody is going to want to tell that story.

This doesn't mean you don't mention what incompetent Rick
makes or that you know you're being paid at the very bottom of the
salary range. But that shouldn't be the focus. They should be paying
you more because they're *excited* about building a future with you.
It's also a better story for them to tell their boss, if they have one.

For example: "I know when I started I didn't have much experience, and you really took a chance on me. I'm so thrilled to be here
and I'm loving the work. I've really grown in this job and I think
it's time for a promotion. You know, I'm the most productive worker
on my team: My productivity is up almost 20 percent over last year.
I have some great ideas and I'm really excited to move forward at
this company. Also, as a Latina, I bring a different perspective to
this work and I know you really value that. I'm at the bottom of
the salary range for my position right now. With the work I've been
doing, that salary isn't really appropriate anymore. I think a salary
of $_____ would better reflect the work I'm doing now. What do
you think?"

Then your unconsciously racist troglodyte of a boss can drag his
knuckles over to *his* boss's office (or the mirror) and say: "You remember when *I* hired Bianca? She didn't have much experience, but
I saw something special in her and she's really proven herself. She's
the most productive member of her team. I think we should have
her in a more senior role and we should get her some more money.
She's a young woman of color and we need to be promoting people
like her. You know, diversity is very important to me."

This story makes your boss look like a total hero and a talent
scout extraordinaire. This is a story your manager will want to tell.
This is a story your manager will want to fight for.

Step 11: Practice Makes Perfect

You know what you want and you have your story. Now, before
you jump into the actual arena, do a few scrimmage rounds. As

salary coach Claire Wasserman puts it, "Practice, practice, practice. Have a friend give you any possible answer or pushback your boss might give, so you know how you're going to navigate it." Claire advises paying attention to your body during practice sessions. "When did your blood feel like it started rising? When did you get sweaty palms and butterflies? Acknowledge it and don't fight it. Say to yourself, 'This will probably happen again.' And when it does, you're not surprised. You can just say, 'Oh, right. This is what happens when I get nervous.'" Claire says this will help you make sure your emotions don't overwhelm you. Play different scenarios out and get used to feeling your feelings and handling them.

Be sure to practice good outcomes and not just the bad ones. I once went into my boss's office to complain that I was underpaid. He stopped me at one point and asked, "How much do you want?" I had no idea. I was so ready for a fight, it hadn't occurred to me to think about what exactly I was fighting for.

Let It Go!

My final piece of advice is a little weird, but I really do believe in it: Before you go into a negotiation, make a list of reasons why it doesn't matter what happens in the negotiation. And then make a list of reasons why it's a *good* thing if you don't get what you're asking for.

This might sound like deeply strange advice, but this helped me solve a conundrum that had been bothering me for years: Why do I only excel in negotiations when I *don't really want* the thing I'm negotiating for? I have successfully negotiated for things I deeply wanted, but the moments when I've really *aced* a negotiation, I didn't really care about what I was negotiating for. Why? I had so much less passion in those negotiations! I barely prepared. In one case, I showed up late; I forgot a pen; and, in the end, I got everything I could even think to ask for. The reason? I walked into those conversations feeling powerful and in control: I wasn't itching for a fight; I didn't feel desperate; I wasn't insecure or scared. I was curious, open-minded, and totally relaxed. I felt my own value and the value of my work. *I was the water in the stream!*

But the great irony here, and what bothered me so much, was that if not caring is the key to being great in negotiations, it meant I would only ever be good at negotiating for things I didn't want! That seemed so cruel. But there's a solution! That is where these lists come in.

Make a list of why it doesn't matter if you don't get what you ask for. For instance:

1. I can still pay my rent for the next six months.
2. I don't *really* need extra money right now.
3. I am pretty sure I can get work I like within a couple of months.
4. Nobody outside my company even understands what that title difference means.

Next, make a list of why it might be the best thing if you don't get what you ask for. For example:

1. I'll know for sure there's no real future for me at this company and it's time to start looking around.
2. I won't feel guilty about taking two weeks off at the holidays.
3. I'll be more rigorous about my expense reports.
4. My current job isn't that challenging. I can use extra time to write that cookbook I've been meaning to write and hang out with my family.
5. This could give me the push I need to finally go back to school.

The final ingredient in a successful negotiation: Not caring a little bit.

The Room Where It Happens

You've made it! You've arrived—the room where it happens! This is it. You are going to walk into your manager's office or get on that video call like the fearless gladiator you are. This is the moment you have trained for! It's time to make your ask.

Let's Get Ready to Rumble

When you walk into the room (or get on the video call), you want to radiate confidence and positive energy. You walk in *knowing* that this is going to go well and they are going to give you everything you want and more. I have a friend who listens to Beyoncé before she negotiates, and another friend of mine swears by power poses. Do what you've got to do to get your blood going and get into a positive frame of mind. Above all, don't walk into a negotiation looking terrified or seething with anger. Walk into the meeting with an attitude of collaboration and good will. Walk into the room *knowing* that you are a powerful, valuable, amazing she-beast and everybody knows it. Walk into the room like you own it and love everybody in it. Walk into the room like a power-posing Beyoncé.

Once you settle in, smile and make small talk: Ask about their kid, their vacation; make some joke about the news. Studies have shown that women are more likely to get what they want using a "social style." This also gives you a moment to compose yourself and get settled in before you get to the tough stuff. It is also an opportunity to see how the person you're negotiating with is doing—are they angry, sad, distracted, stressed out? We're all human beings (even managers). I once went into a negotiation (one I was very nervous about) and asked the person I was negotiating with how they were doing. They replied that they had an extremely ill parent and were dealing with a lot of medical calls. This, of course, completely changed the tone of our conversation. I still asked for what I wanted and addressed everything I had planned on, but my approach was gentler and less brash than what I had prepared. At the end of the conversation, the person told me it was the nicest conversation they had had all day. I got everything I asked for, but more important, I was able to approach the situation with humanity and a sense of perspective, and behave in a way I could feel proud of.

Slow Jams and Candlelight

Now you want to set the mood: Light the candles, turn up the slow jams, and slip into something more comfortable. Don't rush in and start listing off demands. You want to set the stage for your story. A good way to start is to lay out your overarching goal, your "Story of Us." For example, "I want to thank you for meeting with me. I'm really excited about this conversation and about the work I've been doing here. The most important thing to me is the success of this team and this project: I've always felt supported by you in that and I can't tell you how important that is for me. I want to make sure I have the team and the resources I need to make sure the project succeeds and that's what I wanted to talk with you about."

What Do You Think?

You've made your opening statement and laid out your plans. Now it's time to open the floor to them. Ask them what they want. Try something like, "I'd love to hear your thoughts on this. What are you most hoping to see from my team?" or "What are you wanting to see from my work going forward?"

Maybe they really want to get different kinds of clients and they see you as someone who can help. Maybe they see you growing into a role you haven't thought of. Once you know what matters to them and what they want, you will be better able to know what you can offer them. When you open the floor to the person you're negotiating with, you're setting this up as a conversation instead of an angry screed, a list of demands, or a face-off. "You are opening a dialogue," says Dr. Linda Babcock. "Negotiation, in its best form, is a dialogue."

Pro tip: I'm listening. Throughout the negotiation, listening is just as important as talking. Your employer has a story, too. Listen to that story. Respect it. Write things down: What concerns do they have? What are their hopes for the company? What plans do they have? What limitations are they feeling? What is stressing them out? What do they value? This is all helpful for your negotiation and for future negotiations.

Pitfall Alert: You're No Good

There is a risk to opening the floor to the other side: They might come in with a critique or something negative. After all, you've just told them you're going to ask for a promotion or more money and they might want to head you off at the pass and make it harder for you to ask. For instance: "It's great to hear you're so excited to be here. Your positive attitude is really appreciated. Your work has been a little slow lately, though. I've been disappointed by your numbers."

OMG, *crushing*. This would be the end of the game except that *you* have done your homework. This is the moment you have been training for. This is the moment when the homework strikes back!

Pro tip: The hard-data left hook. "Oh, that's interesting. I really appreciate your feedback. Actually, I ran the numbers and my productivity has gone up by 30 percent in the past six months. I am now the second most productive person on my team!" (Remember, this is all about *us*. So you might want to soften things at the end.) . . . "I know that last project was a bear and took a bit longer than projects normally take. I can totally see why you might perceive that my productivity had slowed down. I felt that way, too! But it was an exceptional case and a really important one for our company, I think. I was proud that I could take a case like that and I have some ideas about those kinds of cases that I'd love to get your thoughts on at a future time. But for right now, I feel like I can be really productive for you guys and I'm excited about the work I'm doing here. That is why I've been wanting to talk about a promotion . . ."

Pro tip: The soft-data uppercut. "It's true that my productivity was down in terms of numbers. The last account I took on was a really complicated case and I really did need to put that extra time in. I know you value efficiency and I really do, too! But I wanted to get that right. Actually, I got a nice email about it from the CEO saying this was the kind of account she was hoping to see more of. I'd be open to more cases like this, and it's exciting to be working on projects where I can grow my skills. It will mean I'm doing more complicated projects. That's part of why I wanted to ask about my job title . . ."

Back on Track

Now it's time for you to pivot away from any sidetracks and tell your story. Be positive and assume the very best. It's entirely possible your manager wants to give you more money or at least wants to know what will make you happy.

Name Your Number?

If this is a salary negotiation, now is the moment to decide whether *you* want to name your number or if you want *them* to name the number. Sometimes your employer will name a number right away, before you have a chance to say anything, and sometimes there will be a strange and stressful Kabuki dance. If you are in a position to make this decision, the deciding factor has everything to do with the information you were able to get.

Pro tip: Make the first offer if the company or person you're talking to might not know what someone should get paid for the work you will be doing. When the podcast bubble was at its peak, every company and their sister was starting a podcast, but most of these companies had zero idea what audio work paid. I heard about a lot of ridiculously low offers. In these cases, the companies just didn't know what value to place on that type of work. If this is the case, help them! Name your number.

Also, if this is a salary adjustment (as in you aren't getting paid what you should be), it makes sense for you to name the number.

You have a frame of reference (your current salary) and you probably have a very good idea of what you should be getting paid. In that case, too, name your number.

Pro tip: Do not make the first offer if you don't have much information, if your homework didn't pan out, or if you have no idea what the company typically pays for this kind of work. Youngja Yoo moved to LA from South Korea in her twenties, and says that when she got her first job in the United States, she had no idea what American jobs paid. So when she was interviewing and her employer asked her how much she was expecting to make, instead of making up a number, she tried something radical: "I said, 'I'm a really good worker. Why don't I work for you for a couple of weeks and you can tell me what you think my work is worth? I trust you.'" Youngja put the salary decision entirely in the hands of her employer. It was a salary negotiation trust fall! For Youngja, it paid off. She did her weeks of work and got her employer to name her salary; it seemed fine to Youngja and she accepted it. She later found out she was being paid at the top of the salary range for her position. I love this story, but think the brilliant stroke was Youngja telling her future boss that she trusted her. The boss was suddenly in a position to want to prove herself worthy of that great trust.

Pro tip: All things being equal, if you have solid information about pay and you feel like the company does, too, consider throwing out the number first. Salary coach Claire Wasserman says that, in her experience, naming the number first is a good idea because of a phenomenon called "anchoring." When you name a number, you anchor the negotiation. It also prevents a situation where the company throws out an offer that feels really low, which happens to women quite a bit. Say you're hoping for $90,000 and they offer $55,000. "Now you need to make a comeback from that and from the feeling of disappointment," says Claire. She recommends opening with something like, "So I've done my market research and I know the salary range for this position. I also know that I'm a top performer and a really hard worker: I love this work and you know that about me. So I'm asking for the higher end of that salary range. I think $100,000 would be fair. How does that sound to you?"

Pitfall Alert: Shock and Awe

One reaction I've gotten when I have named a number is a shock-and-awe reaction: "Oh, wow! That's way above what we were thinking. We don't have the budget for that." This is just part of the dance. Don't be fazed. You can counter with "Oh, okay. Well, I have done a lot of market research and I know that what I'm asking for is in line with what this work pays. But tell me, what were you thinking?"

Pitfall Alert: The Lowball Offer

Sometimes a prospective employer will throw out a number that's way lower than you expected. This is terrible! Insulting! A nightmare! WHO DO THEY THINK THEY ARE? WHO DO THEY THINK *YOU* ARE? First things first: Don't panic. Feel free to show your surprise (or, like an iceberg, 10 percent of it).

Pro tip: The diagnostic question. One way to respond to a lowball offer is to put the onus back on them: "I'm surprised. That's quite a bit lower than I was expecting. I've done a lot of market research and I know this position typically pays about double that. I also know this company is a fair place; I've always heard that/felt that. Do you mind telling me how you came up with that number?"

"How . . . ?"

"How . . . ?" is a magical question in a negotiation. It does a couple of things. First, it puts the pressure on them to explain themselves. It's not aggressive, but it is holding them accountable. Often a lowball offer is used as a feeler: They want to gauge your reaction and see if they can get a super-deal or possibly throw you off-balance and get you to give up some valuable information. For example, "What?! I *know* you're paying lazy Jason twice that amount!" or "I'm making $100,000 in my *current* job. I can't go below that!" What you want to hit back with is emotional neutrality, and that is the magic of "How . . . ?" *How* is what is known as a "diagnostic question": You are diagnosing the reason the offer is so much lower than you thought it would be. And after the diagnosis, of course, comes the medicine and the cure.

Let's say they tell you, "Well, you only have three years of work experience and this is what we pay employees with that level of experience." You can say, "You're so right about it being my third year of work. But I do have a master's degree, which, from what I understand, is worth two years of work experience at this company. Also, in my three years of work, I've been promoted twice and I'm now managing a team of ten people. I totally understand your logic and I really appreciate that you're wanting to be fair. But I am already working at a level far beyond what's reflected in my years of work."

If the answer is, "I'm sorry you seem upset, but that's all we have budgeted for the position," try something like, "I understand money is limited. I am surprised, honestly, because that number is quite a bit below what the market is paying right now. And I know this company is a very fair place. A salary of $_____ is more in line with what positions like this are paying. What do you think about that?"

Pro tip: Hear no evil. Another possible solution to a lowball offer is to ignore it. In *Negotiation Genius*, Deepak Malhotra and Max H. Bazerman recommend not dwelling on the low number and basically pretending like they haven't made an offer at all. If you make a big deal out of it, they argue, it legitimizes the offer. You can simply name your own number later, as if their crappy, lowball shenanigans never happened.

Pro tip: they go low, you go high. Another option in the case of a lowball is to make an equally aggressive counteroffer—but frame this counteroffer as a "we" situation rather than a face-off. Let's say they've offered you $50,000 and you want $75,000. You could say,

"I'm incredibly excited about the possibility of working here. I believe this is a good fit. I've done a lot of market research. A salary of $90,000 is the industry standard right now. I realize that's more than you were thinking. Is there some common ground we can find?"

Pitfall Alert: Previous Job Pay

During a job application process or initial interviews, questions may come up about your previous/current salary at another company. Whatever you do, DO NOT TELL THEM HOW MUCH YOU MADE AT YOUR LAST JOB. It's a trap. No good will come of it. This question is part of what perpetuates women and minorities getting paid less. It's totally reasonable for them to ask and it's reasonable for you to say, "None of your damn business!" Except don't say that.

If you are asked about your previous salary, say something like "Oh, you know, they're a very fair company and they pay me really well. I definitely have no complaints about my salary there. But this job is different, and I'd love to focus on a good deal for us and for this job."

Pitfall Alert: They Say, "Sorry, Babe. We'd Love to Pay You More, but That's Really All We Can Offer"

First of all, this is probably not true. Know that. This is a delicate moment, but don't fold! The concessions people make early on in a negotiation are typically the biggest. It's important that you keep your aspirations and goals high. It's equally important that you keep your cool. Be calm and good-natured and keep advocating for what you want. And settle in for a good old-fashioned game of . . .

Hardball

Managers negotiate A LOT. So they may be used to being able to get people (especially lady people) for a low price by saying their crappy offer is the very best they can do and then refusing to budge. But it's all just part of the game. They 100 percent have a salary range they can offer you. In each life, a little hardball must be played. And this is your moment. So step up to the plate like the warrior you are!

Pro tip: Turning tables. If things get hardball-y, Claire Wasserman recommends turning things around on them as much as possible. For example, "I'm surprised to hear that. Seventy-five thousand is so much lower than the industry standard and my research found this company typically pays a lot more than seventy-five. But I'm truly excited about this job and the prospect of working here. I'd love for us to figure this out. What would you suggest?"

Pro tip: Unleash the list! If things are stalling or they come back with a crappy counteroffer, it is now the moment to expand the negotiation. Unleash the list! You can say something like, "I am sympathetic to budgets and it seems like money is a sticking point for you right now. What about this: I am really interested in having some extra time for research. If I could teach one class next semester instead of two, I would be comfortable taking a salary of $_____. I'd also be happy to run the department meetings; I know it can be difficult to find people to do that. What do you think?"

You've done a few really important things here.

1. **You've pulled them out of a you-versus-me mindset.** Instead of just, "You want to pay me $50,000 and I want $80,000" (which is a very narrow conversation that's getting narrower by the second), suddenly it's $75,000 and fewer classes you have to teach, but you've also offered to run the department meetings, which you wouldn't mind doing and which would solve a big problem for them. You have expanded the conversation. Suddenly they're thinking about what they can offer you besides money or in addition to money, and what problems you could solve for them. The more elements you introduce (up to a point, obviously), the better your negotiation is likely to go.

2. **You have expressed empathy.** This makes you look good and gracious. Empathy plays well for women in negotiations.

3. **You have made a concession and you *named* that concession.** When you make a concession, name it. Say it out loud. It might seem like that would make you come across as weak, but it actually makes you more powerful in a negotiation. It's a classic Machiavellian stealth move: It makes you look confident, flexible, and reasonable. It shows you are willing to make efforts to reach an agreement. You came to play! You *are* the water in the stream. It puts pressure on them to step up and make a concession as well.

Pro tip: The sound of silence. Silence is powerful. This is something I've learned from reporting. People can't stand silence; it freaks them out. They will start telling you all kinds of things just to avoid silence. If you can get comfortable with silence, you will have a major upper hand in a negotiation. If you don't know what to say next, consider not saying anything. For example, if they insist, "We just don't have the money," keep your face soft (no bitchy resting face). Maybe smile a little or look off to the side, as if you're deep in contemplation. Sing a song in your head if you need to—just don't speak! And see what happens.

Pitfall Alert: They Threaten to Take the Job Away

The nuclear option! The nightmare! This is the worst-case scenario, and people will tell you it never happens, but it has happened to me TWICE. Once, it scared the bejesus out of me and I folded immediately (and took a salary I knew was way too low); the second time I didn't really want the job, so I said fine. Both scenarios taught me a lot about this particular pitfall.

Pro tip: No fear. The person you are negotiating with is trying to scare you. Don't act scared or sad or offended or angry. Just nod and say something like, "Right. Listen, I am really excited about this job and I think we could do some exciting things together. As you say, it may not work out. Maybe this isn't meant to be. I would be really sad if that happened, of course, and I'm optimistic we can work out a situation we're both happy with. In the interest of that . . . as I said, I have done a lot of research and I know that $_____ is what you typically pay. I would be willing to accept $_____ if I could also get a title bump and could start in October instead of next week. I've been wanting to go see my parents and I'd love the time to do that. Would that work for you?"

Pro tip: Call the bluff. The second time I had a job offer threatened to be rescinded, I was not scared because I didn't want the job. That was truly educational. The person offering me the job said, "It seems like maybe this just won't work out." I said, "Yeah, totally—and that's fine. I really appreciate your considering me for this job." Then we sat there in silence for about thirty seconds. I remember wondering what was going on and whether I should leave and why this person was looking at me so strangely. Then all of a sudden this person started speaking in the warmest, friendliest tone and gave me everything I asked for. I was stunned. My inadvertent bluff calling revealed the tactic for what it is: a tactic. The nuclear option is just a way to scare people into settling quickly. It's like threatening a divorce in order to get your spouse to go to the movie *you* want to see. It's not super admirable, but it can be efficient in a Machiavellian sort of way.

Pitfall Alert: You Start Crying or Shaking

It happens. Negotiations are fraught: All kinds of vulnerabilities and sensitivities can come up. Claire Wasserman says, first, feel no shame: "You're experiencing human emotion. Don't apologize for that!" She recommends using that moment to illustrate how much you care by saying something like "I'm just so invested here. I love what I do. I love this company. This means a lot."

Pitfall Alert: Sweating the Small Stuff

I once spent three days haggling over $3,000. I got the money, but it left a bad taste in everyone's mouth. Whatever you're arguing for, be sure it really matters to you. Go back to your lists and look at the issues you really care about. How are you doing on those? Be careful that you're not giving away a lot of what really *does* matter to you and fixating on small, stupid wins. Or maybe you've gotten what you really wanted and now you're just fussing over details. In that case, DON'T SWEAT THE SMALL STUFF AND TAKE! THE! WIN!

Pitfall Alert: "If I Don't Get This, I'll Quit"

This is totally natural. I have fantasy-quit all the jobs I've ever had about a million times. In a moment of helplessness or fear or frustration, it can feel like quitting is your only real power. But don't say this unless you have to. This is *your* version of the nuclear option. Are you ready to *actually* quit? Okay. Know that. It will change your demeanor and you probably won't have to say anything to get that across. But instead of threatening to quit, offer options. For example, let's say you are in a situation where you are producing a ton of work and are at risk of burnout. Instead of saying, "If you don't hire an assistant for me—no, *two assistants*—I'M OUTTA HERE!" think about saying something like, "I'm not getting the support I need right now to do this job to the best of my abilities. I care deeply about my work and I can't be putting out less than my best. I know you care deeply about the quality of work as well. That's so much of why I love working here. I have a couple of possible solutions: If you limited my caseload to five per month, I could handle that myself. That's less than I've been doing, but it still makes me the most productive person in the department. Or, if that doesn't work and you need me to keep up this workload or possibly even do more, I could absolutely do that, but I would need two assistants. I'm also open to suggestions. I'd love to hear your thoughts and ideas."

Pitfall Alert: Their Offer Is Below Your Floor

It may happen that the employer raises their offer, but that offer is still below your floor. This is the moment for real talk. Be sincere and earnest, but avoid aggression. At some point they need to *know* that this situation is not okay with you. Let's say your floor is $70,000 and they tell you $60,000 is the best they can do. You might try something like, "I understand that money is tight, but $60,000 is below what I can accept. I know what this job typically pays and it's very important to me that I'm fairly compensated for my work. I would be comfortable taking a salary of $75,000 if I could get the title of associate. Anything less than that is really not going to work for me." The fact that you have been fair and made concessions and not blustered or given ultimatums will make this moment very powerful. Be calm and direct, but be firm. Let the employer know that this is important to you.

Pitfall Alert: What if They Still Say No?

It is possible that you will ask for a raise or a promotion and make your best case and tell your story and "the story of us" and smile and throw out your ZOPAs like a champ and they will still say no.

Total defeat?

Hardly. You won by asking. Being *in* the arena was the win. You won't get what you want every time. That's okay! You are playing the long game, and they can't get rid of you that easily.

Remember, you are here to start a conversation, build a relationship, and get information. You have achieved all of those things just by being in the room.

Pro tip: We should do this again! In the case of a no, Claire Wasserman recommends being gracious and relentless: "You know, I'm disappointed because I know how fair this company is. I love working here and I believe I hit it out of the park in this particular way.

Is there a chance we can revisit this conversation before my annual review?" This does a few things: First, it establishes that you aren't crushed or demoralized. Second, you've kept the "we" perspective going—you have kept the rapport collaborative and friendly. Finally, this makes it clear that you won't give up and that *maybe* it's easier just to give you the freaking raise than to tell you no every few months forever.

Pro tip: Getting to yes. This is also a moment to get those concrete goals from your employer that tech unicorn Neha Narkhede talked about: "I'm sorry to hear that. It sounds like you aren't sure I'm ready to be a project leader. What would you need to see from me to feel comfortable giving me a project to lead?" Get specifics. Get things that are quantifiable. Then go back when you've achieved those things and ask for what you want again. Remember Neha's excellent advice about hearing no: "Most people don't ask for the things they need, because they're very concerned that the no is actually the final no . . . I just sort of mentally prepare myself, like 'This is a first no. It's not a permanent one.' And it's completely okay to hear no until it becomes a yes."

Pitfall Alert: Spiking the Football

Let's say their offer is higher than you expected or they agree to what you are asking. WOO-HOO! YOU ARE DOING CART-WHEELS OF JOY AND RELIEF, AND A THOUSAND GOLDEN CANNONS ARE FIRING IN YOUR SOUL! But keep all cartwheels and cannons on the inside. Showing your elation is a very bad idea. In *Negotiation Genius*, authors Deepak Malhotra and Max Bazerman make the point that it's crucial the other side feels successful in their negotiation with you. You're going to be in a business relationship with them and you don't want them resenting you. They will not feel successful if you make it clear they have offered you more than you would have been willing to take. "If you accept too quickly or too enthusiastically, you are likely to upset the other party," they write. "To increase their satisfaction from the deal, you might take some time to ponder the offer." Imagine if you named the salary you were most hoping for in a negotiation and your employer said, "Really? That's it? GREAT! When can you start?" You would probably feel like a total sucker, and even though you had gotten everything you wanted, you wouldn't walk away from that negotiation feeling good. So, in order to make your employer happy, stifle your elation and respond with something like, "Oh. Okay. Thank you for the offer. I really appreciate it. Could I take the night to think about it?"

Mom's Pro tip: Sleep on it. The best piece of advice I ever got about negotiating was from my mom. She advised me to give every big decision "the benefit of a bed and pillow." When my dad proposed to her, she apparently had no doubt that she would say yes, but she told him she needed a night to think it over. Poor Dad! (He got over it: They've been married for forty-five years.) At any point in a negotiation, if you feel exhausted or like things are going in a bad direction, ask for a day or two to think about it. This gives you the benefit of distance and a moment for your emotions to settle. It also gives you time to talk things over with your mentors, friends, and family and to get any additional information you might need. This can also be a time when you come up with creative solutions or alternatives that can get things moving in a better direction. Negotiations can be uncomfortable and emotions often run high, and it can be very tempting to just say yes even if you're not happy with where you've settled, just so you can make the pain and discomfort stop. But make yourself take that time. The impact of the salary or title you settle on could stick with you for years. Take my mom's advice: bed and pillow.

And if everything has gone well and you know you are going to take the job or the raise, use your pondering time as a moment to celebrate! Pop the champagne! Go out on the town! Buy ice cream and roses and that new laptop you've been eyeing! Savor the fruits of all your hard work! You made it! You are A CHAMPION!

Better Together

Negotiation is the culmination of all the time, hard work, and creativity you have put in at your job. It also requires you knowing your value, having the confidence to ask, having the respect and support of the people you're working with, and also having an idea of where you want to go. But, at its core, negotiation is about relationship: You are in a relationship with this company. The two of you are moving forward together in a way that will, hopefully, benefit both of you. Ideally, in a negotiation, there isn't a *winner* and a *loser*; rather, everyone is getting what they need and everyone is feeling properly valued. Succeeding in a negotiation is about understanding and standing up for your own value and for the value of your work. It is also about understanding the value of the company you are working with and the opportunities and resources they are bringing to the table.

Now you are thinking and acting like a prince. And there was no one Machiavelli loved and admired more than a new prince who acted with integrity and honor. In fact, he dedicated the book he wrote after *The Prince*, *Discourses on Livy*, to "not those who are princes, but those who because of their countless good qualities deserve to be."

11

Machiavelli's Final Lesson: Fortune's Gift

Over the past couple of years, as I've been writing this book, I have had a copy of *The Prince* within arm's reach pretty much 24/7—moving from my kitchen table, to my nightstand, to my desk, to my purse. I even smashed a cockroach with it one night, which I felt that Machiavelli—superfan of defending one's territory against intruders of all stripes that he was—would have heartily applauded. The image on the cover is now forever etched in my brain: a portrait of Machiavelli in a red-and-black robe, with twinkling eyes and an unsettling half smile that reminds me of the *Mona Lisa*—who would have been a contemporary of his if she was, in fact, an actual lady. Machiavelli's pale, vulpine face has often been the last thing I saw at night and the first thing I looked at when I woke up in the morning. And the words Machiavelli wrote in those pages have echoed in my head, making me rethink countless events from my career and personal life and coloring my day-to-day experiences. There were many ideas and phrases from *The Prince* that resonated deeply with me, but one stood out and I've probably thought of it a thousand times since I first read it: "Fortune is the arbiter of one-half of our actions, but . . . she still leaves us to direct the other half, or perhaps a little less" (Chapter XXV, MPE).

The reason that phrase stood out to me so much had a lot to do with how Fortune was affecting the world around me as I was writing this book. The COVID-19 pandemic brought the world to its knees, killing millions of people, shutting down cities, decimating economies, and causing huge numbers of people to lose their jobs, businesses, and homes.

For months, the famously lively New York City nights were dark and silent except for the near-constant wail of sirens. Then the cries of Black Lives Matter protesters rose up across the city, demanding justice, equality, and change, while police helicopters whined overhead and cops in riot gear lined the streets. Shops, restaurants, bars, and banks were closed—boarded up and empty. "For Lease" signs were everywhere. Structures that had seemed so solid just months before—multinational corporations, the federal government, New York City, even democracy itself—seemed besieged and in crisis.

At the same time as this turmoil and devastation were unfolding across the country, my own life became very small and quiet. As part of a statewide quarantine, I spent months in near total isolation. The life I had known for years—the rush of midtown Manhattan, daily deadlines, breaking news, lively conversations with coworkers, happy hours, reporting trips, blind dates, coffees, cocktails—all vanished in a flash. In its place was a life of study and solitude, punctuated by Machiavelli's twisted little smile. Every morning I would get up at around 6:00 a.m., make an omelet and a pot of coffee, open *The Prince*, and write for a couple of hours before I "went to work," which used to mean a forty-five-minute commute on a jam-packed subway, scrolling through headlines on my phone all the way to the sensory supernova that is Times Square, but now simply entailed walking down the hall to my broom closet, which I'd converted into a recording studio by nailing a blanket to the wall for soundproofing. Instead of riding boots, blazers, and statement jewelry, I spent my days in pajamas and socks, occasionally throwing on a button-down shirt for video chats.

During those surreal months, Machiavelli felt just as real to me—more real, even—than my friends, family, and coworkers, all of whom came to me filtered through screens and spotty Wi-Fi. At night I would put on my trusty face mask and go for long walks in the park near my apartment with Machiavelli's words running through my head: "Fortune is the arbiter of one-half of our actions, but . . . she still leaves us to direct the other half, or perhaps a little less." Or perhaps a lot less.

Ironically enough, my New York City quarantine had a lot in common with Machiavelli's life at the time he wrote *The Prince*. Machiavelli's existence had also been noisy, social, and harried: midnight strategy sessions, galloping from one town to another to deliver bits of news, scheming, cajoling, outwitting, bacchanal parties, courtly politics, and the occasional torchlit ultimatum. But with a turn of the fates, that life—all the movement, action, and glamour—went up in smoke and was replaced by a quiet, solitary existence in the tiny hilltop town of Sant'Andrea in Percussina, ten miles outside Florence.

The tavern Machiavelli's family owned is still there; it's been converted into a gourmet restaurant that makes its own wine and claims to be the oldest tavern in Tuscany. The ancient wooden beams and giant fireplaces are largely untouched from the days when Machiavelli would order steak and wine and sit in the corner reading his books and chatting up the locals. Across the street are the quarters where Machiavelli lived during the months when he wrote *The Prince*. The rooms are small and austere, with high ceilings and tiny windows. There is a little sink where Machiavelli used to wash up before turning to his nightly studies, and a walled-in garden where he would stroll in the evenings. From the garden you can see the city of Florence spread across the valley below like a glittering carpet. Machiavelli must have been tortured by this view—his beloved Florence! Where all the action was happening.

But the real action, as it turned out, was happening in that tiny stone room on a hilltop in the countryside, where a devastated man who had lost his job was sitting alone in the candlelight, conjuring the ghosts of generals, princes, and emperors of old to extract their wisdom, hoping to claw back a bit of what Fortune had taken from him.

All of those months in quarantine and lockdown made me realize that Fortune plays a strange and complicated role in our lives. After all, if Fortune had been kind to Machiavelli, we would not know him. If Fortune hadn't crushed Machiavelli's dreams and taken most everything away from him, he probably would have died a modestly wealthy, well-thought-of civil servant from a small, politically inconsequential territory in northern Italy. He might have published a few things, but he probably wouldn't have been very bold in his writings—he would have had too much to lose. But Fortune took away all that Machiavelli had to lose and left him with only his sharp mind, his vast knowledge of history, and a set of circumstances that pushed him to write something bold and new—something that would hopefully grab the attention of the most powerful man in Florence and inspire him to action.

Remember, Machiavelli's great ambition when he wrote *The Prince* was to get his government job back and *maybe even* convince the new leader of Florence to unite the whole of Italy. To do this, all Machiavelli needed his book to do was impress one lousy guy: Lorenzo de' Medici. But Lorenzo, it seems, never even read the book. Machiavelli did not get his old job back and Italy would not unite for another three hundred years. But Fortune's plans for the man and his little book were light-years beyond Machiavelli's own highest hopes.

Machiavelli did eventually get back some of what he'd lost: He started writing plays and poetry that got a bit of attention. The pope even hired him to write a history of Florence; he was no longer persona non grata. Still, Machiavelli never regained the social and professional heights he had reached during his heyday in the Florentine Republic. He died pretty broke and pretty broken down in his late fifties. At the time, he thought *The Prince* was a total failure.

Of course, *The Prince* was far from a failure. Although he did not know it, Machiavelli had written one of the most celebrated works of Western literature and his influence has stretched far beyond what he ever could have imagined. *The Prince* is credited with helping create the entire field of political science and a whole new way of looking at human interaction, power dynamics, and global politics. People all around the world continue to read it, consider it, and debate its ideas. Lorenzo may not have been particularly dazzled by Machiavelli's thoughts, but millions of people across centuries have been.

During lockdown, friends of mine lost family members and many lost their jobs. I spoke with people who had seen their businesses, homes, and life-savings vanish—people whose plans, lives, and hearts had been destroyed by Fortune. My own life certainly did not look the way I'd thought it would at forty-three: alone, housebound, and broadcasting business news next to a Swiffer while the suffering of my country deepened by the day. I was often scared, lonely, and sad, but Machiavelli's crooked little smile gave me a strange comfort. As bemused and all-knowing as he looks in that picture, I know something that Machiavelli does not. I know that hundreds of years in the future, people will know his face, his name, and the machinations of his mind, and all because of a piece of writing that emerged like a pearl out of the most vulnerable, terrible, chaotic, and gutting moment of his life—a piece of writing so powerful, honest, and clear, it has echoed through centuries.

"Fortune is the arbiter of one-half of our actions, but . . . she still leaves us to direct the other half, or perhaps a little less." This is the phrase that came to me one torturously humid summer night in the middle of citywide lockdown. I went out on my fire escape to watch the sunset with a glass of wine from Machiavelli's vineyard ("research drinking," as I came to think of it). I sat there for a long time watching the sky darken from pink, to blue, to purple, to black. It was a beautiful night, but I was heartbroken, looking out over my besieged city while a thousand depressing statistics about gender discrimination charged through my head.

And then I thought about Machiavelli—across a few centuries of space and time—at his writing table, studying his books and trying to organize his thoughts while a chaotic world raged all around. I realized at that moment that, yes, Fortune ruins our plans, destroys what we've built, and takes loved ones away from us. But Fortune can also can give us gifts beyond anything our own short lives and limited perspectives can conceive.

This final and most important of Machiavelli's lessons comes, I believe, not from his writing but from his life: We are all always at the mercy of Fortune in some form—some sexist middle manager won't promote you; some small-minded investor won't back your idea; an evil colleague steals credit for your work; a virus devastates your planet and confines you to a one-bedroom apartment in Brooklyn. But sometimes Fortune's cruelest turns give us gifts we don't understand at the time. I wonder what Machiavelli would think if he knew that, five hundred years after his death, a forty-three-year-old woman would be drinking wine from his vineyard and studying his words just as he had studied the words of Plato, Tacitus, and Plutarch.

I imagine he would smile.

Experiencing discrimination at work is gut-wrenching and traumatizing. Having to fight so hard to be hired, paid properly, promoted, respected, and given a fair shake is exhausting. But these hardships also bond us together and create empathy. Discrimination makes our companies and our country worse, but I believe we can use it to make things better. As women gain power and position in the U.S. economy, it is my hope that we will use what these difficult circumstances have taught us to create a new kind of workplace: a workplace where everyone can experience the joys, challenges, rewards, and growth that come with doing work you love; a workplace where everyone can grow into their very best personal and professional selves; a workplace where everyone can *be able*. Maybe that is Fortune's gift to us.

"Fortune is the arbiter of one-half of our actions, but . . . she still leaves us to direct the other half, or perhaps a little less. I compare her to one of those raging rivers, which when in flood overflows the plains, sweeping away trees and buildings, bearing away the soil from place to place; everything flies before it, all yield to its violence, without being able in any way to withstand it . . ."

Acknowledgments

First and foremost, I must thank my wonderful parents. My father, James W. Smith, encouraged me to take on this project. He and my mother, Mary B. Smith, were a constant source of encouragement and inspiration.

Larry Weissman, my agent, believed I had a book in me even when I was very certain I didn't. He and his wonderful business partner and wife, Sascha Alper, provided amazing edits and insights.

I also must credit my brilliant and visionary editor, Karyn Marcus, who came up with the central idea for this book and also provided many of the fundamental concepts.

Robert Smith's structural ideas and all-around editorial genius truly helped shape the book.

Laurie Farrell's encouragement, love, laughter, and excitement about this project were constant. I owe her a huge debt of gratitude.

My research assistant, Sarah Ellis, contributed in so many ways: Her incredible interviews, diligence, kindness, intelligence, and great ideas were absolutely indispensable. The book would not be the same without her.

The fact-checking prowess of Hilary McClellen was likewise indispensable.

Anya Kamenetz and Hilke Schellmann were both enormously helpful when it came to getting started on this project, which felt so daunting! I can't thank them enough.

Eve Troeh, Allison Schrager, Aarti Shahani, Sally Herships, and Molly Thomas-Jensen contributed great ideas and edits, as well as their wonderful friendship.

My dearest lifelong friend, Heather Jones, provided constant and invaluable support, counsel, and conversation, and may have single-handedly saved my sanity throughout the writing process.

Jonathan Lyons's sage advice helped in so many ways.

I would love to thank my aunt Judy Lea Smith and my cousin Kandice Knigge for their support.

Matteo Saraceni and Marta were enormously generous in showing me around Machiavelli's apartments and their lovely taverna and vineyards. That visit gave my book a context, depth, and empathy it would never have otherwise had. Thank you, too, for the *I ♥ Machiavelli* coffee mug, which I use every day.

I also want to thank my NPR colleagues, especially Cardiff Garcia, Paddy Hirsch, Alex Goldmark, Neal Carruth, and Anya Grundmann, for giving me time and space to write this book.

Bonafini café in Brooklyn and Karma Café in San Francisco let me sit and sip coffee and write for hours. There would be no book without them.

Finally, I want to thank all the women who shared their experiences with me: I was so moved by their stories. It takes enormous courage to share difficult experiences, and I was inspired by how brave and strong they were and often delighted and impressed by their fabulous Machiavellian work-arounds. It is my highest hope that this book can help them in some way.

Notes

Introduction

3   *Consider this: In school:* Enrico Gnaulati, "Why Girls Tend to Get Better Grades Than Boys Do," *Atlantic*, September 18, 2014, https://www.theatlantic.com/education/archive/2014/09/why-girls-get-better-grades-than-boys-do/380318/.

3   *women graduate from high school and attend college:* Joel McFarland et al., *Trends in High School Dropout and Completion Rates in the United States: 2018 Compendium Report* (NCES 2019-117), U.S. Department of Education, Washington, DC: National Center for Education Statistics, https://nces.ed.gov/pubs2019/2019117.pdf.

3   *there are more women than men in medical school and law school:* Linda Searing, "The Big Number: Women Now Outnumber Men in Medical Schools," *Washington Post*, December 23, 2019, https://www.washingtonpost.com/health/the-big-number-women-now-outnumber-men-in-medical-schools/2019/12/20/8b9eddea-2277-11ea-bed5-880264cc91a9_story.html; Ian Pisarcik, "Women Outnumber Men in Law School Classrooms for Third Year in a Row, but Statistics Don't Tell the Full Story," *Jurist*, March 5, 2019, https://www.jurist.org/commentary/2019/03/pisarcik-women-outnumber-men-in-law-school/.

3   *Nearly 40 percent of businesses:* Guadalupe Gonzalez, "New Research Finds Women Are Starting 1,821 New Businesses a Day, but There's a Catch," *Inc.*, August 22, 2018, https://www.inc.com

/guadalupe-gonzalez/state-women-owned-businesses-report-2018
.html.

3   *(including at NPR . . . sexual harassment):* "Top NPR News Executive
Mike Oreskes Resigns Amid Allegations of Sexual Harassment,"
All Things Considered, hosted by Mary Louise Kelly, National
Public Radio, November 1, 2017, transcript and radio segment at
https://www.npr.org/2017/11/01/561427869/top-npr-new-executive
-mike-oreskes-resigns-amid-allegations-of-sexual-harassment.

3   *80% of CEOs are men:* McKinsey & Company, *Women in the
Workplace: 2020* report, https://www.mckinsey.com/featured-insights
/diversity-and-inclusion/women-in-the-workplace; C200, Catalyst,
Women Business Collaborative, *2020 Women CEOs in America Report:
Changing the Face of Business Leadership,* http://womenceoreport.org/.

3   *Corporate boards are more than 80% male:* Deloitte, *Women in the
Boardroom: A Global Perspective, 6th ed.,* 2020, https://www2.deloitte
.com/global/en/pages/risk/articles/women-in-the-boardroom-global
-perspective.html.

3   *Women make about 80¢:* Nikki Graf, Anna Brown, and Eileen
Patten, "The Narrowing, but Persistent, Gender Gap in Pay," *Fact
Tank,* Pew Research Center, March 22, 2019, https://www.pew
research.org/fact-tank/2019/03/22/gender-pay-gap-facts/.

3   *Two-thirds of federal judges:* Women in Business Law Initiative, Roundtable Series, "Addressing Development and Retention:
Gender Parity in U.S. Law Firms: Recommendations," University of California, Berkeley School of Law, September 20, 2019,
https://www.law.berkeley.edu/wp-content/uploads/2019/10/Gender
Parity_Recommendations-for-Law-Firms.pdf; Danielle Root, Jake
Faleschini, and Grace Oyenubi, "Building a More Inclusive Federal Judiciary," Center for American Progress, October 3, 2019,
https://www.americanprogress.org/issues/courts/reports/2019/10/03
/475359/building-inclusive-federal-judiciary/.

3   *75% of elected representatives:* "Women in Elective Office: 2020,"
Center for American Women and Politics, Eagleton Institute of
Politics, Rutgers University, fact sheet, accessed November 2020,
https://cawp.rutgers.edu/women-elective-office-2020.

NOTES

3 *Women start 40%:* American Express, "The 2019 State of Women-Owned Businesses Report," Summary of Key Trends, https://s1.q4cdn.com/692158879/files/doc_library/file/2019-state-of-women-owned-businesses-report.pdf.; Hayden Field, "98 Percent of VC Funding Goes to Men. Can Women Entrepreneurs Change a Sexist System?," *Entrepreneur*, October 23, 2018, https://www.entrepreneur.com/article/315992.

5 *Psychologists have even developed:* Eugenia Mandal and Dagna Kocur, "The Machiavellianism and Manipulation Tactics Used by Patients with Borderline Personality Disorder in Everyday Life and in Therapy," *Psychiatria Polska* 47, no. 4 (July 2013): 667–78, pmid:24946473.

5 *"I love my native city more than my own soul":* Niccolò Machiavelli to Francesco Vettori, 1527, letter, in Maurizio Viroli, *Niccolò's Smile: A Biography of Machiavelli*, trans. Antony Shugaar (New York: Farrar, Straus and Giroux, 2000), 254.

5 *"The streets were filled with the parts of men":* Paul Strathern, *The Artist, the Philosopher, and the Warrior: Da Vinci, Machiavelli, and Borgia and the World They Shaped* (New York: Bantam, 2009), 39, citing Niccolò Machiavelli, *Florentine Histories*, trans. Laura F. Banfield and Harvey C. Mansfield, Jr. (Princeton, NJ: Princeton University Press, 1988), chap. VIII, secs. 7–9.

7 *If a woman has a cranky demeanor:* M. E. Heilman and J. J. Chen, "Same Behavior, Different Consequences: Reactions to Men's and Women's Altruistic Citizenship Behavior," *Journal of Applied Psychology* 90, no. 3 (2005): 431–41, https://doi.org/10.1037/0021-9010.90.3.431.

Chapter One: Machiavelli's Playbook

9 *"Since it is my intention":* Paul Strathern, *The Artist, the Philosopher, and the Warrior: Da Vinci, Machiavelli, and Borgia and the World They Shaped* (New York: Bantam, 2009), 376, quoting Niccolò Machiavelli, *The Prince*, Chapter XV.

10 *Machiavelli himself was a bit:* Strathern, *The Artist, the Philosopher, and the Warrior*, 37–40.

11 *Its original Anglo-French root:* Robert K. Barnhart, *The Barnhart Concise Dictionary of Etymology: The Origins of American English Words* (New York: HarperCollins, 1995), 590.

12 *They talk a lot, make decisions:* C. L. Ridgeway and C. Bourg, "Gender as Status: An Expectation States Theory Approach," in *The Psychology of Gender,* eds. Alice H. Eagly, Anne E. Beall, and Robert J. Sternberg (New York: Guilford Press, 2004), 29–31.

13 *Those are the emotions:* Julie E. Phelan and Laurie A. Rudman, "Prejudice Toward Female Leaders: Backlash Effects and Women's Impression Management Dilemma," *Social and Personality Psychology Compass* 4, no. 10 (October 2010): 807–20, https://doi.org/10.1111/j.1751-9004.2010.00306.x.

13 *(Studies show basically everybody agrees on that):* A. H. Eagly et al., "Gender Stereotypes Have Changed: A Cross-Temporal Meta-Analysis of U.S. Public Opinion Polls from 1946 to 2018," *American Psychologist* 75, no. 3 (2020), 301–15, http://dx.doi.org/10.1037/amp0000494.

14 *The powerful Medici family seized:* Machiavelli to Giuliano de' Medici, in Strathern, *The Artist, the Philosopher, and the Warrior,* 399.

14 *Machiavelli confided to a close correspondent:* Ibid., 402.

15 *He looks at things with an honest:* Maurizio Viroli, *Niccolò's Smile: A Biography of Machiavelli,* trans. Antony Shugaar (New York: Farrar, Straus and Giroux, 2000), 158.

15 *It seems Lorenzo:* Ibid., 160.

16 *"I shall continue, then, among my lousy doings":* Machiavelli to Francesco Vettori, June 10, 1514, in Corrado Vivanti, *Niccolò Machiavelli: An Intellectual Biography,* trans. Simon MacMichael (Princeton, NJ: Princeton University Press, 2019), 103.

16 *His conclusion: Fully facing:* Quentin Skinner, *Machiavelli: A Very Short Introduction,* 2nd ed. (Oxford, UK: Oxford University Press, 2000), 18.

17 *Institutions that claim:* Emilio J. Castilla and Stephen Benard, "The Paradox of Meritocracy in Organizations," *Administrative Science Quarterly* 55, no. 4 (December 2010), https://doi.org/10.2189/asqu.2010.55.4.543.

17   *Carly Fiorina:* Carly Fiorina, *Tough Choices: A Memoir* (New York: Portfolio, 2006), xii.

19   *In one study (that made . . .):* M. I. Norton, J. A. Vandello, and J. M. Darley, "Casuistry and Social Category Bias," *Journal of Personality and Social Psychology* 87, no. 6 (2004): 817–31, https://doi.org /10.1037/0022-3514.87.6.817.

19   *In a study out of Yale:* Corinne A. Moss-Racusin et al., "Science Faculty's Subtle Gender Biases Favor Male Students," *Proceedings of the National Academy of Sciences* 109, no. 41 (October 9, 2012): 16474–79, https://doi.org/10.1073/pnas.1211286109.

19   *In a study by Harvard:* Claudia Goldin and Cecilia Rouse, "Orchestrating Impartiality: The Impact of 'Blind' Auditions on Female Musicians" (working paper 5903, National Bureau of Economic Research, January 1997), https://doi.org/10.3386/w5903; Claudia Goldin and Cecilia Rouse, "Orchestrating Impartiality: The Impact of 'Blind' Auditions on Female Musicians," *American Economic Review* 90, no. 4 (2000): 715–41, https://pubs.aeaweb.org/doi/pdfplus /10.1257/aer.90.4.715.

21   *People have strong preconceived notions:* Virginia E. Schein, "A Global Look at Psychological Barriers to Women's Progress in Management," *Journal of Social Issues* 57, no. 4 (Winter 2001): 675–88, https://doi.org/10.1111/0022-4537.00235.

21   *An ideal man is supposed to be:* Frank Newport, "Americans See Women as Emotional and Affectionate, Men as More Aggressive: Gender Specific Stereotypes Persist in Recent Gallup Poll," Gallup News Service, February 21, 2001, https://news.gallup.com/poll /1978/americans-see-women-emotional-affectionate-men-more -aggressive.aspx; P. T. Costa Jr., A. Terracciano, and R. R. McCrae, "Gender Differences in Personality Traits Across Cultures: Robust and Surprising Findings," *Journal of Personality and Social Psychology* 81, no. 2 (2001): 322–31, https://doi.org/10.1037/0022 -3514.81.2.322.

22   *Of course, if the woman messes up:* Therese Huston, "Research: We Are Way Harder on Female Leaders Who Make Bad Calls," *Harvard Business Review*, April 21, 2016, https://hbr.org/2016

/04/research-we-are-way-harder-on-female-leaders-who-make-bad-calls; Victoria L. Brescoll, Erica Dawson, Eric Luis Uhlmann, "Hard Won and Easily Lost: The Fragile Status of Leaders in Gender-Stereotype-Incongruent Occupations," *Psychological Science* 21, no. 11 (2010): 1640–42, https://gap.hks.harvard.edu/hard-won-and-easily-lost-fragile-status-leaders-gender-stereotype-incongruent-occupations.

23   *Here's how it works:* Mary Ann Cejka and Alice H. Eagly, "Gender-Stereotypic Images of Occupations Correspond to the Sex Segregation of Employment," *Personality and Social Psychology Bulletin* 25, no. 4 (April 1, 1999): 413–23, https://journals.sagepub.com/doi/10.1177/0146167299025004002.

23   *If a woman displays "leadership":* Emily T. Amanatullah and Catherine H. Tinsley, "Punishing Female Negotiators for Asserting Too Much . . . or Not Enough: Exploring Why Advocacy Moderates Backlash Against Assertive Female Negotiators," *Organizational Behavior and Human Decision Processes* 120, no. 1 (January 2013): 110–22, https://doi.org/10.1016/j.obhdp.2012.03.006; A. H. Eagly and S. J. Karau, "Role Congruity Theory of Prejudice Toward Female Leaders," *Psychological Review* 109, no. 3 (2002): 573–98, https://doi.org/10.1037/0033-295X.109.3.573.

25   *Women of color will also get:* Robin Bleiweis, "Quick Facts About the Gender Wage Gap," Center for American Progress, March 24, 2020, https://www.americanprogress.org/issues/women/reports/2020/03/24/482141/quick-facts-gender-wage-gap/; Sarah Coury et al., "Women in the Workplace 2020," McKinsey & Company, https://www.mckinsey.com/featured-insights/diversity-and-inclusion/women-in-the-workplace.

26   *Unemployment rates for LGBTQ workers:* Sharita Gruberg and Michael Madowitz, "Same-Sex Couples Experience Higher Unemployment Rates Throughout an Economic Recovery," Center for American Progress, May 5, 2020, https://www.americanprogress.org/issues/lgbtq-rights/news/2020/05/05/484547/sex-couples-experience-higher-unemployment-rates-throughout-economic-recovery/.

26   *More than a third of LGBTQ workers:* Ibid.

27   *Consider this: Young, single women:* Belinda Luscombe, "Workplace Salaries: At Last, Women on Top," *Time*, September 1, 2010, http://content.time.com/time/business/article/0,8599,2015274,00.html.

27   *So much so that:* "New Report Paints a Grim Picture of Older Women in Poverty," Association of Health Care Journalists, blog entry by Liz Seegert, January 8, 2019, https://healthjournalism.org/blog/2019/01/new-report-paints-a-grim-picture-of-older-women-in-poverty/.

Chapter Two: Money

29   *Women earn roughly 80 cents:* "The Simple Truth About the Gender Pay Gap: Fall 2019 Update," American Association of University Women, https://www.aauw.org/app/uploads/2020/02/Simple-Truth-Update-2019_v2-002.pdf.

29   *The pay gap closed:* Francine D. Blau and Lawrence M. Kahn, "The Gender Wage Gap: Extent, Trends, and Explanations" (working paper 21913, National Bureau of Economic Research, January 2016), https://www.nber.org/papers/w21913.pdf.

31   *One famous study:* Linda Babcock et al., "Nice Girls Don't Ask," *Harvard Business Review*, October 2003, https://hbr.org/2003/10/nice-girls-dont-ask.

31   *The kicker:* Linda Babcock and Sara Laschever, *Women Don't Ask: The High Cost of Avoiding Negotiation—and Positive Strategies for Change* (Princeton, NJ: Princeton University Press, 2003), 11.

32   *I know this might sound like:* Emily T. Amanatullah and Michael W. Morris, "Negotiating Gender Roles: Gender Differences in Assertive Negotiating Are Mediated by Women's Fear of Backlash and Attenuated When Negotiating on Behalf of Others," *Journal of Personality and Social Psychology* 98, no. 2 (February 2010): 256–67, https://doi.org/10.1037/a0017094.

32   *Here's the painful truth:* Linda Babcock et al., "Propensity to Initiate Negotiations: A New Look at Gender Variation in Negotiation Behavior" (April 15, 2002), ResearchGate, https://www.researchgate.net/publication/228182496_Propensity_to_Initiate_Negotiations_A_New_Look_at_Gender_Variation_in_Negotiation_Behavior.

32 *Most women feel:* Babcock and Laschever, *Women Don't Ask*, 95;
    M. L. Williams, M. A. McDaniel, and N. T. Nguyen, "A Meta-
    Analysis of the Antecedents and Consequences of Pay Level Satis-
    faction," *Journal of Applied Psychology* 91, no. 2 (2006): 392–412,
    https://doi.org/10.1037/0021-9010.91.2.392.

33 *Men tend to focus on:* A. D. Galinsky, V. H. Medvec, and T. Muss-
    weiler, "Disconnecting Outcomes and Evaluations: The Role of Ne-
    gotiator Focus," *Journal of Personality and Social Psychology* 83, no. 5
    (2002): 1131–40, https://doi.org/10.1037/0022-3514.83.5.1131.

33 *Men are raised to embrace it:* Priya Fielding-Singh, Devon Magliozzi,
    and Swethaa Ballakrishnen, "Why Women Stay Out of the Spot-
    light at Work," *Harvard Business Review*, August 28, 2018, https://
    hbr.org/2018/08/sgc-8-28-why-women-stay-out-of-the-spotlight-at
    -work; Muriel Niederle and Lise Vesterlund, "Do Women Shy Away
    from Competition? Do Men Compete Too Much?" *Quarterly Jour-
    nal of Economics* 122, no. 3 (August 2007): 1067–1101, https://web
    .stanford.edu/~niederle/Niederle.Vesterlund.QJE.2007.pdf.

33 *In one study, women were asked:* Devavrat Purohit and Harris
    Sondak (2001), in conversation with the authors about their study
    "Fear and Loathing at the Car Dealership: The Procedural Justice
    of Pricing Policies," cited in Babcock and Laschever, *Women Don't
    Ask*, 127.

34 *If you are underpaid:* Robin L. Pinkley and Gregory B. Northcraft,
    *Get Paid What You're Worth: The Expert Negotiators' Guide to Salary
    and Compensation* (New York: St. Martin's Press, 2014).

34 *That belief makes it real:* Lenny Bernstein, "An 'Expensive' Placebo
    Is More Effective Than a 'Cheap' One, Study Shows," *Harvard
    Business Review*, January 28, 2015, https://hms.harvard.edu/news
    /expensive-placebo-more-effective-cheap-one-study-shows.

35 *Research has found:* Hannah Riley Bowles, Linda Babcock, and
    Lei Lai, "Social Incentives for Gender Differences in the Propen-
    sity to Initiate Negotiations: Sometimes It Does Hurt to Ask,"
    Organizational Behavior and Human Decision Processes 103, no. 1
    (May 2007): 84–103, https://doi.org/10.1016/j.obhdp.2006.09.001;
    Emily T. Amanatullah and Catherine H. Tinsley, "Punishing

Female Negotiators for Asserting Too Much . . . or Not Enough: Exploring Why Advocacy Moderates Backlash Against Assertive Female Negotiators," *Organizational Behavior and Human Decision Processes* 120, no. 1 (January 2013), 110–22.

35 *Add to that the fact:* Dina Gerdeman, "Why Employers Favor Men," Harvard Business School, September 11, 2017, https://hbswk.hbs .edu/item/why-employers-favor-men.

35 *The man might not get more money:* Benjamin Artz, Amanda Goodall, and Andrew J. Oswald, "Research: Women Ask for Raises as Often as Men, but Are Less Likely to Get Them," *Harvard Business Review*, June 25, 2018, https://hbr.org/2018/06/research-women -ask-for-raises-as-often-as-men-but-are-less-likely-to-get-them.

37 *In an interview a decade later:* "Happy Birthday, Linda Evangelista! The Original Supermodel Turns 50 and Is Happy About Aging," *HuffPost*, May 8, 2015, https://www.huffpost.com/entry /happy-birthday-linda-evangelista-the-original-supermodel-turns -50-and-is-happy-about-aging_b_7242534.

37 *"I paid twenty-nine million dollars":* Glenn Plaskin, "The Playboy Interview with Donald Trump," *Playboy*, March 1, 1990, https://www.playboy.com/read/playboy-interview-donald-trump -1990?utm_source=fark&utm_medium=website&utm_content =link&ICID=ref_fark.

38 *As a result, a huge number:* "New Report Paints a Grim Picture of Older Women in Poverty," Association of Health Care Journalists, blog entry by Liz Seegert, January 8, 2019, https://healthjournalism .org/blog/2019/01/new-report-paints-a-grim-picture-of-older-women -in-poverty/.

38 *One effect of women earning less:* Stacy Francis, "Money Stress Traps Many Women into Staying in Unhappy Marriages," CNBC, August 13, 2019, https://www.cnbc.com/2019/08/13/money-stress -traps-many-women-into-staying-in-unhappy-marriages.html.

38 *This, in fact, is a tactic:* Pinkley and Northcraft, *Get Paid What You're Worth.*

39 *I nearly burst into tears:* L. A. Rudman, "Self-Promotion as a Risk Factor for Women: The Costs and Benefits of Counterstereotyp-

ical Impression Management," *Journal of Personality and Social Psychology* 74, no. 3 (1998): 629–45, https://doi.org/10.1037/0022 -3514.74.3.629.

40 *Machiavelli felt so passionately:* Paul Strathern, *The Artist, the Philosopher, and the Warrior: Da Vinci, Machiavelli, and Borgia and the World They Shaped* (New York: Bantam, 2009), chap. 25.

41 *Women do much better:* Katie Shonk, "Women and Negotiation: Narrowing the Gender Gap in Negotiation," Program on Negotiation, Harvard Law School (blog), July 23, 2020, https://www.pon .harvard.edu/daily/business-negotiations/women-and-negotiation -narrowing-the-gender-gap/.

43 *Women don't tend to get what they want:* "Negotiations, Gender, and Status at the Bargaining Table," Program on Negotiation, Harvard Law School (blog), August 20, 2020, https://www.pon.harvard .edu/daily/leadership-skills-daily/men-women-and-status-in -negotiations/; Cristina Rouvalis, "Gender Divide," *Carnegie Mellon Today,* Carnegie Mellon University, March 7, 2016, https://www .cmu.edu/cmtoday/artsculture_business/gender-pay-gap-research /index.html.

43 *Research shows us:* Linda L. Carli, "Gender and Social Influence," *Journal of Social Issues* 57, no. 4 (Winter 2001): 725–41, https://doi .org/10.1111/0022-4537.00238; Bowles, "Social Incentives for Gender Differences," 84–103; M. LaFrance, M. A. Hecht, and E. L. Paluck, "The Contingent Smile: A Meta-Analysis of Sex Differences in Smiling," *Psychological Bulletin* 129, no. 2 (2003): 305–34, https:// doi.org/10.1037/0033-2909.129.2.305.

44 *Silver lining:* Anastasia Buyalskaya, "Keep Learning to Ask," *Economist, Career Hacks* (blog), accessed October 2020, https://execed .economist.com/blog/career-hacks/keep-learning-ask.

47 *When news of the deal:* Emily VanDerWerff, "Report: Crazy Rich Asians Sequels Offered an Asian Writer 1/8th of Her White Co-Writer's Salary," *Vox,* September 4, 2019, https://www.vox.com /culture/2019/9/4/20850026/crazy-rich-asians-sequels-pay-gap -adele-lim-peter-chiarelli.

Chapter Three: Confidence

50 *Less confident people:* Katty Kay and Claire Shipman, "The Confidence Gap," *Atlantic*, May 2014, https://www.theatlantic.com/magazine/archive/2014/05/the-confidence-gap/359815/.

50 *Studies have shown:* Ernesto Reuben, Pedro Rey-Biel, Paula Sapienza, and Luigi Zingales, "The Emergence of Male Leadership in Competitive Environments," *Journal of Economic Behavior & Organization* 83, no. 1 (June 2012): 111–17, http://dx.doi.org/10.1016/j.jebo.2011.06.016.

50 *The men paid themselves:* B. Major, D. B. McFarlin, and D. Gagnon, "Overworked and Underpaid: On the Nature of Gender Differences in Personal Entitlement," *Journal of Personality and Social Psychology* 47, no. 6 (1984): 1399–412, https://doi.org/10.1037/0022-3514.47.6.1399.

51 *Women didn't tend to nominate themselves:* Georges Desvaux, Sandrine Devillard-Hoellinger, and Mary C. Meaney, "A Business Case for Women," *McKinsey Quarterly*, September 2008, 4, https://annazavaritt.blog.ilsole24ore.com/wp-content/uploads/sites/54/files/studio-mckinsey-sulle-donne.pdf.

51 *Women, on the other hand:* Linda L. Carli, "Gender and Social Influence," *Journal of Social Issues* 57, no. 4 (Winter 2001): 725–41, https://doi.org/10.1111/0022-4537.00238.

51 *Cesare was a formidable general:* Paul Strathern, *The Artist, the Philosopher, and the Warrior: Da Vinci, Machiavelli, and Borgia and the World They Shaped* (New York: Bantam, 2009), 104–5.

52 *"This lord is truly splendid":* Ibid., 104–5, 202.

54 *In their book:* Katty Kay and Claire Shipman, *The Confidence Code: The Science and Art of Self-Assurance—What Women Should Know* (New York: HarperCollins, 2014), 50.

56 *"I know that many say a policy":* Niccolò Machiavelli to Francesco Vettori, 1514, letter, in Maurizio Viroli, *Niccolò's Smile: A Biography of Machiavelli*, trans. Antony Shugaar (New York: Farrar, Straus and Giroux, 2000), 178.

57 *It comes from a study:* Julia B. Bear and Linda Babcock, "Negotiation Topic as a Moderator of Gender Differences in Negotiation," *Psycho-*

logical Science 23, no. 7 (June 2012): 743–44, https://doi.org/10.1177
/0956797612442393; Gary E. Bolton and Rachel T. A. Croson,
eds., *The Oxford Handbook of Economic Conflict Resolution* (Oxford,
UK: Oxford University Press, 2012), chap. 5; Hannah Riley Bowles,
Linda Babcock, and Kathleen L. McGinn, "Constraints and Trig-
gers: Situational Mechanics of Gender in Negotiation," *Journal of
Personality and Social Psychology* 89, no. 6 (2005): 951–65, https://
doi.org/10.1037/0022-3514.89.6.951, https://projects.iq.harvard.edu
/files/hbowles/files/situational_mechanics.pdf.

60　*The new pope overpowered:* Strathern, *The Artist, the Philosopher, and
the Warrior,* 368.

Chapter Four: Respect

65　*A study of Supreme Court transcripts:* Tonja Jacobi and Dylan
Schweers, "Justice, Interrupted: The Effect of Gender, Ideology,
and Seniority at Supreme Court Oral Arguments," *Virginia Law
Review* 103 (2017): 1379–496, https://www.virginialawreview.org
/sites/virginialawreview.org/files/JacobiSchweers_Online.pdf.

66　*Kenneth Steven Geller:* Ibid.

66　*When men are in a mixed-gender group:* Christopher F. Karpowitz,
Tali Mendelberg, and Lee Shaker, "Gender Inequality in Deliberative Participation," *American Political Science Review* 106, no. 3 (August 2012): 533–47, https://doi.org/10.1017/S0003055412000329.

67　*So when a woman speaks up:* Zuhairah Washington and Laura Mor-
gan Roberts, "Women of Color Get Less Support at Work. Here's
How Managers Can Change That," *Harvard Business Review,*
March 4, 2019, https://hbr.org/2019/03/women-of-color-get-less
-support-at-work-heres-how-managers-can-change-that; Amanda
K. Sesko and Monica Biernat, "Prototypes of Race and Gender:
The Invisibility of Black Women," *Journal of Experimental Social
Psychology* 46, no. 2 (March 2010): 356–60, https://doi.org/10.1016
/j.jesp.2009.10.016.

71　*Consider this: When men are in meetings:* Karpowitz, Mendelberg,
and Shaker, "Gender Inequality in Deliberative Participation." Lydia
Smith, "The Stark Reality of How Men Dominate Talking in Meet-

ings," Yahoo Finance UK, April 10, 2019, https://finance.yahoo.com /news/stark-reality-men-dominate-talking-meetings-113112910 .html; Adrienne B. Hancock and Benjamin A. Rubin, "Influence of Communication Partner's Gender on Language," *Journal of Language and Social Psychology* 34, no. 1 (January 2015), https://doi.org /10.1177/0261927X14533197.

72 *Tina learned the:* Juliet Eilperin, "White House Women Want to Be in the Room Where It Happens," *Washington Post*, September 13, 2016, https://www.washingtonpost.com/news/powerpost/wp/2016/09/13 /white-house-women-are-now-in-the-room-where-it-happens/.

73 *We're perfectly happy:* Julia B. Bear and Linda Babcock, "Negotiation Topic as a Moderator of Gender Differences in Negotiation," *Psychological Science* 23, no. 7 (2012): 743–44, https:// doi.org/10.1177/0956797612442393; Emily T. Amanatullah and Michael W. Morris, "Negotiating Gender Roles: Gender Differences in Assertive Negotiating Are Mediated by Women's Fear of Backlash and Attenuated When Negotiating on Behalf of Others," *Journal of Personality and Social Psychology* 98, no. 2 (February 2010): 256–67, https://doi.org/10.1037/a0017094.

73 *Machiavelli is careful:* "A Prince should be careful never to join with one stronger than himself in attacking others . . . For if he whom you join prevails, you are at his mercy," Niccolò Machiavelli, *The Prince*, trans. N. H. Thomson (New York: Dover, 1992), 61.

74 *Studies have shown that when women use softeners:* Melannie Matschiner and Sarah K. Murnen, "Hyperfemininity and Influence," *Psychology of Women Quarterly* 23, no. 3 (1999): 631–42, https:// doi.org/10.1111/j.1471-6402.1999.tb00385.x; Cecilia L. Ridgeway and Lynn Smith-Lovin, "The Gender System and Interaction," *Annual Review of Sociology* 25 (August 1999): 191–216, https://doi.org /10.1146/annurev.soc.25.1.191.

78 *Studies estimate more than 80 percent:* Rhitu Chatterjee, "A New Survey Finds 81 Percent of Women Have Experienced Sexual Harassment," NPR, *The Two Way* (blog), February 21, 2018, https://www.npr.org /sections/thetwo-way/2018/02/21/587671849/a-new-survey-finds -eighty-percent-of-women-have-experienced-sexual-harassment.

78 *Stefanie points out that women:* Heather McLaughlin, Christopher Uggen, and Amy Blackstone, "Sexual Harassment, Workplace Authority, and the Paradox of Power," *American Sociological Review* 77, no. 4 (August 2012): 625–47, https://doi.org/10.1177/0003122412451728; Meredith A. Newman, Robert A. Jackson, and Douglas D. Baker, "Sexual Harassment in the Federal Workplace," *Public Administration Review* 63, no. 4 (July 2003): 472–83, https://doi.org/10.1111/1540-6210.00309.

78 *She is quick to add:* Robert A. Jackson and Meredith A. Newman, "Sexual Harassment in the Federal Workplace Revisited: Influences on Sexual Harassment by Gender," *Public Administration Review* 64, no. 6 (November 2004): 705–17, https://doi.org/10.1111/j.1540-6210.2004.00417.x.

79 *LGBTQ workers are frequent targets:* Sharita Gruberg, Lindsay Mahowald, and John Halpin, "The State of the LGBTQ Community in 2020," Center for American Progress, October 6, 2020, https://www.americanprogress.org/issues/lgbtq-rights/reports/2020/10/06/491052/state-lgbtq-community-2020/.

80 *Stefanie says sociologists:* National Academies of Sciences, Engineering, and Medicine; Policy and Global Affairs; Committee on Women in Science, Engineering, and Medicine; and Committee on the Impacts of Harassment in Academia, *Sexual Harassment of Women: Climate, Culture, and Consequences in Academic Sciences, Engineering, and Medicine,* eds. Frazier F. Benya, Sheila E. Widnall, and Paula A. Johnson (Washington, DC: National Academies Press, June 12, 2018), chap. 2, https://www.ncbi.nlm.nih.gov/books/NBK519455/.

80 *Nobel Prize–winning biochemist:* Dan Bilefsky, "Women Respond to Nobel Laureate's 'Trouble with Girls,'" *New York Times,* June 11, 2015, https://www.nytimes.com/2015/06/12/world/europe/tim-hunt-nobel-laureate-resigns-sexist-women-female-scientists.html.

80 *There was the infamous "Google memo":* Louise Matsakis, Jason Koebler, and Sarah Emerson, "Here Are the Citations for the Anti-Diversity Manifesto Circulating at Google," *Vice,* August 7, 2017, https://www.vice.com/en/article/evzjww/here-are-the-citations-for-the-anti-diversity-manifesto-circulating-at-google.

81 *And in 2005, famed economist:* Sam Dillon, "Harvard Chief Defends His Talk on Women," *New York Times*, January 18, 2005, https://www.nytimes.com/2005/01/18/us/harvard-chief-defends-his-talk-on-women.html.

81 *This might not seem like:* Indiana University, "Stereotypes Lower Math Performance in Women, but Effects Go Unrecognized," *ScienceDaily,* March 26, 2015, https://www.sciencedaily.com/releases/2015/03/150326162600.htm.

81 *In one case, a math test was given:* C. S. Sims, F. Drasgow, and L. F. Fitzgerald, "The Effects of Sexual Harassment on Turnover in the Military: Time-Dependent Modeling," *Journal of Applied Psychology* 90, no. 6 (2005): 1141–52, https://doi.org/10.1037/0021-9010.90.6.1141; "Select Task Force on the Study of Harassment in the Workplace, Report of Co-Chairs Chai R. Feldblum and Victoria A. Lipnic; Executive Summary and Summary of Recommendations," U.S. Equal Employment Opportunity Commission, June 2016, https://www.eeoc.gov/select-task-force-study-harassment-workplace.

81 *When a different group:* Steven J. Spencer, Claude M. Steele, and Diane M. Quinn, "Stereotype Threat and Women's Math Performance," *Journal of Experimental Social Psychology* 35, no. 1 (January 1999): 4–28, https://doi.org/10.1006/jesp.1998.1373.

82 *The words most strongly:* Alice H. Wu, "Gender Stereotyping in Academia: Evidence from Economics Job Market Rumors Forum" (undergraduate honors thesis, University of California, Berkeley), August 2017, https://www.dropbox.com/s/v6q7gfcbv9feef5/Wu_EJMR_paper.pdf?dl=0.

83 *Also, responding can come with consequences:* Mindy E. Bergman et al., "The (Un)reasonableness of Reporting: Antecedents and Consequences of Reporting Sexual Harassment," *Journal of Applied Psychology* 87, no. 2 (2002): 230–42, https://doi.org/10.1037/0021-9010.87.2.230.

84 *Speaking out about:* Julia Skinner, "Recovery from Trauma: A Look into the Process of Healing from Sexual Assault," *Journal of Loss and Trauma* 14, no. 3 (2009): 170–80, https://doi.org/10.1080/15325020902724537.

84 *And it's gotten much easier:* Ksenia Keplinger et al., "Women at Work: Changes in Sexual Harassment Between September 2016 and September 2018," *PLoS ONE* 14, no. 7 (July 17, 2019): e0218313, https://doi.org/10.1371/journal.pone.0218313.

85 *Her UC Berkeley research:* Justin Wolfers, "Evidence of a Toxic Environment for Women in Economics," The Upshot, *New York Times*, August 18, 2017, https://www.nytimes.com/2017/08/18/upshot /evidence-of-a-toxic-environment-for-women-in-economics.html.

85 *The website started to be monitored:* 2018 AEA Annual Meeting Webcasts of Selected Sessions, https://www.aeaweb.org/conference /webcasts/2018.

Chapter Five: Support

91 *In a study out of Yale University:* Corinne A. Moss-Racusin et al., "Science Faculty's Subtle Gender Biases Favor Male Students," *Proceedings of the National Academy of Sciences* 109, no. 41 (October 2012): 16474–79, https://doi.org/10.1073/pnas.1211286109.

92 *This probably helps explain why:* Stephanie Neal, Jazmine Boatman, and Linda Miller, "Women as Mentors: Does She or Doesn't She? A Global Study of Businesswomen and Mentoring," Development Dimensions International, Inc. (2013), https://media.ddiworld.com /research/women-as-mentors_research_ddi.pdf.

92 *This lack of mentorship:* Rochelle DeCastro et al., "Mentoring and the Career Satisfaction of Male and Female Academic Medical Faculty," *Academic Medicine* 89, no. 2 (February 2014): 301–11, https:// doi.org/10.1097/ACM.0000000000000109.

92 *If the higher-ups in your workplace:* Paul A. Gompers, Kevin Huang, and Sophie Q. Wang, "Homophily in Entrepreneurial Team Formation" (working paper 23459, National Bureau of Economic Research, May 2017), https://www.nber.org/papers/w23459.

92 *Women of color have an especially:* Zuhairah Washington and Laura Morgan Roberts, "Women of Color Get Less Support at Work. Here's How Managers Can Change That," *Harvard Business Review*, March 4, 2019, https://hbr.org/2019/03/women-of-color-get-less -support-at-work-heres-how-managers-can-change-that.

93 *Research has shown:* "Working Relationships in the #MeToo Era: Key Findings," LeanIn.org (2020), https://leanin.org/sexual-harassment-backlash-survey-results#key-finding-1.

94 *"It's kind of like finding a friend":* Chip Conley, *Wisdom at Work: The Making of a Modern Elder* (New York: Crown, 2018): 36–37.

97 *In 1999, MIT did a review:* Committee on Women Faculty in the School of Science at MIT, "A Study on the Status of Women Faculty in Science at MIT," *MIT Faculty Newsletter* 11, no. 4, special edition (March 1999), http://web.mit.edu/fnl/women/women.html.

98 *Women head about 17 percent:* Gené Teare, "In 2017, Only 17% of Startups Have a Female Founder," TechCrunch, April 19, 2017, https://techcrunch.com/2017/04/19/in-2017-only-17-of-startups-have-a-female-founder/; Emma Hinchliffe, "Funding for Female Founders Stalled at 2.2% of VC Dollars in 2018," Fortune.com, January 28, 2019, https://fortune.com/2019/01/28/funding-female-founders-2018/.

98 *That is an alarmingly low number:* Rohit Arora, "The Lending Gap Narrows for Women Business Owners, but It's Still 31% Less Than for Men," CNBC.com, March 7, 2019, https://www.cnbc.com/2019/03/07/the-lending-gap-narrows-for-women-business-owners-nationwide.html.

100 *They represent extraordinary:* Austin Stofier and Bennett Quintard, "Diversity in U.S. Startups: A Report on the Diversity in U.S. Venture-Backed Startups," RateMyInvestor and DiversityVC, 2018, https://ratemyinvestor.com/pdfjs/full?file=%2FDiversityVCReport_Final.pdf.

101 *It's also where a lot of racism:* Rebekah Bastian, "How (and Why) to Make Venture Funding More Equitable," *Forbes,* October 28, 2020, https://www.forbes.com/sites/rebekahbastian/2020/10/28/how-and-why-to-make-venture-funding-more-equitable/?sh=51fc8e344b70.

102 *When women reach leadership:* Martin Abel, "Do Workers Discriminate Against Female Bosses?," IZA Discussion Papers no. 12611, Institute of Labor Economics (IAZ), Bonn, Germany, September 2019, https://www.econstor.eu/bitstream/10419/207436/1/dp12611

.pdf; Kieran Snyder, "The Abrasiveness Trap: High-Achieving Men and Women Are Described Differently in Reviews," Fortune.com, August 26, 2014, https://fortune.com/2014/08/26/performance -review-gender-bias/.

104 *Managers, male and female:* Annette Towler, "Transformational Leadership: What Works and What Doesn't Work?," CQ Net website, June 1, 2019, https://www.ckju.net/en/dossier/transformational -leadership-what-works-and-what-doesnt-work.

104 *One of my very favorite photographs:* Pater Tenebrarum, "A Convocation of Interventionists, Part 1," Stocktalk, SiliconInvestor.com, September 7, 2016, https://www.siliconinvestor.com/readmsgs.aspx ?subjectid=36817&msgnum=24570&batchsize=10&batchtype =Next. (Scroll down to view photo.)

Chapter Six: Title

111 *"It is not the title that honors the man":* Niccolò Machiavelli, *Discourses on Livy,* trans. Harvey C. Mansfield and Nathan Tarcov (Chicago: University of Chicago Press, 1996), chap. 38, p. 296.

111 *About 80 percent of company CEOs:* McKinsey & Company, *Women in the Workplace: 2020* report, https://www.mckinsey.com/featured -insights/diversity-and-inclusion/women-in-the-workplace; C200, Catalyst, Women Business Collaborative, *Women CEOs in America Report: Changing the Face of Business Leadership,* http://womenceoreport.org/.

111 *Women make up fully half:* Women in Business Law Initiative, Roundtable Series, "Addressing Development and Retention: Gender Parity in U.S. Law Firms," University of California, Berkeley School of Law, September 20, 2019, https://www.law.berkeley.edu /wp-content/uploads/2019/10/GenderParity_Recommendations-for -Law-Firms.pdf; Danielle Root, Jake Faleschini, and Grace Oyenubi, "Building a More Inclusive Federal Judiciary," Center for American Progress, October 3, 2019, https://www.americanprogress .org/issues/courts/reports/2019/10/03/475359/building-inclusive -federal-judiciary/.

111 *This is in spite of the fact that companies:* Marcus Noland and Tyler Moran, "Study: Firms with More Women in the C-Suite Are More

Profitable," *Harvard Business Review*, February 8, 2016, https://hbr.org/2016/02/study-firms-with-more-women-in-the-c-suite-are-more-profitable.

111 *If women do get a shot:* Herminia Ibarra, Nancy M. Carter, and Christine Silva, "Why Men Still Get More Promotions Than Women," *Harvard Business Review*, September 2010, https://hbr.org/2010/09/why-men-still-get-more-promotions-than-women; Morten T. Hansen, Herminia Ibarra, and Urs Preyer, "The Best-Performing CEOs in the World," *Harvard Business Review*, January–February 2010, https://hbr.org/2010/01/the-best-performing-ceos-in-the-world.

113 *In one massive study involving:* Wal-Mart Stores, Inc., v. Dukes et al., 564 U.S. 338 (2011), https://www.supremecourt.gov/opinions/10pdf/10-277.pdf.

114 *The result: When a position:* M. José González, Clara Cortina, and Jorge Rodríguez, "The Role of Gender Stereotypes in Hiring: A Field Experiment," *European Sociological Review* 35, no. 2 (April 2019): 187–204, https://doi.org/10.1093/esr/jcy055.

114 *Part of the reason for this is that:* Kieran Snyder, "The Abrasiveness Trap: High-Achieving Men and Women Are Described Differently in Reviews," Fortune.com, August 26, 2014, https://fortune.com/2014/08/26/performance-review-gender-bias/.

114 *In a 2014 study of job performance reviews:* Ibid.

119 *For women of color:* Aysa Gray, "The Bias of 'Professionalism' Standards," *Stanford Social Innovation Review*, June 4, 2019, https://ssir.org/articles/entry/the_bias_of_professionalism_standards.

122 *Studies have found that people: Discrimination in America: Experiences and Views of LGBTQ Americans*, National Public Radio, Robert Wood Johnson Foundation, and Harvard T.H. Chan School of Public Health, report (November 2017), https://legacy.npr.org/documents/2017/nov/npr-discrimination-lgbtq-final.pdf.

122 *When Ginni Rometty:* Pat Vaughan Tremmel, "IBM Chief Gets Standing Ovation at Commencement," Northwestern University, June 19, 2015, https://news.northwestern.edu/stories/2015/06/ibm-ceo-gets-standing-ovation-at-northwestern-commencement/.

124   *Research does back up some:* Janice D. Yoder and Thomas L. Schleicher, "Undergraduates Regard Deviation from Occupational Gender Stereotypes as Costly for Women," *Sex Roles* 34 (February 1996): 171–88, https://doi.org/10.1007/BF01544294.

124   *Also, when women hold higher-status:* Alyson Byrne and Julian Barling, "Does a Woman's High-Status Career Hurt Her Marriage? Not if Her Husband Does the Laundry," *Harvard Business Review*, May 2, 2017, https://hbr.org/2017/05/does-a-womans-high-status -career-hurt-her-marriage-not-if-her-husband-does-the-laundry.

125   *In fact, these entrenched cultural norms:* Kathleen Gerson, *The Unfinished Revolution: Coming of Age in a New Era of Gender, Work, and Family* (Oxford, UK: Oxford University Press, 2010), 105.

125   *And families in which the breadwinning:* Ibid., 45; Kathleen Gerson, "Changing Lives, Resistant Institutions: A New Generation Negotiates Gender, Work, and Family Change," *Sociological Forum* 24, no. 4 (December 2009), https://doi.org/10.1111/j.1573-7861.2009.01134.x.

128   *80 percent of social workers:* "Labor Force Statistics from the Current Population Survey," *U.S. Bureau of Labor Statistics*, accessed November 20, 2020, https://www.bls.gov/cps/cpsaat11.htm.

Chapter Seven: The Parent Trap

137   *Women with children are paid less:* Shelley J. Correll, Stephen Benard, and In Paik, "Getting a Job: Is There a Motherhood Penalty?," *American Journal of Sociology* 112, no. 5 (March 2007): 1297–338, https://doi.org/10.1086/511799; Sarah Coury et al., "Women in the Workplace 2020," McKinsey & Company, https://www.mckinsey .com/featured-insights/diversity-and-inclusion/women-in-the -workplace.

138   *Mothers are consistently sidelined:* Kathy Gurchiek, "The Wage Gap Is Wider for Working Mothers," Society for Human Resource Management, October 21, 2019, https://www.shrm.org/resources andtools/hr-topics/compensation/pages/wage-gap-is-wider-for -working-mothers.aspx.

138   *In one particularly interesting study:* Correll, Benard, and Paik, "Getting a Job: Is There a Motherhood Penalty?"

138 *(Never mind that nearly one-quarter . . . are women):* "Religion and Living Arrangements Around the World," Pew Research Center, Religion and Public Life, December 12, 2019, https://www.pewforum.org /2019/12/12/religion-and-living-arrangements-around-the-world/.

141 *Even in established programs:* Alison Wynn and Aliya Hamid Rao, "The Stigma That Keeps Consultants from Using Flex Time," *Harvard Business Review,* May 2, 2019, https://hbr.org/2019/05/the -stigma-that-keeps-consultants-from-using-flex-time.

142 *The result of this discrimination is striking:* Nanette Fondas, "The Many Myths About Mothers Who 'Opt Out,' " *Atlantic,* March 25, 2013, https://www.theatlantic.com/sexes/archive/2013/03/the -many-myths-about-mothers-who-opt-out/274354/; Lisa Belkin, "The Retro Wife Opts Out: What Has Changed, and What Still Needs To," *HuffPost* (blog), March 19, 2013, https://www.huffpost .com/entry/retro-wife-opt-out_b_2902315.

142 *The phenomenon . . . (for example, of the women . . . full-time):* Sylvia Ann Hewlett and Carolyn Buck Luce, "Off-Ramps and On-Ramps: Keeping Talented Women on the Road to Success," *Harvard Business Review,* March 2005, https://hbr.org/2005/03/off-ramps-and -on-ramps-keeping-talented-women-on-the-road-to-success.

143 *The reason for this seemed:* Jenny Anderson, "Better-Educated Women Pay a Steeper Price for Motherhood," Quartz, August 23, 2016, https://qz.com/764174/better-educated-women-pay-a-steeper -price-for-motherhood/.

143 *Many of these women wanted to continue:* Hewlett and Luce, "Off-Ramps and On-Ramps."

143 *Anne-Marie was rocketed:* Anne-Marie Slaughter, "Why Women Still Can't Have It All," *Atlantic,* July/August 2012, https://www .theatlantic.com/magazine/archive/2012/07/why-women-still-cant -have-it-all/309020/.

147 *Even as men started reentering:* Alisha Haridasani Gupta, "Why Did Hundreds of Thousands of Women Drop Out of the Work Force?," In Her Words, *New York Times,* October 3, 2020, updated October 13, 2020, https://www.nytimes.com/2020/10/03/us/jobs-women -dropping-out-workforce-wage-gap-gender.html.

147   *In fact, during the pandemic, mothers were:* Coury et al., "Women in the Workplace 2020."

147   *First of all, these women are losing:* "Still a Man's Labor Market: The Long-Term Earnings Gap," Institute for Women's Policy Research, June 11, 2020, https://iwpr.org/publications/still-a-mans-labor-market-the-long-term-earnings-gap/.

151   *The thought is that men who are active:* "Fathers Face Higher Penalties for Taking Parental Leave Than Mothers Do," *Economist*, July 20, 2019, https://www.economist.com/united-states/2019/07/20/fathers-face-higher-penalties-for-taking-parental-leave-than-mothers-do; Katherine Weisshaar, "From Opt Out to Blocked Out: The Challenges for Labor Market Re-Entry After Family-Related Employment Lapses," *American Sociological Review* 83, no. 1 (February 2018): 34–60, https://doi.org/10.1177/0003122417752355.

Chapter Eight: Women and the Dark Arts

155   *As the great Madeleine Albright:* Madeleine Albright, "My Undiplomatic Moment," Opinion, *New York Times*, February 12, 2016, https://www.nytimes.com/2016/02/13/opinion/madeleine-albright-my-undiplomatic-moment.html.

155   *It's the "queen bee syndrome":* Olga Khazan, "Why Do Women Bully Each Other at Work?," *Atlantic*, September 2017, https://www.theatlantic.com/magazine/archive/2017/09/the-queen-bee-in-the-corner-office/534213/; Peggy Drexler, "The Tyranny of the Queen Bee," *Wall Street Journal*, March 6, 2013, https://www.wsj.com/articles/SB10001424127887323884304578328271526080496.

156   *Dealing with a bully:* Shellie Simons, "Workplace Bullying Experienced by Massachusetts Registered Nurses and the Relationship to Intention to Leave the Organization," *Advances in Nursing Science* 31, no. 2 (April–June 2008): E48–59, doi: 10.1097/01.ANS.0000319571.37373.d7; Roberta Alexander, "Anxiety, Depression and Suicide: The Lasting Effects of Bullying," Healthline, last modified December 20, 2019, https://www.healthline.com/health-news/bullying-affects-victims-and-bullies-into-adulthood-022013#Far-reaching-impacts.

157 *When a Highlander gets into a position:* Molly Cain, "7 Ways To Spot a Bully at Work," *Forbes*, August 23, 2012, https://www.forbes.com/sites/glassheel/2012/08/23/7-ways-to-spot-a-bully-at-work/?sh=6e8c572c2b33.

158 *Here are a few ways to deal with:* Amy Gallo, "How to Deal with a Mean Colleague," *Harvard Business Review*, October 16, 2014, https://hbr.org/2014/10/how-to-deal-with-a-mean-colleague.

161 *They can be a charming and magnetic lot:* Mayo Clinic Staff, "Narcissistic Personality Disorder: Symptoms and Causes," Mayo Clinic, https://www.mayoclinic.org/diseases-conditions/narcissistic-personality-disorder/symptoms-causes/syc-20366662.

163 *One good way to approach a QOH:* Susan Krauss Whitbourne, "8 Ways to Handle a Narcissist," *Psychology Today*, August 30, 2014, https://www.psychologytoday.com/us/blog/fulfillment-any-age/201408/8-ways-handle-narcissist.

165 *It kind of breaks my heart:* Dale Hartley, "Meet the Machiavellians," *Psychology Today*, September 8, 2015, https://www.psychologytoday.com/us/blog/machiavellians-gulling-the-rubes/201509/meet-the-machiavellians; "15 Signs You Work with a Narcissist, Machiavellian, or Psychopath," *Academy of Management Insights* (July 2019), https://journals.aom.org/doi/10.5465/amp.2017.0005.summary.

169 *Remember, Machiavelli's very favorite Machiavellian, Cesare:* Paul Strathern, *The Artist, the Philosopher, and the Warrior: Da Vinci, Machiavelli, and Borgia and the World They Shaped* (New York: Bantam, 2009), 368.

169 *Women report having far more complicated:* Heather A. Daniels et al., "Navigating Social Relationships with Mentors and Peers: Comfort and Belonging Among Men and Women in STEM Summer Research Programs," *CBE: Life Sciences Education* 18, no. 2 (Summer 2019), https://doi.org/10.1187/cbe.18-08-0150; Sharon E. Straus et al., "Characteristics of Successful and Failed Mentoring Relationships: A Qualitative Study Across Two Academic Health Centers," *Academic Medicine* 88, no. 1 (January 2013): 82–89, doi: 10.1097/ACM.0b013e31827647a0.

175   *"Many times, indeed, having been good":* Corrado Vivanti, *Niccolò Machiavelli: An Intellectual Biography,* trans. Simon MacMichael (Princeton, NJ: Princeton University Press, 2013), 159–60.

Chapter Nine: You Can Go Your Own Way

177   *"I want you to get this pleasure from my distresses":* Machiavelli to Francesco Vettori, 1513, in Corrado Vivanti, *Niccolò Machiavelli: An Intellectual Biography,* trans. Simon MacMichael (Princeton, NJ: Princeton University Press, 2013), 159–60.

183   *Betsey Stevenson and her partner:* Betsey Stevenson and Justin Wolfers, *Principles of Economics* (New York: Worth Publishers, 2020).

184   *Women over sixty-five:* Zhe Li and Joseph Dalaker, "Poverty Among Americans Aged 65 and Older," Congressional Research Service report, R45791, July 1, 2019, https://crsreports.congress.gov/product /pdf/R/R45791.

186   *Hundreds of people came:* "Pacific Ballroom Dance Studio Expanding, Sets Grand Opening Jan. 4," *Auburn Reporter,* December 12, 2019, https://www.auburn-reporter.com/news/pacific-ballroom -dance-studio-expanding-sets-grand-opening-jan-4/.

Chapter Ten: A Lady's Guide to Negotiation

196   *In their excellent book:* Deepak Malhotra and Max Bazerman, *Negotiation Genius: How to Overcome Obstacles and Achieve Brilliant Results* (New York: Bantam, 2007), 38.

197   *As Machiavelli wrote in a letter:* Niccolò Machiavelli, *Machiavelli: The Chief Works and Others, Vol. II,* trans. Allan H. Gilbert (Durham, NC: Duke University Press, 2013), 1,004.

201   *According to Glassdoor:* Glassdoor Team, "How to Calculate Cost-Per-Hire," *Glassdoor for Employers* (blog), July 5, 2019, https:// www.glassdoor.com/employers/blog/calculate-cost-per-hire/.

209   *Studies have shown that women are more likely:* Linda L. Carli, "Gender and Social Influence," *Journal of Social Issues* 57, no. 4 (Winter 2001): 725–41, https://doi.org/10.1111/0022-4537.00238; Hannah Riley Bowles, "Why Women Don't Negotiate Their Job Offers," *Harvard Business Review,* June 19, 2014, https://hbr.org/2014/06

/why-women-dont-negotiate-their-job-offers; Cameron Anderson and Leigh L. Thompson, "Affect from the Top Down: How Powerful Individuals' Positive Affect Shapes Negotiations," *Organizational Behavior and Human Decision Processes* 95, no. 2 (November 2004): 125–39, https://doi.org/10.1016/j.obhdp.2004.05.002; Emily T. Amanatullah and Michael W. Morris, "Negotiating Gender Roles: Gender Differences in Assertive Negotiating Are Mediated by Women's Fear of Backlash and Attenuated When Negotiating on Behalf of Others," *Journal of Personality and Social Psychology* 98, no. 2 (February 2010), 256–67, https://doi.org/10.1037/a0017094; L. J. Kray, L. Thompson, and A. Galinsky, "Battle of the Sexes: Gender Stereotype Confirmation and Reactance in Negotiations," *Journal of Personality and Social Psychology* 80, no. 6 (June 2001): 942–58, pmid:11414376.

215 *In* Negotiation Genius, *Deepak Malhotra and Max H. Bazerman:* Malhotra and Bazerman, *Negotiation Genius*, 32.

222 *In* Negotiation Genius, *authors Deepak Malhotra and Max Bazerman:* Ibid, 46.

224 *In fact, he dedicated the book:* Niccolò Machiavelli, *Discourses on Livy*, trans. Harvey C. Mansfield and Nathan Tarcov (Chicago: University of Chicago Press, 1996).

Selected Bibliography

In writing this book, my readings went in three very different directions: historical books about Machiavelli and Renaissance Italy, books about gender, and books about negotiation. I have included here the books I referenced most frequently.

History/Machiavelli

Machiavelli, Niccolò. *The Prince.* Trans. N. H. Thomson. New York: Dover, 1992.

———. *The Prince.* Trans. W. K. Marriott. Middletown, DE: Millennium, 2014.

Strathern, Paul. *The Artist, the Philosopher, and the Warrior: Da Vinci, Machiavelli, and Borgia and the World They Shaped.* New York: Bantam, 2009.

Viroli, Maurizio. *Niccolò's Smile: A Biography of Machiavelli.* Trans. Antony Shugaar. New York: Farrar, Straus and Giroux, 2000.

Vivanti, Corrado. *Niccolò Machiavelli: An Intellectual Biography.* Trans. Simon MacMichael. Princeton, NJ: Princeton University Press, 2013.

Gender

Babcock, Linda, and Sara Laschever. *Women Don't Ask: The High Cost of Avoiding Negotiation—and Positive Strategies for Change.* Princeton, NJ: Princeton University Press, 2003.

Eagly, Alice, and Linda L. Carli. *Through the Labyrinth: The Truth About How Women Become Leaders.* Boston: Harvard Business School, 2007.

Kay, Katty, and Claire Shipman. *The Confidence Code: The Science and Art of Self-Assurance—What Women Should Know.* New York: Harper-Collins, 2014.

Ridgeway, Cecilia L. *Framed by Gender: How Gender Inequality Persists in the Modern World.* New York: Oxford University Press, 2011.

———. *Status: Why Is It Everywhere? Why Does It Matter?* New York: Russell Sage Foundation, 2019.

Williams, Joan C., and Rachel Dempsey. *What Works for Women at Work: Four Patterns Working Women Need to Know.* New York: New York University Press, 2014.

Negotiation

Babcock, Linda C., and Sara Laschever. *Ask for It: How Women Can Use the Power of Negotiation to Get What They Really Want.* New York: Bantam, 2008.

Malhotra, Deepak, and Max H. Bazerman. *Negotiation Genius: How to Overcome Obstacles and Achieve Brilliant Results at the Bargaining Table and Beyond.* New York: Bantam, 2007.

Wasserman, Claire. *Ladies Get Paid: The Ultimate Guide to Breaking Barriers, Owning Your Worth, and Taking Command of Your Career.* New York: Gallery Books, 2021.

Index

261

About the Author

STACEY VANEK SMITH is a longtime public radio reporter and host. She currently cohosts NPR's *The Indicator* from *Planet Money*, a daily podcast covering business and economics. She has also served as a correspondent for NPR's *Planet Money* and *Marketplace*. A native of Idaho, Smith is a graduate of Princeton University, where she earned a BA in comparative literature and creative writing. She also holds an MS in journalism from Columbia University.